The Second Oldest Profession

THE
SECOND
OLDEST
PROFESSION

*An Informal History of
Moonshining in America*

BY

JESS CARR

PRENTICE-HALL, INC.
Englewood Cliffs
N.J.

The Second Oldest Profession: An Informal History of Moonshining in America
by Jess Carr
Copyright © 1972 by Jess Carr
All rights reserved. No part of this book may be
reproduced in any form or by any means, except for
the inclusion of brief quotations in a review, without
permission in writing from the publisher.
ISBN: 0-13-797563-5
Library of Congress Catalog Card Number: 70-172277
Printed in the United States of America 3
Prentice-Hall International, Inc., London
Prentice-Hall of Australia, Pty. Ltd., North Sydney
Prentice-Hall of Canada, Ltd., Toronto
Prentice-Hall of India Private Ltd., New Delhi
Prentice-Hall of Japan, Inc., Tokyo
Design by Janet Anderson

OLD MOUNTAIN DEW

I know a place 'bout a mile down the road
Where you lay down a dollar or two.
If you hush up your mug, they will slip you a jug
Of that good old mountain dew.

They call it that old mountain dew
And them that refuse it are few.
You may go 'round the bend, but you'll come back again
For that good old mountain dew.

What can compare with the fragrance so rare
Which your nostrils detect from the flue?
So you pucker your lips for to take a few sips
Of that good old mountain dew.

High on a hill, there's a secluded still,
And it's run by a hard working crew.
You can tell very well as you sniffle a smell,
It's that good old mountain dew.

My brother Paul, he is tiny and small,
And he measures about four foot two,
But he thinks he's a gi'nt when they give him a pint
Of that good old mountain dew.

Ol' Parson Brown was feelin' low down,
'Cause his wife had a case of the flu.
So we told him the cure which would fix her for sure,
It's that good old mountain dew.

Speak if you will 'gainst that still on the hill,
We'll agree that your words may be true,
And, in fact, there's no doubt—you can well do without
This here good old mountain dew.

Miss Jane MacHume tried a brand new perfume,
It had oh such a sweet smelling pu,
Was that lady surprised when 'twas just analyzed
As that good old mountain dew.

Used by permission of Ashley Publications, Inc., 39 West 60th Street, New York, N.Y. 10023.

Foreword

It seems, in retrospect, that I have been writing *The Second Oldest Profession* all my life. It is not a certainty that the subject about which I write was not the world's oldest profession but since the "oldest profession" is so firmly fixed in the minds of the populace at large, I will concede the fact in the interest of historical harmony. Pursuing the matter further would result in the old which-came-first argument—the chicken or the egg? Or, somewhat better defined, which needed to be satisfied first—the sex urge or the craving in the belly for strong drink?

I say I have been compiling this history all my life for a number of reasons. I was born and reared in a geographical location which history has proven to be one of the breeding grounds of moonshining activity. Southwest Virginia, my place of birth, is only a short distance from West Virginia, eastern Kentucky, and Tennessee, where moonshining in some regions is still an honorable occupation. To the south, and only a short distance, is North Carolina whose record for moonshining activities still ranks the third highest in the nation. More specifically defined, a mountain walk fifty to a hundred miles from here in any direction would likely be rewarded with at least a sniff of mountain dew drifting up from some secluded hollow. No one in my immediate family was active in the distilling art during my boyhood, but some of the more distant relatives could make no such claim. As a small child, I can remember family whisperings about these elusive men, operating both in the neighborhood and more distantly removed. My first view of an actual distilling site in the mountains came about accidentally while on a mountain hike. I was only nine or ten at the time, and the still site had been abandoned. I remember standing in awe beside the ashes of the still furnace and plunging my head deeply into one or two remaining barrels, which I reasoned had contained some of the necessary ingredients of the whole process. The scene merely hinted at what had transpired in days, or perhaps years, gone by. The setting was typical of others I would come to visit in years to come. The site was located between two steep ridges, both running southeast to northwest. Between the ridges ran a small limestone branch which flowed out of a shallow cave further back in the mountains. There was a heavy growth of tall timber, and an abundance of rhododendron and small hemlock trees. Numerous fallen trees, some of which had reached an advanced state of decay, lay pointing in all directions. Some had the limbs chopped off, evidently for firewood.

I never forgot the scene, and at the time, the excitement of coming upon it swelled my boyish brain to great heights of euphoria. When I revealed the discovery to my father, he passed it off as something I was just as well off not knowing too much about. Mine was a nondrinking family, and the prohibition against strong drink—and the persons who either made or consumed it—had been firmly set forth.

When I reached the age of twelve, I began to work full time in the fields and mountains with the older men, where the subject of moonshining was discussed quite often. It was not hard to guess that some of those doing the talking were either present or past masters of the art. In spite of their talk, much of what they said was a mystery to me but I held on to every strange term and expression with childlike delight. The talk was always in overtones of secrecy and frequently halted when I showed too much interest. That is another part of a bygone age which would be hard for the young of today to understand. There was an unwritten code of ethics among hired farm hands, neighbors, older members of a family, or tenants that things possibly damaging to the moral health of a young boy or girl were not to be discussed in his or her presence.

As every young person knows, an atmosphere of secrecy and strict prohibition against participation in a particular activity are as much a stimulus as a deterrent. But increased interest was as far as the matter went. Again it was an age when children obeyed their parents.

My interest waned a little in my early teen years possibly because I lacked the opportunity to investigate the matter. Most likely World War II and the absence of many men of service age from the community had a great deal to do with it, as well as my own advancing years and the interests of school and related activities. But a seed once planted may lie dormant for a while and grow belatedly. Such was the case with the subject of moonshining. There were many times when I wondered what it would be like to be in the inner circle and enjoy the fellowship that I was sure prevailed around the light of the stilling fire. There were a thousand questions which plagued my brain. How was the whiskey made? Would one small glassful really knock a man cold as I had heard from my school chums? What actually were the ingredients and how were they properly mixed? How did the worm really function and how did a moonshiner make it? What was the function of the yeast that I had heard the men speak of when they were sure I wasn't listening? Why was a still better if made from copper? Why would "doublin'" help the drink? The questions were endless, and the answer to one only raised two more. When did moonshining begin and why did the government prohibit such a seemingly pleasant occupation? I believe, since those very early days, I have consciously or unconsciously cataloged everything I ever heard about this subject. From the very threshold of awareness, the moonshiner himself never ceased to fascinate me. He was a unique individual—the man you saw and the man you didn't see. There was an aura of mystery—a certain feeling of fearful respect—for such men even among members of the community who disapproved entirely of such illicit activity.

Little did I realize the epic drama behind the minute specks of knowledge I had gained as a child of the mountains, until the decision was made to write the moonshiner's story, hopefully in all its most intricate detail. It is a fascinating and surprising story, for it is as much a part of America as George Washington or the Civil War.

J. C.

Acknowledgments

No book of this scope would be possible without many people who contributed unselfishly to the cause of the author and his reading public. I will ever be grateful to the small army of helpers who went far beyond the usual response to requests for assistance or provided shreds of information that seemed at times lost to history.

To reference librarians, assistants, agency heads and their assistants, enforcement personnel, members of the academic community, government, and industry, and people in various walks of life—I can never praise them sufficiently for their professionalism and their spirit of enthusiasm on my behalf.

It will be obvious from the text that the contribution of two widely contrasting sources is the real strength of the book. Without the help of either, the work would have been futile. I therefore deem it a privilege to thank these two sources first: Mr. Harold Serr, former director of the Alcohol, Tobacco and Firearms Division of IRS, who opened the doors of ancient and present-day documents that I might have a prolonged look at the moonshiner of yesteryear and his modern contemporary. To assist me through a maze of never-ending government documents and bound volumes, I had the assistance of a dedicated professional in the person of William D. Behen, chief, Operations Branch, ATFD, of IRS. "Bill," as I came easily to call him, guided my footsteps to the proper departments of IRS and made the very first day of my stay in Washington a most productive one. My thanks are extended also to the following people of the Internal Revenue Service: Mr. Scott Waffle and Richard M. Wilkins, Public Information Division, and Warren McConnell, ATFD, for reviewing the manuscript and technical advice relating thereto; Mr. John McCarren, director, Legal Division, ATFD; Mr. Robert C. Watson, assistant chief, National Office Laboratory of ATFD; Mr. Thurmond Shaw, former assistant director, Legal Division, ATFD; Mr. Richard L. Painter, executive assistant to the director, ATFD; Mr. Chic Bonger, librarian, Legal Library, ATFD; Mr. Al Jacobs, assistant librarian, Legal Library, ATFD; Mrs. Alberta B. Jones, secretary in the ATFD; who rendered invaluable service to me in the handling of a multitude of both important and mundane details; Mrs. Bernice Kohlmeier, secretary, ATFD, who seemed always to be making copies of this or that for me and always with a smile. Lastly, to all of those government employees with whom only a short but vital moment was spent—file clerks, statisticians, divisional library assistants, secretaries, and copy-machine operators—I extend my heartfelt thanks.

The second source of helpfulness must, of necessity, remain nameless, faceless, and unidentified. Without the help and co-operation of the moonshiner himself, the work would be sadly lacking in authenticity and spirit. He was not always a cooperative assistant—as often as not intricate arrangements to obtain his acquaintance and knowledge were aborted for one reason or an-other. But the percentages of failure were overridden by percent-ages of success in which a vast knowledge of the man and his method of operation was gained. Of near equal importance to the moonshiner himself were present and former supply men, boot-leggers—active and retired—transporters of today and yesteryear. Often the key to successful contact with the moonshiner lay in the knowledge of some long-forgotten practitioner of an earlier day who still had contacts and a good memory. Of all such men from Florida to Ohio and Texas to Virginia, the old moonshiners in their seventies, eighties, and occasionally in their nineties are the most memorable. They were also the most helpful. Some could remember fifty to seventy-five years of moonshining history that is to be found in no book of record. Perhaps in their dotage, a nostalgia for their "occupation" and experiences provided so sharp a focus that a nearly forgotten age was recreated for me with a clarity beyond belief.

Some of them will be hard to forget, and the faces of their families, children, and grandchildren will be no less easily erased when their simple kindnesses come to mind. But there were other varieties too—those who compose the majority and represent col-lectively a great and dangerous threat to society. All were, or had been, guilty of violation of national laws that made no man exempt. To have shared their secrets, earned their trust, and on occasion to have broken bread with them makes me less hostile to this cancer of our society than I should be. It should not be so, but it is. It is a paradox felt by many a writer who has become close to his subject, whether he is a murderer or a moonshiner. Somehow the man close up does not look nearly so bad as his image; yet the murderer has his victim and the moonshiner his glass jar of potential poison.

My thanks are also due to a number of scouts who were law-abiding men and who trudged the hills, hollows, swamps, and mountains of the Southern states to show me areas of once-prosperous moonshining activity. Trips to working stills were, without exception, conducted by active participants or trusted associates and with a great deal of apprehension on both of our parts. There were times when all of us felt the flies, wood ticks, gnats, and all crawling things were the real victors.

A hearty pat on the back is hereby given to my general office secretary, Gennett Strength, and manuscript secretary, Peggie Boggess. To Peggie especially, I am grateful for efficient handling of my garbled typescript, coming out of Washington much faster than she might have been inspired to work on it, in the then one-hundred-degree weather. And to Gennett who turned out an avalanche of letters to sundry people and places and performed a thousand tasks always pleasantly, I promise the next great work will be a novel. Thanks are also extended for research assistance to Henry Mitchell, Virginia Polytechnic Institute, and Jim Lyon IV, University of Tennessee. Thanks to Dr. Preston Durrell, professor of chemistry, Radford College; Dr. Edward Jervey, professor of history at Radford College; Mr. Andrew Ingles, associate professor of biology, Radford College, and Mr. Joseph Mitchell, library director, Radford College. Other hometown folk were a real help and inspiration which I acknowledge with gratitude: Mrs. Dot McConnell, assistant librarian, City of Radford Public Library; Judge Richard W. Davis, who read the manuscript and offered criticism, advice, and counsel, as well as interesting bits of history from childhood recollections of the elusive man of the mountains; Congressman Richard H. Poff and his Washington office staff who paved the way for extended research into various departments of government.

Indispensable, too, was the professional help extended by numerous people at the Library of Congress in Washington, D.C. It was extremely hard to leave that imposing national treasure, and should I ever be confined for life between masonry walls, I hope it will be there. In particular I would like to thank the following people of the library staff: Dudley B. Ball, chief, Stack and Reader Division; William Sartain, head, Reader Service Section; Lewis C. Coffin, law librarian; George Hobart, cataloger, Rare Prints and Photo Division; Robert Costenbader, assistant supervisor, Microfilm Division; Oliver W. Maynor, Law Library Reading Room; Wayne D. Shirley, Music Library assistant; Dorothy Gene Richardson, administrative assistant, Law Library; John F. Thomas, Issue Desk supervisor; and Augustus Melton, Issue Desk assistant.

There are others who made some special contribution. Some are individuals; others, institutions of learning and related personnel. Many are public servants or members of the newspaper and magazine field. A few are fellow authors who know well the sweat and tears of such an undertaking as this. I would like to list them as follows in demonstration of my esteem:

Florence E. Blakely, head, Reference Department, William R. Perkins Library, Duke University;

Jane Milligan, Rights and Permissions Department, *The Saturday Evening Post* Company;

Maveret Buenfil, reference assistant, Alderman Library, University of Virgina;

Harry J. Sandrus, assistant regional commissioner, ATFD, Internal Revenue Service;

W. B. Hamilton, managing editor, *The South Atlantic Quarterly*;

George Stevenson, library assistant, North Carolina Collection, University of North Carolina;

Valerie J. Edessis, picture editor, Encyclopaedia Britannica;

Ardie L. Kelly, librarian, University of Richmond, Virginia;

Audrey L. Forbes, manager, Reader Service, *U.S. News & World Report*;

Rebekah L. Pratzman, reference assistant, Milton S. Eisenhower Library, Johns Hopkins University;

V. A. Stenberg, director of research, Encyclopaedia Britannica;

John Kobler, writer, New York City;

E. L. Inabinett, librarian, University of South Carolina;

Marie Ellis, assistant reference librarian, Earl Gregg Swem Library, College of William and Mary;

Milton C. Russell, head, Reference Section, Virginia State Library;

Samuel M. Boone, head, Photographic Service, University of North Carolina;

Adele Kozan, Archives Department, Sears, Roebuck & Co.;

Rebecca Walker, reference librarian, Richmond (Virginia) Public Library;

Edward Leslie Herbert, Consumer Products Division, U. S. Department of Commerce;

S. Robert Andersen, publications manager, Licensed Beverage
     Industries, Inc.;
Nina Schoenemann, Editorial Department, *Nation's Business*
     magazine;
Albert Gamse, editor, Ashley Publications, Inc., New York City;
Peter Finley, Licensed Beverage Industries, Inc.;
W. M. Houchins, general manager, Biggs-Johnston-Withrow
     Publishing Co. (West Virginia);
Stuart Itter, associate scientific director, Fleishmann Laboratories,
     Standards Brands, Inc.;
The American Historical Association, Washington, D.C.;
B. A. Davis, Jr., attorney at law, Rocky Mount, Virginia;
Charles R. Peterson, assistant regional commissioner, ATFD,
     Internal Revenue Service;
S. E. Gaulding, director, Division of Enforcement, Virginia
     Alcoholic Beverage Control Board;
A. L. Fulcher, supervisor, Western District, Virginia ABCB;
Paul Gavaghan, director of public information, Licensed
     Beverage Industries, Inc.;
Charles Merz, author, Falmouth, Massachusetts;
Charles Stanley, Alcoholic Beverage Commission, State of
     Tennessee;
Bufford Pusser, sheriff, McNeary County, Tennessee;
Howard Hammersley, Photographic Department, Roanoke
     (Virginia) *Times and World News*;
Kermit Salyer, publisher, *Franklin* (Virginia) *News Post*;
Edward M. Riley, director of research, Colonial Williamsburg,
     Virginia;
Frank Cahoon, sheriff, Dare County, North Carolina;
Bob Powell, special investigator in charge, ATFD, Internal
     Revenue Service, Wilkesboro, North Carolina;
John Hubbard, reporter, *The Journal Patriot*, Wilkesboro,
     North Carolina;
Ruth Osborne, head, Reference Section, Charlotte (North
     Carolina) Public Library;
Elizabeth Pharr, assistant director, Wilkesboro, (North
     Carolina) Public Library;
Marvin O. Shaw, assistant chief, Enforcement Branch, ATFD,
     Internal Revenue Service, Atlanta, Georgia;
D. F. Colvard, sheriff, Etowah County, Alabama;

Fred Goswick, owner, Moonshiner's Museum, Dawsonville, Georgia;

C. S. Felts, agent, (retired), ATFD, Internal Revenue Service, Wilkesboro, North Carolina;

Joe Owings, deputy sheriff, Wilkes County, North Carolina;

Bill Triplett, deputy sheriff, Wilkes County, North Carolina;

William Arland, Hamptonville, North Carolina;

Gene Gibson, sheriff, Hancock County, Tennessee;

John Hix, agent, Virginia ABCB, Franklin County, Virginia;

Morris Stephenson, reporter, *Franklin* (Virginia) *News Post*;

Jean D. Ward, librarian, Dare County, North Carolina;

Mary H. Raitt, Washington, D.C.;

Helen M. Midgett, assistant librarian, Dare County, North Carolina;

Honorable Ted Dalton, federal judge, Western District of Virginia;

Jack Anderson, syndicated columnist, *Washington Post*;

George Donehoo, resident general manager, National Distillers & Chemical Corp., Frankfort, Kentucky.

I acknowledge the help of Mrs. H. M. Sutherland, who made available to me her deceased husband's lifelong collection of mountain folklore dealing in part with the infare wedding customs.

In conclusion, two groups are yet to be thanked. First, the widely separated group of educators who encouraged this work and were convincingly serious about the need for such a history of this vital bit of Americana. When the going was rough, such encouragement was a profoundly sustaining force. And lastly, to my dear wife and three little girls to whom the subject of moonshining became a daily household word. Hopefully they will also forgive me for my frequent absences from their midst in the pursuit of the man at the still and look back upon this time as one of adventure together and a worthy contribution to society.

Radford, Virginia   J. C.

CONTENTS

The Second Oldest Profession

CHAPTER ONE

The Ancestors of the Moonshiner and Their Gift from the Gods

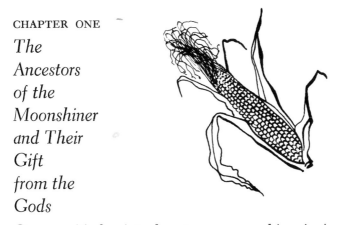

On one critical point, almost every moonshiner in America is in agreement: Since the coming of mankind upon the earth, little time elapsed before he had tasted some form of alcoholic beverage he found to his liking. A favorite moonshiners' belief is that the Almighty was not really so wrathful with Adam and Eve for taking the apple—it was what they did with it that caused the anger of their Creator. Whether or not such far-fetched conjecture is believable, ample evidence exists that mankind's taste for intoxicating substances extends as far back as recorded history and beyond.

The Bible is rich in references to early man's taste for wine and records that his interest often went beyond "taste," until the magic spirits lifted him above the drabness of ordinary life and carried him into a delightful, exhilarating stupor. Genesis documents the life of Noah after the flood and his wine making—and the sampling of his own product until he becomes drunken. Drunken parties abounded in those ancient times, enjoyed by such men as Ben-hadad, King of Syria, Belshazzar, King of Babylon, and a multitude of other notables.

The ancient peoples of Mesopotamia inherited from some unnamed tribe of early man the secrets of fermentation, and evidence exists that in Mesopotamia beer from malted grain was being brewed as far back as 6000 B.C. It is interesting to speculate how prehistoric man might have found the secret of intoxicants. Perhaps in his wanderings over the land of his domain, wild fruit was gathered and placed temporarily in a container and left to spoil and ferment while he pursued some other interest or distraction. Or possibly ancient man attempted to store other foods for periods when no fresh supply would be available and later discovered rapid decay taking place. In his effort to eat such food in a spoiled condition, perhaps he was more delighted than dismayed at the goodness of it. In times of food scarcity, it is almost a certainty that he sampled every herb and plant found growing. One cannot help but wonder how long it took our caveman relative to remember what particular herb or plant gave him his "highs" and which merely rewarded him with a bellyache or even worse, and the exact spot in which he found it.

In geographical areas where wild fruit was not abundant or nonexistent, ancient man must have discovered that wild grain, such as barley or rice, would also produce a homemade "brew." Other foodstuffs would also have been prime ingredients for fermented liquids: animal milk, honey and dates, and sap extracts from plants and trees. Fermentative yeasts form naturally in vegetable matter, a quirk of nature that man can be thankful for every time he takes a drink.

From this beginning, nebulous as it must be, alcoholic beverages were to spread over the then known world. By the fourth or fifth millennium B.C., brewing was well established and *several types* of beer were widespread in Babylon about 1800 B.C. At a later date brewing began in Egypt and is thought to have developed independently of the Babylonian brewing art. In addition to being the national beverage of that time, it also played a part in religious worship and medicine. Most likely the champion distributor up until his day was Ramses III who is claimed to have distributed the equivalent of more than 500,000 gallons. It is interesting to note that most of the original brewmasters were bakers by trade—the product was derived from grain and yeast, so bakers were considered best qualified to pursue this occupation. Their methods of workmanship and formulation were simple: Barley was soaked until it germinated and then was roughly ground. Yeast was added to this malted material and molded into cakes, which were partially baked. These were then crumbled, put into a jar of water, and left to ferment. This method is similar to that still used in Egypt in the making of bosa, one of the many names from which it is suspected our modern day "booze" might have derived.

The Greeks learned the art of brewing from the Egyptians but added something of their own by way of furthering the science.

The Greeks grew hops, although they do not appear to have used them primarily in brewing. Young shoots were also eaten like asparagus and occasionally used as medicine. Additional references to the use of hops appears sparsely in history until the eighth century. The Greeks passed on their knowledge of brewing to the Romans, and at the same time the craft became known in Gaul and Spain.

The races of northern Europe have a less clear history of the brewing craft, but history does establish that the earliest Teutonic and Celtic beverages were made from a mixture of grain and honey and approximated mead—an alcoholic drink made by fermentation of honey and other substances. Brewing progressed more speedily in lands having a plentiful grain supply, whereas wine seemed more prevalent in lands abundant in grapes.

Other ancient civilizations contributed to the advance of alcoholic-beverage making and produced their own favorite concoctions from available base products. Sometime around 800 B.C., *several* countries had brought about a major breakthrough; this new development was the art of distilling, and Chinese knowledge of the subject dates back even further to 1100 B.C.

The people of China, Ceylon, India, Asiatic Tartary, Caucasia, and Japan had learned the art of distilling beverages about this time. China, by using the raw materials rice and millet, produced a fermented liquor called tchoo and from that, a distilled beverage called sautchoo. Japan used rice to make a fermented beer called sake and distilled off a drink called sochu. Ceylon and India both used rice and molasses (or palm sap) and from that made a fermented liquor called toddy; the resulting distillate was called arrack. Caucasia used mare's milk as a base substance and produced therefrom a fermented liquor called kefir, the distillate being skhou. Asiatic Tartary also used mare's milk to produce a distillate called arika. The fermented liquor from which it was made was called koumiss.

Distilling of alcoholic beverages in antiquity is not nearly so well documented as the history of brewing and winemaking. Though history does not establish with certainty whether Britain knew the brewing art prior to the Roman occupation, by A.D. 500, Britain had joined the ranks of the Old World's distillers. Their first distillate was obtained by the use of honey which, mixed with other substances, provided mead. By A.D. 1000, Italy was distilling brandy from wine. In A.D. 1100, Ireland joined the ranks of the other distillers by using oats and barley beer from which they distilled a product called usquebaugh. Spain was only one hundred years in following the example of Italy; Spaniards distilled aqua vini from grape wine in A.D. 1200, France followed in A.D. 1300 with cognac, also distilled from grape wine. Just prior to A.D. 1500, Scotland made beer from malted barley and distilled from it aqua vitae whiskey.

Elementary distilling of the simplest nature was described by the Roman writer Pliny the elder (A.D. 24–79). His record of the art, while not specifically applicable to distilling alcoholic beverages, does describe what was to become the limited, elementary mechanics of extracting a distillate from steam. His writing describes the hanging of fleeces over boiling resin to collect turpentine from the rising vapors. Alexander of Aphrodisias, the Greek lecturer and writer of the second century A.D., described the distillation of freshwater from seawater in his writings. Aristotle, the Greek philosopher, described the same process in 384–322 B.C. This was accomplished by boiling the seawater and collecting the freshwater by hanging sponges over the steam, then wringing them out.

Albukassen, the Arabian alchemist, was another who described early distilled beverage making in his writings of the tenth century. By A.D. 1260 his countrymen were distilling great quantities of such a product and passing on advanced knowledge to Spain. Early man thought of this potent liquid as a gift from the gods, possessing mystic powers and healing properties beyond imagination. One of the early physician-chemists so awed by this "liquid of the gods" was Arnaldus Villanovanus who wrote about it in the thirteenth century.

The earliest account of whiskey ("whisky" in Scotland and Canada) making in Scotland is to be found in the Scottish exchequer rolls of 1494. Here we are introduced to a step in the evolution of whiskey making, from mead (derived from honey and other substances) in A.D. 500, to grain whiskey. Ireland, too, improved upon the earlier grain distillate usquebaugh to rival Scotland in a slightly differing formula of whiskey making.

Early stills (or alembics, as they were called in some parts of the world) reflected most profoundly the ingenuity of man. Improvements in distilling progressed from crude apparatus, the first design of which can never be known, to the use of a large bowl filled with cold water and from the outer surface of which the condensate dripped into a vessel within the still pot (see Figure 1). The Tibetan and Bhutan people were among the earliest to use this invention. The Peruvians made an advance which rendered this ancient still more efficient in operation. The method they employed was to funnel off the steam drippings to an external receiving jar (see Figure 2). By getting the condensate away from the heat and into a separate container, undesired vapor loss was reduced and a higher yield was the result. By forcing the vapors through a still longer pipe into a receiving vessel, which allowed a longer cooling period, the Kalmuck Tartars added one more step in the evolution. Neither, however, saw the possibilities of cooling the vapor by water as it traveled from the still to the receiver. Such an omission of engineering observation merely points out the slow development of scientific advance. The Sinhalese did come up with the idea of immersing the receiving jar in cool water, but the natives of Tahiti really got the right idea by chilling the hot vapors while still in the connecting pipe and before vapors reached the receiver (see Figure 3). Output of distillate naturally increased substantially, and vapor loss was reduced by astounding proportions. Such a breakthrough was actually the forerunner of the Dariot or Liebig condenser which has been used and modified in modern times to serve humanity in many ingenious forms.

Water cooling was still further harnessed by circulation around the specially constructed head of an Alexandrian still. This still was the forerunner of the Mysore still which was reinvented in later years as the Kodak and Sheldon condensers came into use. Figure 4 illustrates more advanced design ideas.

The art of distilling spread rapidly, but no more rapidly than was required to keep pace with the thirst for the new product. From the early inventions and further improvements and modifications, the Scotsman and the Irishman had the know-how and equipment to launch their countries into a new industry, the heights of which are still unseen.

Robert Stein's invention in 1826, of the column still, provided a continuous distillation process, and commercial distilling began its long climb upward. The alcoholic beverage the world would soon come to know as Scotch whiskey was fast coming into its own. In 1832 Aeneas Coffey improved the column still, increas-

Figure 1   Ancient form of still used in Tibet

Reproduced from the article "Alcohol Beverages, Distilled," in the *Encyclopaedia Britannica*, 1967.

Figure 2   Ancient form of still used in Peru

Reproduced from the article "Alcohol Beverages, Distilled," in the *Encyclopaedia Britannica*, 1967.

Figure 3   Still of ancient type as used in Tahiti

Reproduced from the article "Alcohol Beverages, Distilled," in the *Encyclopaedia Britannica*, 1967.

Figure 4   Design for distilling apparatus from Braunschwicks Das Buch Distillieren (1512).

Reproduced from the article "Alcohol Beverages, Distilled," in the *Encyclopaedia Britannica*, 1967.

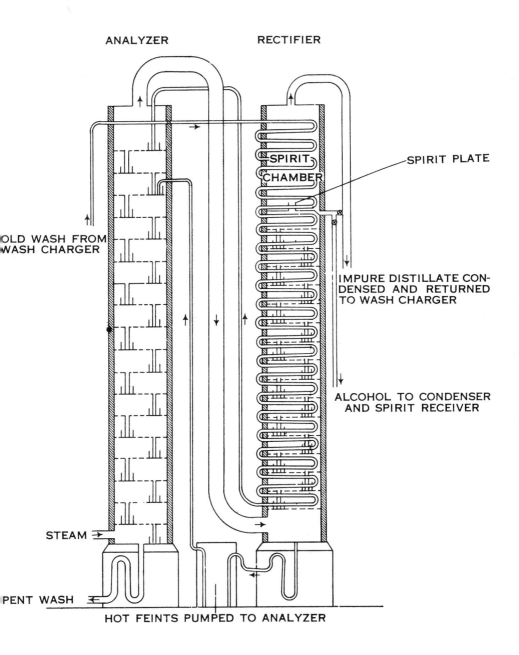

Figure 5   Diagram of a Coffey still

Reproduced from the article "Alcohol Beverages, Distilled" in the
Encyclopaedia Britannica, 1967.

ing production and improving the quality (see Figure 5). Scotch whiskey was to become unique to Scotland in more ways than equipment or technique could account for. The water used had a quality perhaps not duplicated in any other section of the world, for it rises through red granite formations and passes through peat-moss country, giving a taste and character unique to itself.

Official trouble appeared for the small, local distiller in 1814 when commercial distillation began. Territorial monarchs had taxed whiskey making before but now widespread excise taxes* were levied and and stills of less than five hundred gallons were prohibited. England also had the equivalent of the man to become known as the American moonshiner. In an effort to evade English excise taxes on distilling, Scotsmen and Irishmen began to operate pot stills illegally. Such illegal whiskey was called poteen or potheen from the Irish word *poitin* which means a small pot.

---

* Excise taxes as we know them today dated back to 1643 in England when both the tax and the name were borrowed from the Dutch. Excise taxing privileges in that era were often passed on by sovereigns to private monopolists who paid a fixed sum for the right to levy taxes.

CHAPTER TWO

Alcoholic Beverage Making in New America

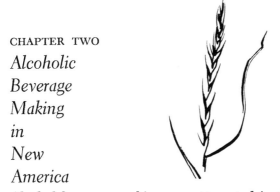

Alcohol beverage making was attempted in the newly discovered America at the same time first colonization attempts were made. The English made beer from Indian corn (maize) in 1584 while trying to establish the first colony in the New World. The very first explorers were served wine made from wild grapes and persimmons during their first contact with the Indians of the Atlantic Coast. History also substantiates that various kinds of alcoholic beverages were made by some of the Indian tribes long before the advent of Europeans in North America. We have already seen evidence of manufacturing activity of distilled spirits among peoples of the South American continent. There were tribes other than those discovered on the eastern coast in North America who had already become expert makers of fermented spirits before the coming of the white man. The Cahita Indians, who were located in the southwest area of what was to become a part of the United States, made wine from the pitahaya cactus. In the same area the Tarahumara tribes made wine from agave plants. Maize beer was made in the area south of the Mexican border. This fermented drink was made in three varieties: from the corn grains, from sprouted corn grain, or from the corn stalks. The alcoholic content of this beer ran to 4 to 5 percent—amazingly near to some modern beer. This drink spread northward to the San Carlos, Chiricahua, Mescalero, and Lipan Apaches. Great varieties of plants for brewing were used by Indian tribes throughout Mexico and the Southwest: mesquite and screw-bean plants, pitahaya cacti, tuna cacti, sotols, magueys, manzanita berries, and wild plums, among others.

Captain John G. Burke, writing in *The American Anthropologist* of July 1894, asserted that natives of northern New Spain (or Mexico) were not only good makers of fermented spirits but did in fact possess the knowledge and experience of distilling. Although the equipment they used was an aboriginal type of apparatus and not in any way traceable to the still designs of Europeans, it did appear to function well, particularly under the skilled hands of the Aztecs.

Captain Burke supports his belief by citing words of Charles V (Holy Roman emperor from 1519 to 1556 and king of Spain as Charles I from the year 1516) who noted for historians that

> Indians of New Spain make use of a drink called pulque which is distilled by [from] the magueys, plants of great value for certain purposes, and when drunk in moderation its use may be tolerated, since they have always been accustomed to it; but it has been noted that great harm and danger have been occasioned by their manner of doctoring it by the introduction of various ingredients noxious to spiritual and temporal health, since under pretense of preserving it and keeping it from corruption, they mix with it certain roots, boiling water and lime which impart so much additional strength that it deprives them of their senses. . . .

Captain Burke believed this observation was the early making of mescal since the sap (or miel) of the maguey, when allowed to ferment, becomes the beerlike pulque. He believed the center stalk or heart of the plant was first baked, allowed to ferment, and then distilled into mescal. The possibility that invading Spaniards under Cortez could have taught the natives this new art is questioned by Captain Burke on the grounds that the Spaniards could not have known so thoroughly the various formulations of berries, roots, and plants used by the aborigines in their fermenting and distilling.

No less a figure than Columbus also adds credibility to this theory, for he too seems to have believed the observation of sufficient importance that his son Fernando makes mention of it in the *Life of Columbus* (Paris, 1571).

From this and other evidence it appears that knowledge of distilling existed in Mexico and the southwestern portion of the United States before 1600. Other geographical areas and tribes, however, would not know the secrets and existence of distilled beverages until the coming of the white man.

After the settlement of Jamestown in 1607, there is no evidence that the transplanted Europeans lost their taste for a frequent dose of spirits in some form. In fact, history indicates there was no prolonged lapse at all in the need or the supply other than transportation difficulties. The Mayflower crew allowed adequate shipping space for a healthy supply of spirits, and such foresightedness appears to be well documented on the voyages of other passenger and supply ships. As the early colonists went busily about the task of carving out a new world from the wilderness which faced them, the work and hardship were monumental—but there always seemed a time or occasion for a drink of some available spirit. Beer, wine, or ale continued to be supplied from England or other countries of the older world. The physically hard days and the lonesome, long nights only seemed to whet the appetite of the early settler for the exhilarating uplift of his favorite drink if he could get it, and any kind of drink if he could not. From New England to Virginia the forests kept being pushed back and new land claimed for planting and home building. From England came new seed and a multitude of suggestions for improved economic growth. In addition to the native crab apple, imported apple trees bloomed in newly cleared fields and such nearly forgotten things today as silk culture were being introduced into the infant America. As the colonists pushed inland, their appetite for spirited drink did not subside at all. Each new enterprise, social gathering, or even a burial called for a generous supply of spirits to promote the occasion. One elderly planter of early Virginia refused to allow such "goings on" at his funeral and so stated in his burial instructions.

As settlers moved further and further inland from the coast, access to a supply of imported spirits became more of a problem. Whether early colonial man was prompted by his creative instinct to provide his own needs or simply overcome by his thirst, he did find the wild grapes and grain necessary to start his own winemaking and brewing in Virginia around 1615–1620. He was supported and encouraged by the English government in such an enterprise, for this too reflected much wanted economic growth.

At about the same time, Dutch colonists set up a brewing house on the southernmost point of Manhattan Island. Home-grown barley, supplemented by imported grain, provided the source of the American-made brew. America's first saloon opened in Boston in 1625, and soon this type of establishment would gain popularity throughout the colonies.

The first grain distilling in the 1620's, from Indian corn, took place along the James River in Virginia. Captain George Thorpe, a Cambridge University scholar and socioreligious worker among the Indians, developed the art in that region. He was killed by the Indians, who either got too much of his whiskey or his religion, or got the two confused. Except for the lack of any law prohibiting such an act, this could have been the first act of moonshining in the New World. The year 1640 found the Dutch making further advances in the manufacture of spirits when William Kieft, director general of New Netherlands, distilled the first grain spirits in the northern area of new America. Rye and barley became the grain source for mash, and spirits distilled from rye remained the most plentiful distilled beverage until rum was to overtake it in popularity prior to the American Revolution.

Overindulgence in drink became such a problem in the early 1600's that the English-controlled Virginia Company accused Virginia colonists of drunkenness (a charge vehemently denied, verbally and in writing) at the time of the Indian massacre around 1622. Years later, Governor Harvey of Virginia added to English suspicion by revealing that one half of the tobacco profits received by the planters was being spent on drink. Considering that tobacco was at the time the colony's principal commodity, some insight is gained into the consumption of that day. As the problem grew, so did efforts at curtailing it. Ship captains were given strict instructions not to open casks or other containers for the dispensation of any beverage until the entire shipment reached its proper destination and was in the hands of a controlling agent or official. Such old customs of "meeting the ship" were to become a thing of the past.

The institution of additional controls became necessary in the growing new country. In 1633 Massachusetts required a permit for the sale of spirits. As early as 1657 beer prices came under control in Massachusetts. Regulations pertaining to ingredients of the different varieties were laid down and fines imposed on maltsters whose output contained too many impurities or consistently poor quality. Production was not meeting demand, a factor always calculated to reduce quality. More than *that* single problem existed. The amount and quality of home-grown barley soon became inadequate. The importation of grain, malt, and flour was prohibited in the hope that home production would be improved and thereby add to the fledgling economy. Part of that law of

1660 was repealed to allow the importation of malt. This amendment was predicated on the fear that lack of malt, and as a result lack of beer, would make the people turn more heavily to drinking spirits.

By the year 1685 alcoholic beverages, although not plentiful, were made in some form, throughout the entire length and breadth of the populated areas of the new America. William Penn erected the first brewery in Pennsylvania in 1683. In addition, applejack was being distilled in New Jersey in 1698. Variety as well as quantity became the byword as the pioneers had their eye on westward movement. The roll call of domestic and imported varieties must have sounded pretty modern for a new land hardly a hundred years old: hard and soft cider, wine, peach and apple brandy, beer, rum, applejack, occasional grain whiskey, and others.

Distilled and undistilled spirits continued to touch the lives of our founding fathers in somewhat ambiguous ways as the seventeenth century moved onward. On the one hand there was official concern as to the overindulgence of some of the population, and conversely, there seemed to be semi-official sanction of the use of spirits at any and every occasion. On many official meeting days of various assemblies, a nip of brandy seemed an essential part of the acts of the day. In old records, the requisitioning of a gallon of brandy for official meetings of any description was documented time and again. Colonists thought nothing of a heavy to moderate consumption of spirits, and some of the very earliest practitioners of the beverage-making art were ministers and church leaders. If there had been any sizable degree of moral stigma attached to the practice of imbibing, such a stand would have been weakened by the active participation and overt approval of the most forward-looking leaders of that day and those who waited for another day to dawn.

George Washington was one such future leader who would cast his stamp of approval by operating his own still at his Dogue farm near Mount Vernon. His output of rye whiskey seems never to have presented a serious storage problem.

Thomas Jefferson would be another of the influential breed of men who possessed both the talent of leadership and the know-how to produce good rye whiskey.

The distiller, brewer, or winemaker continued to be a relatively unencumbered operator, and he wanted to remain as such. Though

Figure 6   This still is on display in the lobby of the Internal Revenue Service building on Constitution Avenue in Washington, D.C. It was seized in 1939 by federal agents and may have been the personal still of George Washington. At the time of seizure it was being operated by a family descended from George Washington's slaves. The unit was made in Bristol, England, and the 1787 model has been described by coppersmiths as "a masterpiece of coppersmith art."

Internal Revenue Service

most spirits had prices fixed when sold at taverns and ordinaries, for the producer it was for the time being a free-wheeling business. The law officer who kept his ear and eye to the tavern door and knew his current price regulations by heart bothered the producer only on rare occasion.

By the latter half of the seventeenth century, early colonists in the area of New England began a prosperous trade in rum from the isles of the Caribbean. The appetite for this drink and recipro-cal-trade possibilities that accompanied its importation provided the impetus for more rapid development of the coastal areas of New England. With a source of supply for molasses from the West Indies and the scattered islands of French and Spanish domain, early American rum making became a fast-growing enter-prise. Mother England was not unmindful of colonial ingenuity in action. Especially was she not unmindful of the colonial inde-pendence in buying the supply of molasses for rum making from any source chosen. In an effort to curb such independent pur-chasing and free-wheeling trade, as well as to gain a source of revenue, England in 1733 passed the Molasses Act. This act was designed to impose a duty on molasses imported into the colonies from any country other than British-owned or British-controlled territory.

The colonists stewed in anger at the mere existence of a paper document which would pose such a stumbling block to their economic growth. It seemed to them that the English parliament sat watching from across the Atlantic, taking note of what products were most in demand and directing their parliamentary law-making where it would hurt the most. The colonial answer was nonobservance. Importation of rum, molasses, and sugar continued from areas of non-British domain but the far-sighted saw their rebellion as merely a temporary alleviation of the problem.

The Molasses Act was not to die as an ignored document of little effectiveness. Parliament seemed only to be streamlining the levying of duty when the Sugar Act of 1764 came into being. This new act cut the tariff on molasses in half but raised duty on refined sugar imported into the colonies. This more far-reaching duty was also placed on wines and coffee, textiles, and other imports, unless these products were moved by way of England. The economic squeeze play was backed by strict measures of compliance regardless of injury to colonial traders. Commerce with the French West Indies in particular was largely destroyed, and the much-sought-after Madeira wine, a favorite of colonial Americans, no longer flowed directly by way of the Azores.

If revolutionary spirit was now lacking in the colonies, it was only among those pioneers who, moving so rapidly west, were not aware of the oppressive action of the mother country.

In 1765, the Stamp Act, previously introduced by George Grenville, was passed by the British parliament. A further act to draw revenue from the prospering new America, the act set stamp duties on every skin or piece of vellum or parchment. Every sheet of paper used for legal documents, academic degrees, commercial instruments, pamphlets, newspapers, almanacs, etc., was to be the object of this tax. Duties were also placed on advertisements and liquor licenses.

Opposition was again so great as to render hoped-for revenue an unprofitable venture in light of collection costs, which wiped out any real gain for the English government.

The rum trade suffered after such an onslaught of prohibitive legislation. The heyday of rum in the period 1740–1760 seemed destined for a downward spiral without the promise it might have enjoyed free of the prohibitive duties which were placed on the ingredients and base products.

It is a correct assumption that with the crippling of an industry and the enslavement of self-reliant people by oppressive taxation in one form or another, alternative action would be contemplated. Part of the citizenry would push farther west in the vain hope that distance would isolate them from the acts of a British parliament; others would stand their ground and drink a toast of rum to the growing spirit of colonial independence.

A colonial army supplemented by a legal issue of rum wrested the yoke of oppression from a young America bent on self-determination. With the spirit of 1776 for freedom from taxation without representation came a new zest for economic freedom as well. Already, in Pennsylvania, the first grain distillery was in business at Pittsburgh, and settlers had started opening up the wilderness of Kentucky, planting corn and rye and watching the cool limestone water push the plantings heavenward toward a nourishing sun.

In 1783, corn whiskey was being distilled in Kentucky by Evan Williams and later in 1789 by a Baptist minister named Elijah Craig, who made the pages of history by being credited with the founding of the world-renowned bourbon whiskey of Kentucky. Former settlers from the east were already making rye and wheat whiskey they had been accustomed to making in the coastal areas. Newly arrived settlers to Kentucky found that Indian corn grew better than the less hardy grains of rye and wheat, so it was natural that corn would become the increasingly popular base grain for whiskey distillation.

Neighboring Quebec in 1769 boasted of Canada's first distillery. By 1787 Montreal had added two more distilleries for the propagation of the industry in that region. The Canadians had not yet distilled from grain; rum alone was their product, and as in early New England, the molasses required for it was imported from the West Indies. Grain distilling was not to come to Canada before the early nineteenth century.

CHAPTER THREE

The Whiskey Makers and Their Rebellion

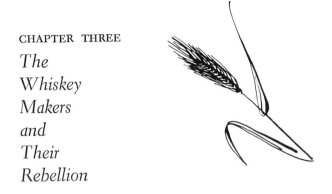

Whiskey making in new America spread into various regions partially because of geological facts often overlooked. Because of the necessity for—or certainly the desirability of—good cool limestone water (50–60 degree F. range, preferably), the whiskey making practitioners tended to move to the regions offering such desirable natural resources. They followed the patterns of the limestone mantles which ran along the areas of western Pennsylvania, cutting across southern Indiana and over into Kentucky and Tennessee. Other mantle outcroppings in Maryland and the length of Virginia and into North Carolina provided bold limestone springs of the purest water. Such areas provided a bonus as well; rye and wheat grain, the base product of distilling, grew healthily. Corn prospered with a deep rich greenness in the limestone soil, and gristmills dotted the cleared wilderness countryside. Corn did so well, in fact, that the older grains soon lost ground in demand for this product, which was easier to raise and required less ground preparation and much easier harvesting. This was particularly true in states with less cleared land and more mountainous terrain.

The making of grain whiskey was on the rise. The veterans of the Revolution, who had whetted their fighting spirit with an issue of rum, found more and more to their liking an increasingly available product called corn or rye whiskey. As rum declined in availability at bargain prices, a greater demand for corn whiskey in particular was sought to cut the dust from the throats of hard pushing pioneers.

By 1790 whiskey output in western Pennsylvania reflected a phenomenal growth for a young country still feeling the pangs of postwar revolutionary times. For an industry that had hardly developed its walking legs before the Revolution, the future now loomed brighter, with corn and rye for "makin' " coming from every conceivable direction.

Many of those possessing the whiskey-making skill and the know-how of still construction moved to the new scenes of the action. The rye whiskey makers of the east and the Scotch-Irish practitioners with old country know-how feathered out to Kentucky or Pennsylvania or south through the valley of Virginia to North Carolina and Georgia.

The newly established federal government under George Washington was not unmindful of the prosperous new whiskey industry. The debts incurred by the Revolutionary War plagued the national treasury to a point where new revenue was desperately needed. In addition to this more immediate need, the federal government felt that its authority ought to be asserted among the newly freed citizenry. On March 3, 1791, Alexander Hamilton, then Secretary of the Treasury, proposed a tax on the domestic manufacture of alcoholic spirits. Distillers could pay a yearly levy on their distilling operation or a tax on the gallonage output of the still. (This tax amounted to fifty-four cents per gallon capacity of each still, plus seven cents per gallon of whiskey produced.)

Violent opposition broke out the length and breadth of the whiskey-making areas. To some, the law infringed their right of free enterprise. To others the government interference into their personal habits and methods of livelihood was a personal insult. To the small farmers of the interior it was an interruption of an income derived from converting their surplus grain into whiskey. There were those who speculated that their own new government was little better than the English parliament which had presumed to capitalize on the fruits of their labors, and from such men they had thought to be free.

Some resolved to stay and fight this contrived menace. Others, disgruntled past the point of reconciliation, moved on into Indian territory, hoping to be beyond the reach of tax collectors.

Hostile resistance continued in Virginia, North Carolina, Kentucky, and with even greater zeal in Pennsylvania. So vehement was the mood in Pennsylvania that federal authorities thought a plan of defiance toward the national government itself was the real motive of the chief resisters. Resistance to the tax became bolder as the distillers became more defeated in their hope of permanent repeal. Federal revenue agents sent out to collect the

Figure 7   Small pot still of the 1700's. Known use of the small unit continued until well past the 1900's.

Lyndall Mason

tax were assaulted and insulted. Distillers who refused to pay turned on other distillers who had reluctantly agreed to pay to stay in business; their stills were wrecked or shot full of holes and their families ostracized.

Armed rebellion was the outgrowth of personal frustration and anger. The tax seemed broader in scope with each day its effects were contemplated. Even the exemption of whiskey for private use seemed to reflect a contemptible arrogance on the part of government—a dole of appeasement. And the whiskey used to pay the preacher—was that to be contributed and then a tax added as well?

A young but determined federal government refused to back down in spite of almost certain local war. A law of June 5, 1794, was passed to give teeth to the collection of the tax. Fury among the distillers resulted, and to show their contempt, five hundred armed themselves and attacked the home of General John Neville, regional inspector of the excise, and burned it. President Washington ordered the rebels to return to their homes and abide by federal law or suffer the consequences. To augment his order, federal troops were being assembled throughout the states and readied to march. The armed attack in July by the insurgents merely led to other more daring adventures, and Washington was compelled to use the force of the militia. In October of 1794, a sizable army was on the march into Pennsylvania for the showdown. Within a few weeks the rebellion was crushed and the main instigators dealt with according to law. The occupation of Pittsburgh (first by the insurgents, then by the militia) and the overpowering forces the federal government had to call out established once and for all that power was needed to uphold the laws of a new nation. Though the whiskey tax failed to produce the hoped-for revenue, a new day had dawned on the whiskey maker and his chosen land.

Bitterness gradually receded among some of the distillers but not all, and such energies as might have been used for nursing a grudge against the government turned more constructively toward living with the law and making more and better whiskey. Areas of the South would suffer the most under burdensome taxation. The interruption of whiskey making during the first days of the tax and during the Whiskey Rebellion caused grain spirits to be in short supply. The far South, lacking the skills, equipment, and flush grain fields of the more developed areas felt a contempt of government that was to last for more than a century. Vast orchards and berry fields were things yet to come with time and economic improvement, but in the interim, hard days, higher priced whiskey, or long dry spells would have to be endured; that or illicit makin'.

Although the government had taken steps to lighten the tax burden on alcoholic spirits in 1792 and 1794, eight more years were to elapse before the repeal of the tax in 1802. A partial reduction of the Revolutionary War debt incurred by the states, desire of the government for an upward-moving economy, and pleadings for relief from the whiskey makers no doubt helped to bring such welcome news into being. With hard cash needed to pay the tax, and that being a scarce item in the midst of a weak confederation of states, the government sought a period of reconstruction in the years following the Revolution in which the country might recover from postwar hardships.

Grain-whiskey making got another shot in the arm with the

passage of the Embargo Act of 1807–1808, cutting off the supply of imported molasses. Rum had been losing favor steadily in post-war years, and this act would automatically cut some of the competition with rum, in favor of grain spirits.

For a while at least, the whiskey makers of America must have felt their troubles to be over. Kentucky had stills numbering in the hundreds, and Pennsylvania seemed to have outlived the effects of the Whiskey Rebellion. New England still provided a healthy output of rum in spite of a decreasing national market for it. The drink was a prime product for trade and barter and used extensively for purchasing slaves (who might be sold or re-traded) and/or more base products for rum making. The drinking pro-portion of America's 7 million citizens seemed unable to get enough of "that wonderful stuff." Up and down many a navigable stream, rye whiskey, corn whiskey, Kentucky whiskey, Western whiskey, or by whatever name it was known moved to a market of some kind. Traveling peddlers from the north and east would barter everything from a Bible to a kitchen skillet for the exhil-arating liquid. Mules and horses trudged the hills and hollows, laden down with casks of converted corn or rye to be exchanged for goods or simply sold to provide some ready cash. Only the surplus moved to market. No shortage existed at home for a barn raising or a wedding. For the most part, a preacher would feel such pay to be premium wages. On the latter point, a growing discom-fort at acceptance seemed to be emerging. Thus far it was more instinct than fact, for few of the far-flung churches had established a firm policy on the moral issues of drinking. But it had been dis-cussed even before 1800, and scattered groups and denominations saw a big issue arising. Baptists and Methodists especially were pushing hard toward a doctrine of temperance or, better still, abstinence.

In 1814 the dreaded excise tax on spirits was again a thing of reality rather than history. Revived to assist the U.S. Treasury in reducing the debt of the War of 1812, it was to stay in effect for three years, when the law was repealed in 1817. It must have appeared to every distiller in the land that each new war brought further burden to his industry. The fever of war seemed to whet the national appetite, but at the same time government interest in distillers' activities increased accordingly.

Whether the national conscience was being further aroused

after the war, or a bad social pattern seen to be emerging as the drinking habits of fellow citizens were observed, temperance sentiment was beginning to be felt. States individually had begun to tighten the laws regulating drinking. Retail prices had long been a matter under control where any manner of civil authority existed; now some states looked with close scrutiny on other regulatory areas. As early as 1798, North Carolina legislative action declared that an ordinary keeper or retailer of liquor who entertained slaves against the will of his master should forfeit his liquor license. (Formerly, slaves could purchase spirits.) This same legislature prohibited slaves from selling liquor, prescribing thirty-nine lashes for any person found guilty of such offense. In other acts passed before 1833, the legislature made it unlawful to sell intoxicants to a known slave under any circumstances whatever. Prior to this period, free Negroes could sell liquor but this too presented ever-increasing problems. The slave, determined to get liquor one way or another, fell victim to the free Negro who would encourage the slave to steal goods from his master's house and receive payment for the bounty in whiskey. Woe to the plantation owner at Christmas time when the slave's thirst was the greatest and his free hours most numerous.

National conscience at this period went much deeper than American drinking habits. The issue of slavery required a national settlement, for that question alone began to divide Americans sufficiently to demand the emergence of stout-hearted leaders. Many literate Americans knew by fact or instinct that national crisis was on the horizon. As the slave issue moved nearer to a point of climax, drinking and ideas of temperance seemed to move along in unison. Temperance societies had helped to bring about limited state-wide prohibition in the State of Indiana in 1816. This limited victory made the sale of liquor on Sunday illegal. Local-option laws began to emerge in 1829 in the state of Maine; in Indiana by 1832, followed by Georgia in 1833. Other moves were happening as an accurate gauge of the times; in 1830 the government abolished the whiskey ration of army enlisted personnel.

It is not to be assumed that some nationwide movement toward temperance was causing the grinding to a halt of the whiskey-making industry. Early temperance sentiment was felt, but paradoxically, the first absolute state prohibition law of 1846 in Maine was in effect at about the same time bourbon whiskey was being recognized by that name in Kentucky. While the prohibition law of Maine was being improved upon and strengthened (by June 1851), exactly the same thing was happening to bourbon whiskey.*

Some improvements came by accident. The virtues of aging seem to have been discovered in whiskey which had been shipped a long distance or stored a long period of time. Bourbon grew in reputation (as did Bourbon County, Kentucky, the name source), and demand for the Kentucky product spread across the land of its birth and to foreign shores as well.

The rapidity with which the temperance movement gained momentum was not altogether expected. As early as 1833 over six thousand local societies of the temperance movement were organized and active. Churches exerted pressure within their domain, and by the 1850's thousands of signatures appeared on petitions in support of prohibition.

Adding to the social and moral clouds of gloom, economic thunderbolts were gathering by 1860. For forty-three years the production and sale of distilled spirits had remained unhampered by federal taxes. The distilling industry had progressed steadily to a point where there were 1,138 distilleries in operation, producing over 88 million gallons of distilled spirits annually. Kentucky led in whiskey production, followed closely by Pennsylvania. Whiskey prices were low, being approximately fourteen cents per gallon in Ohio and about twenty-four cents per gallon in New York. With the outbreak of the Civil War, the economy and normal trade patterns of the entire nation were interrupted. Grains, beasts of burden, manpower, transportation facilities, capital, and human energies were diverted to the war effort. Prices in general and war costs spiraled sharply upward. The federal government

---

* The story of bourbon whiskey is a fascinating story within itself. Debate yet rages between Virginians and Kentuckians as to whether Rev. Elijah Craig can be justly credited with the founding of the bourbon industry of Kentucky in 1789 after settling there; or whether George Thorpe, a Virginia distiller of the 1620 era who distilled the first corn whiskey along the James River, was really the founder of what is now known as bourbon whiskey. The question will not be dwelt upon further in this history of moonshining in America. For the interested reader, Gerald Carson's *The Social History of Bourbon* (New York: Dodd, Mead & Co., 1963) will make fascinating reading.

under Lincoln moved almost immediately toward a plan to collect more revenue. In 1862 the Office of Internal Revenue was established to collect taxes on liquor and other commodities. Whiskey taxes at this period were based on twenty cents per proof gallon. Officially, the ration of spirits in the U.S. Navy was abolished.

Kentucky stills, both legal and illegal, served both sides in the war, and on occasion field commanders would exercise their privilege of issuing a few drams to the thirsty soldier.

The Yankee enlisted man seemed not to have encountered the difficulty of whiskey procurement that his Southern counterpart did. Travel routes south often took the Union army through areas of abundant supply, and if they could arrange purchase time and live with the consequences, the opportunity was there. Unofficially, soldiers and sailors of both North and South managed to procure intermittent supplies of spirits from one source or another. Stills in most states, legal and illegal, were yet in business to some degree, and illicit operations throughout the war zones kept a fluctuating supply moving to buyers both within and without the military ranks. Other states stopped whiskey making altogether to preserve food supplies. Liquor prices continued to mount along with other goods, but supply dropped sharply, and grain was needed more for food than for whiskey. Between 1863 and 1864 whiskey prices in Southern war zones were thirty-five to sixty dollars per gallon, depending on conditions and availability at a given time. Flour had reached prices of two hundred dollars per bushel; corn sold at fifty dollars per bushel and sugar at ten dollars per pound.

By 1864 Confederate money was worthless, and by 1865 at the war's end, most of the South's economy stood in a state of chaos. Industry was seriously hampered, or in some cases, at a standstill. Railroads had been destroyed by war; barns and houses and grain fields had been laid waste; work animals had been killed by the thousands or eaten in desperation. It was a time to nurse the wounds of war and bury the last of the dead. Many families had lost their wealth in investment bonds, slaves were free, and numerous homesteads lay in ruins—a picture of solemn discouragement.

Many distillers along with other businessmen were ruined. Final tallies of the war debt were astronomical, and the taxes on spirits enacted in 1862 at twenty cents per proof gallon were raised to

$1.50 per proof gallon in 1864, and still again in 1865 to two dollars per proof gallon.

At the conclusion of the war, many distillers found themselves bankrupt or undercapitalized, understaffed, underequipped, or simply unable to meet the demands of postwar industrial requirements. Many family operations sold out to larger corporate interests or newly formed stock companies, which could better weather the storm of being both distillers and national distributors. Perhaps, too, larger and more solidly backed companies could withstand the onslaught of the increasingly powerful temperance societies and competition of illegal distillers. Whiskey sales were down from prewar years, and a great amount of alcohol had been used during the 1860's in the preparation of burning fluid (25 million gallons estimated for that purpose alone), and red tape in tax collection posed further new problems such as stamp taxes and new penalties for tax evasion.

The close of the Civil War would now be left to the historians, but another war continued. The mandate of 1862 requiring every distiller to pay the tax or tear down the still had turned into a game, costing the government millions of dollars. The game was being played by members of government working in concert with unscrupulous distillers to defraud the national treasury of whiskey taxes. Such a conspiracy succeeded by means of falsifying distillery records, distilling without government supervision, and shipping illegally without benefit of records and/or gauging.

This "Whiskey Ring," as it came to be known, reached into the highest levels of government and operated from 1864 to 1875 before its operation was brought to a close, and the dishonest government officials and distillers were dealt with by the laws of their land.

Battling the illicit distillers was beginning to look like the Whiskey Rebellion of an earlier era all over again. In 1867 it became necessary to send a detachment of marines to Philadelphia to aid the civil forces attempting to destroy illicit distilleries. In 1869, in Brooklyn, New York, the opposition of the illicit distillers was so great that a marine detachment attempting to destroy illicit stills was beaten off by a mob. A charge with fixed bayonets was finally required to finish the job.

By 1875 the lines of the legal and the illegal industry were being vaguely drawn. The legal industry had its own ideas about how to live with the law, and its actions in the years to follow would take the form of various pools and trusts. Legal distillers would not be completely reconciled to government authority, but they recognized it as a permanent fixture. None of the problems looked insurmountable, and a feeling seemed to prevail that even the temperance forces, who were beginning to be heard again, could be held in tow. The Office of Internal Revenue wasn't exactly a friend, but it could come nearer to such a status by enforcing the law equally. If the fledgling, war-weary whiskey industry paid the tax, the Scotch-Irish mountaineer had better do the same. It was a fair proposition to make. Everybody would pay the tax, or the federal men would simply clean him out. There would be no problem. Or would there?

CHAPTER FOUR

The
Moonshiner
and His
Adversary

Webster's Third New International Dictionary defines a moonshiner as "one that makes or sells illicit whiskey." The term does not seem to have been coined with the advent of such a man or his nefarious pastime in America alone. The origin of the term more than likely found its beginning in various occupational pursuits which necessitated night work, or work by the light of the moon. The term originated in the Old World and was known to be in use in England in the 1700's. Most likely the word* predated this period by years, but at that time "moonshiner" applied to the manufacturer of white or illicit brandy smuggled by night into England from France and Holland. Early western use in America referred to a cattle drive done at night. Regardless of varying historical applications and definitions, "moonshiner" will hereafter be used solely in its reference to the illicit whiskey maker and/or seller. By the strictest definition, the moonshiner (occasionally called "wildcatter") is the illegal maker; the "bootlegger" the seller of illegal whiskey; the "wholesaler" the man who buys from the moonshiner and resells to the bootleggers (usually in smaller quantities) and the "runner" (or "blockader") who transports the illegal whiskey. These are divisions of responsibility normally found in the larger moonshine operations of the 1920–1960 periods. Quite often, and especially among the very small moonshining operations of the rural areas and the cities as well, the moonshiner, bootlegger, runner, and wholesaler are one and the same person. Likewise the runner and bootlegger are sometimes the same person. The moonshiner and runner also are quite often the same person. This manufacturing, distributing, and selling operation is always based on the type and size of illicit operation and its location.

The origin of the term "bootlegger" is an interesting bit of history. This term originated in early colonial days when the sell-

---

* To be found in Grose's A *Classical Dictionary of the Vulgar Tongue* (1785) and other eighteenth-century dictionaries.

ing of intoxicating beverages to Indians was officially discouraged. To the unscrupulous operator who still sought his opportunity to trade with the Indians (and who found a drunken Indian easier and more profitable to deal with) would conceal a bottle of spirits in the top of his boot and cover the bottle with his pants leg; hence the term "bootlegger."

"White lightnin'," one of the many terms applied to the illegal distillate, has an interesting origin. Aside from being clear-white, which is one possible source of the name, still another explanation is believed to be the original. Many early people, up to and including some nineteenth century Americans, believed there were two kinds of lightning, one being white, the other red or blue-red. They believed that a fire started by white lightning could not be extinguished by any means, while a fire by red or blue-red lightning could be extinguished. Anybody who has ever taken a healthy swallow of white lightnin' will concur that, for a while at least, he has a fire in his belly which simply cannot be extinguished!

Other names for illegal whiskey, which have been passed down and which are still recognizable, would include the following: "moon," "tiger's sweat," panther's breath," "white mule," "stump whiskey," "mountain dew," "corn squeezin's," "alky" (used by city moonshiners in prohibition era), "squirrel whiskey," "pop-skull" or "sugarhead" (a more recent name applicable to whiskey made from a high percentage of sugar and said to cause splitting headaches to the drinker), "soda pop moon" (usually bottled in discarded soft-drink bottles), etc. These are just a few of the general names for illegal whiskey. There were hundreds of others which designated various whiskey types, both legal and illegal, that never implied an official brand name.

The reader will also find, as the history and activity of the moonshiner/bootlegger evolves, a general division of types will be noticed. After the period of the Whiskey Ring and the shutdown of large illicit operations near more heavily populated areas, the rural moonshiner became the chief problem. With the whiskey tax down to a fairly low level, the legal industry made progress steadily and left the illegal distilling to the man in the mountains. The city moonshiner and the mountain moonshiner have always been distinguishable, but we will see how they become more closely intertwined in the twentieth century. Differences were in method of operation, equipment, personality, habits, social customs, philosophy of life, and geographical location.

Where and when, then, did our moonshiner/bootlegger start his long history of operation? Two sources pinpoint this question. Keeping in mind our definition of "one that makes or sells illicit whiskey" and giving such an act the most strict and sweeping connotation, we are inclined to go back to the restrictions of the Molasses Act of 1733 and the prohibition of hard liquors in Georgia by the English Parliament.* Our young country prior to the Revolution was still under English influence. In the broadest sense then, any American distiller making or using rum from molasses and sugar of non-British origin was doing so illicitly, acting in defiance of the imposed prohibition upon the colonies. It should be kept in mind that these periods were slightly similar to the American prohibition era of the 1920's.

Although one kind of moonshining was born during the period of the 1730's (making moonshine rum) and cut its teeth during the period of the Sugar Act of the 1760's, the moonshiner had not yet developed his walking legs.

The coming of 1791 was to be a different matter. On that date the Revolution was over, and a new nation with homemade laws existed. Aside from those who would abide by the law for a short duration, then decide to break the law by tax evasion and become illicit distillers, there were those who never had any intention of observing the distilling laws in the first place. These were many of the Scotch-Irish and their descendents who had made illicit whiskey in England before settling in America. Many of the mountain moonshiners practicing today can trace their ancestry back to those early-day practitioners. The moonshiner, then, emerges from not one but two sources: those who were connected with the early legal industry and defected to the illicit ranks for one reason or another; and those who, like the early Scotch-Irish immigrants, had made illicit whiskey in their home countries and continued to do so in America.

One of those laws of 1791 set forth an excise tax on the domestic manufacture of alcoholic spirits. Many distillers defected in a very

---

* Under James Edward Oglethorpe, colonial resident trustee of Georgia, rum and Negro slaves were forbidden the settling colonists, whose task it was to protect South Carolina from invasion by the Spaniards from Florida and by the French from Louisiana.

short while and continued to make whiskey in violation of the excise. Though this moonshiner was not widely so-called at the time, and it is not likely that he worked his illicit business by the light of the moon all the time, this nevertheless was the date of his emergence to national attention. The excise was shortlived and abolished in 1802. Another period of 1814 to 1817, when the excise was revived, gave this type of moonshiner a few more years of practice in his illicit occupation.

In 1862, however, the moonshiners of both origins were to inherit a twenty-four-hour-a-day adversary; the Office of Internal Revenue was established to collect taxes on spirits and given broad powers to prosecute violators who tried to evade the tax of twenty cents per proof gallon for every gallon made. Twenty cents per gallon today might seem a small amount over which to risk violating the law, but violations increased—not only by the small operators, but by some established distillers and members of government in collusion with them, as well.

Civil War days gave the illegal distiller a vast market for his product. The moonshiner in this period was working not only against the tax issue but in some cases against state prohibition on the use of grains for anything but feeding the population. The economy of the times was disrupted, and the availability of spirits and other products posed a serious consumer problem. Often buyers who were nondrinkers used the beverage to effect other purchases. Buyers came mostly to the distiller in each area of his operation, for it was not yet the time when distant transportation of the product would be a government problem. Soldiers and traveling men bought the water-clear spirits greedily, and either consumed them or used the product for the barter of food or other necessities. The moonshiner seldom had a twinge of conscience about his violation of the tax law. For the Southern moonshiner, his patriotism demanded that he produce to supply Confederate troops, and often, if his home was in the pathway of Union forces, his ability to calm the temper of the enemy with some corn squeezin's meant saving his house and barns. In countless interviews with old moonshiners of the South, I heard many a rich tale, handed down to them from their fathers and uncles, of the continuance of their occupation while in the ranks of the Confederate army. One old moonshiner related the ingenuity of his father who "mashed in" in the bed of a wagon and made the components of the still from two mess tubs and topped it off with a bugle for the cap!

After the end of the Civil War, whiskey-tax laws covered the Southern states with renewed impact, and every area within the domain of the U.S. government became fair game for the men whom the moonshiners would tag as "revenooers." While such sweeping authority existed on paper, the enforcement would not be an easy task, especially with so few men for territorial policing.

Arrests for moonshining activities started to climb sharply though, as Reconstruction got underway. Southern moonshiners, who would comprise the majority of illicit operations from the 1875 period to the present, continued to offer the major difficulty and demonstrated an unwavering contempt for government authority. Many believed after the war's end that only their state and local laws were binding. Some moonshiners would swear to apprehending federal authorities that they never heard of any law against makin'. Revenue agents and collectors were resented for more reasons than interference with whiskey-making activity. Southerners looked upon the presence of federal officials as a continuing device for tyrannizing over a defeated people and upon the whiskey tax as a federal, and hence a "foreign," monopoly. Politics became embroiled in the issue with the appointment of revenue officers who, the Southerner believed, were always pro-Northern and unsympathetic to genuine reconciliation between North and South. Further accusations against the revenue men became popular, with the widespread belief that they were essentially corrupt and parties to bribery and intimidation.

Even with all the pressure on the moonshiner, he remained a formidable foe with considerable home support, as witness this excerpt from the annual report of the commissioner of Internal Revenue, dated 1878:

> It is with extreme regret I find it my duty to report the great difficulties that have been and still are encountered in many of the Southern States in the enforcement of the laws. In the mountain regions of West Virginia, Virginia, Kentucky, Tennessee, North Carolina, South Carolina, Georgia, and Alabama, and in some portions of Missouri, Arkansas, and Texas, the illicit manufacture of spirits has been carried on for a number of years, and I am satisfied that the annual loss to the government from this source has been very nearly if not quite

equal to the annual appropriation for the collection of the internal revenue tax throughout the whole country. In the regions of country named there are known to exist about five thousand copper stills, many of which at certain times are lawfully used in the production of brandy from apples and peaches but I am convinced that a large portion of these stills have been and are used in the illicit manufacture of spirits. Part of the spirits thus produced has been consumed in the immediate neighborhood; the balance has been distributed and sold throughout the adjacent districts. This nefarious business has been carried on, as a rule, by a determined set of men, who in their various neighborhoods league together for defense against the officers of the law, and at a given signal are ready to come together with arms in their hands to drive the officers of internal revenue out of the country.

CHAPTER FIVE

The
Moonshiner
at Bay

While government men took stock of an increasingly hostile situation and planned their strategy, the moonshiners were doing the same. The strategy of the moonshiner was comparatively uniform throughout the largest moonshining states (no organized collective plan is implied) and consisted of two major methods of fighting government intruders. The first was an agreement among moonshiners who operated closely enough geographically to assemble on short notice when the need arose and form a small guerrilla band. If government men were going to raise posses and outnumber them, the moonshiners would meet force with force. The second scheme pursued by the moonshiners was to secure neighborhood sympathy—silence or participation—regarding his illegal business. The moonshiner did not have the entire community on his side (with rare exceptions), and he was smart enough to know this, but he was not beyond maneuvering every citizen he could into a position of keeping his mouth shut. To aid the cause a man too law-abiding might find his barn burned as a lesson to others who were too progovernment. The intimidation did not stop here. The bigger operators, who were usually the more intelligent moonshiners, let it be known that ambitious aspirants to county elective office might do well to treat them kindly and with due respect.

For what the government side of the conflict was planning, we need only return to the commissioner of Internal Revenue's report for the year 1878:

> So formidable has been the resistance to the enforcement of the laws that in the districts of fifth Virginia, sixth North Carolina, South Carolina, second and fifth Tennessee, second West Virginia, Arkansas, and Kentucky, I have found it necessary to supply the collectors with breech-loading carbines. In these districts, and also in the States of Georgia, Alabama, Mississippi, in the fourth district of North Carolina, and in the second and fifth districts of Missouri, I have authorized the organization of posses ranging from five to sixty in number, to aid in making seizures and arrests, the object being to have

a force sufficiently strong to deter resistance if possible, and, if need be, to overcome it.

Sympathy of Citizens and State Officers with Violators of Law.

In some of the districts where illicit distilling was carried on to any great extent leading citizens were either directly interested in the business, or else were in active sympathy with the distillers, and the officers of the law have usually received but little aid or encouragement from the people in their efforts for the collection of the revenue and the arrest and punishment of offenders. This state of things has been extremely discouraging, and added to it is the fact that in some cases State officers, including judges on the bench, have sided with the illicit distillers and have encouraged the use of the State courts for the prosecution of the officers of the United States upon all sorts of charges, with the evident purpose of obstructing the enforcement of the laws of the United States. The illicit distillers have on numerous occasions fired upon our officers. . . . I regret to have to record the fact that when the officers of the United States have been shot down from ambuscade, in cold blood, as a rule no efforts have been made on the part of the State officers to arrest the murderers; but in cases where the officers of the United States have been engaged in the enforcement of the laws, and have unfortunately come in conflict with the violators of the law, and homicides have occurred, active steps have been at once taken for the arrest of such officers, and nothing would be left undone by the State authorities to bring them to trial and punishment.

Two Cases in Point.

Two cases occurring in the State of South Carolina forcibly illustrate this position. In April last, Rufus H. Springs, a United States deputy marshal, accompanied a posse of deputy collectors in their search for an illicit still among the foot hills of the Blue Ridge. Without the slightest provocation, or any overt act of his against the person of his assassin, he was fired upon from ambush and instantly killed. This deed scarcely created a ripple on the surface of the public mind. There has been no attempt on the part of the State authorities to ferret out the murderer or to bring him to trial and punishment. The murdered man was an excellent officer, of unimpeachable personal character, and left a widow and one child.

In strong contrast with this case are the circumstances attending the arrest of Hugh P. Kane, William Durham, and R. P.

Scruggs in the same State. They were deputy collectors and deputy marshals who were intrusted with a warrant for the arrest of one Amos Ladd, who had been long engaged in the business of illicit distilling and formed one of a band of lawless men in Pickens County who had openly defied and attacked the officers of the United States. Ladd resisted arrest, gun in hand, and the officers, acting as I believe upon a well-grounded apprehension of danger to their own lives, fired upon him and killed him. No sooner had this unfortunate act occurred than great excitement prevailed throughout the State. The local newspapers denounced the officers as murderers, and, though they promptly surrendered to the nearest State authorities outside of Pickens County, where they deemed their lives would be unsafe, bail was refused them and they were committed to jail. At the next sitting of the State court they were indicted for murder, and the State judge, in an elaborately prepared opinion, refused to recognize the transfer of their cases to the United States circuit court. . . .

The Root of the Evil.

Much of the opposition to the enforcement of the internal revenue laws is properly attributable to a latent feeling of hostility to the government and laws of the United States still prevailing in the breasts of a portion of the people of these districts, and in consequence of this condition of things the officers of the United States have often been treated very much as though they were emissaries from some foreign country quartered upon the people for the collection of tribute. The courts of the United States have come in for a due share of suspicion and abuse, upon the ground that they are organized for the oppression of the citizen and for the protection of the officers of the United States in oppression and wrong. I have endeavored to disabuse the minds of the people upon these questions by having our officers point out that the laws of the United States are enacted by the representative of the whole people; that the law providing for the imposition of a tax upon distilled spirits is uniform throughout the country, and realizes to the government nearly sixty million of dollars per annum, and that while the law remains upon the statute book it is the duty of every good citizen to observe it, and of every officer of the United States assigned to that duty to enforce it. I have stated to them that the pains and penalties for violation of this law are severe, that no man can with safety infringe its provisions, and that any community in which violations of the law become general must soon be given over to anarchy and disorder. I have further endeavored to extend to the people in the mountain districts where illicit distilling has mostly prevailed every facility for the establishment of small distilleries in conformity with law. . . .

Character of the Officers Employed.

It has been my wish, and I have so directed collectors, that in the employment of special deputies, as well as in the appointment of their regular force, they should select men of integrity, character, and discretion, and I am satisfied that in the main they have been able to procure the services of men of this description. It must be borne in mind, however, that operations against illicit distillers for the seizure of their distilleries and the arrest of their persons are extremely hazardous, and in fact, an officer who goes upon a mission of this kind feels that he takes his life in his hand. For this desperate work it has not been found practicable to obtain the services of the most educated and refined citizens, especially in view of the fact that the service is temporary and the pay not large. I am, however, glad to be able to report that, with very rare exceptions, the officers so employed have proven themselves trustworthy, courageous, and discreet, and although they have often been resisted and fired upon by violators of the law, and though frequently their characters have been traduced by the local press, they have gone forward earnestly in the discharge of their duties, and have received the commendation of the collectors and of this office.

Conditional Amnesty to Offenders.

Open violations of law in the manufacture and sale of illicit spirits have gone on in some districts, from year to year, until whole neighborhoods, and in some cases hundreds of men in a single county, became involved, so that it seemed wholly impracticable to bring all the violators of the law to trial and punishment. Consequently, after demonstrating to the minds of these men, by vigorous efforts to suppress the frauds with strong bodies of armed officers, that the government had not only the disposition but the abiilty to put an end to these violations of the law, offenders, who have not been actually engaged in resisting the officers by force, have been permitted to come forward and plead guilty, and have their sentences suspended during good behavior. This course has been pursued with your approbation and with that of the honorable the Attorney General and the President. The object has been to induce illicit distillers to abandon their evil practices, and also to arouse in the breasts of law-abiding citizens a sentiment favorable to the observance and enforcement of the laws. I am not without hope that some good results may follow the course that has been pursued. One advantage that has been derived from the amnesty accorded is seen in the fact that whereas, previously, our officers could scarcely enter the infected countries without being fired upon, they are now able, in most cases, to police the districts with comparative safety. I am, however, opposed to a repetition of this business of wholesale amnesty. . . .

Ways and Means.

The usual force of deputies heretofore allowed collectors for the collection of the revenue in the districts where illicit distilling has mostly prevailed, has been found totally inadequate for the suppression of frauds, and with your approval I have adopted the plan of giving collectors authority to employ, from time to time, a suitable number of special deputies to aid in making seizures. . . . To meet the extraordinary expenses thus incurred I have found it necessary to cut down the salaries of officers throughout the country, so as to be able to set aside from the general appropriation a sum of money for that purpose, which has been supplemented by the use of a considerable portion of the appropriation for the suppression of frauds. But, with the best care I could bestow upon the subject, I have been unable to provide a suitable sum for paying these extraordinary expenses during the present fiscal year. I am of opinion that if active measures can be kept up against illicit distillers for twelve months more the business will be substantially broken up, and that violations of internal revenue laws in the districts named will be scarcely more frequent than in other portions of the country.

From 1875 to 1880 federal seizures of illegal stills were running over an average of one thousand per year. Arrests for offenders were averaging almost two thousand per year. Even these figures are unrealistic compared to the total number of stills most likely in operation and the thousands who participated in some way toward turning out the illicit product. The bands of revenue agents operating during any of these years were pitifully small for the task at hand and the almost boundless geographical territory they were expected to police. Even with the authority to organize posses and call upon other federal agents, marshals, and deputy marshals, the number of seizures made, compared to violators in existence, was slight. Occasionally the situation got so bad Internal Revenue collectors were forced to requisition, through their superiors, escort troops of the federal government as illustrated by the letter (on facing page) to L. C. Carpenter, collector of Internal Revenue, Columbia, South Carolina, in May of 1875:

The long-term effect of troop intervention was akin to withdrawing one's hand from a pail of water and expecting the hole to remain. Another army man had the same degree of success with the man of the mountains. Lt. Colonel George Custer tried cleaning out the moonshiners in Kentucky during the 1870's. Perhaps he thought the Sioux at Little Big Horn would be a pushover after the frustration of guerrilla tactics employed by the moonshiners. A Kentucky moonshiner would have opined that "a little jug of squeezin's woulda made bein' whopped a downright pleasure."

Leaders in the offending Southern states in the year of 1879, listed in order of highest number of violations downward, were as follows: North Carolina, Georgia, Tennessee, South Carolina, Alabama, Kentucky, Virginia, West Virginia, Arkansas, and Missouri.

Moonshining was still going on in the North, though on a much smaller scale. Northern states having still seizures within their boundaries in the same year were Illinois, Indiana, Massachusetts, Maryland, New Jersey, New York, Ohio, Pennsylvania, and Wisconsin.

Illicit-still seizures were up sufficiently in 1879 to prompt the commissioner of Internal Revenue in his 1880 report to be more optimistic than later history would justify:

. . . during the last four years and four months, 4,061 illicit distilleries have been seized, 7,339 persons have been arrested for illicit distilling, 26 officers and employes have been killed and 57 wounded, in the enforcement of the internal-revenue laws. During the past sixteen months 1,120 stills have been seized, 1,265 persons arrested, and 10 officers wounded in the enforcement of the laws. While the number of stills seized and persons arrested since my last annual report is very large, *I am satisfied that there will be a decrease henceforward in the number of such seizures and arrests.*

In January of the present year a combined movement was made, by armed bodies of internal-revenue officers, from West Virginia southward through the mountains and foothills infested by illicit distillers, which resulted in the seizure of a

United States Internal Revenue,

Supervisor's Office, District of Virginia, Carolinas, Georgia, and Florida.

Raleigh, N.C., May 5th, 1875.

L. Cass Carpenter, Esq.,
 Collector Int. Revenue,
  Columbia, S.C.

Sir:

Referring to your letter of April 27th relative to the Existance of illicit distilleries and other Classes of frauds in your district I have to state that a requisition made by you on the Post Commandant at Columbia for a military escort for the Officers of your district should, and no doubt would be filled immediately. The principal difficulty Experienced in the use of troops, is furnishing transportation for them off the lines of Rail Road, and you should make the best arrangement possible relative thereto before starting out.

I recommend that you make application for a detachment and make a raid on the illicit distilleries at once, and I have so Expressed myself to the Hon. Commissioner of Internal Revenue.

I return to you the letter of Mr Earle.

Very Respectfully,

P.W. Perry
Supervisor

number of illicit distilleries, and the arrest of many persons engaged therein. The effect of this movement was to convince violators of the law that it was the determination of the government to put an end to frauds and resistance to authority, and since that time it has been manifest to all well-meaning men in those regions of country that the day of the illicit distiller is past. Public sentiment has been gradually setting in against these frauds, and I feel assured that if continued efforts are made for the enforcement of the laws the taxes upon whiskey and tobacco can soon be collected in the districts where frauds have been so rife without the use of armed posses of men.

For the purpose of preventing old offenders from resuming the business of illicit distilling, I have deemed it advisable to maintain a special force of deputies in many of the districts to police the districts and seize illicit distilleries. These officers are armed and move in small posses so as to deter resistance. They are instructed to establish friendly relations with the people and to encourage the observance of the laws. . . .

Encouragement of Legal Distilleries.

It has been the policy of this office to encourage the establishment of legal distilleries in those collection districts where illicit distillation has heretofore prevailed, and there are now 469 licensed grain distilleries in those districts against 380 in 1879, and 177 in 1878. I have felt that if the manufacture of whisky was to be carried on at all in this section of country it was much better that it should be done openly and in full compliance with the requirements of law rather than secretly in violation and defiance of law, and with the demoralizing influences of dishonesty, turbulence, outlawry, and murder, which invariably prevail in a community where illicit distilling is carried on unchecked. The policy thus adopted has worked well. In every country where legal distilleries have been established in any number, illicit distilling has almost entirely ceased, violent resistance to law has become almost unknown, and there has been a large increase of revenue.

It must be understood that many of the legal distilleries thus established have no greater capacity than ten gallons per day, and that it is necessary for the protection of the rights of the government to have a storekeeper and gauger assigned to each distillery. It is thus obvious that the expense of collecting the taxes upon the spirits so made is very heavy, and necessarily increases the estimates for this year for the pay of storekeepers and gaugers. It is, however, unquestionable that it is far preferable to incur this expenditure to secure the collection of the revenue and an orderly observance of the laws than to spend large sums of money in the employment of raiding parties for the seizure of illicit distilleries and the arrest of illicit distillers. So long as the government looks to the tax upon distilled spirits for a large proportion of its revenues, it is just and right that every producer of distilled spirits shall be held to the payment of his legal tax, and such appropriations should be made as will enable the executive branch of the government to enforce the tax law so as to collect the revenues justly from all alike.

In 1881 the commissioner's optimistic outlook seemed to be coming true. Still seizures dropped sharply in that year and still further in 1882, prompting a statement in his 1882 report that obviously gave him great satisfaction.

It affords me great pleasure to report that the supremacy of the laws of the United States for the collection of its internal revenues has been established in all parts of the country. Frauds in the manufacture and sale of whisky and tobacco in the districts where they have hitherto most prevailed have become the exception rather than the rule. There is no longer organized resistance to the authority of the government, the people render obedience to the laws, and the taxes are collected without unnecessary friction and with but little litigation. To maintain this favorable condition of things and to prevent the recurrence of frauds it will be necessary to continue the system of careful policing which has brought about this result.

I have to record with extreme regret, as signalizing the closing hours of the long struggle maintained against the enforcement of the internal-revenue laws, the murder of Deputy Collector James M. Davis, near McMinnville, Tenn., in March last. Captain Davis was one of the bravest and most efficient officers engaged in the suppression of illicit distilling. Whilst on his way from court he was waylaid on the public highway in broad daylight by ten or more assassins, concealed behind an ambush of logs and bushes specially constructed for the purpose, and was deliberately murdered under circumstances of peculiar atrocity whilst bravely defending himself to the last. The place where this crime was committed is in the midst of a well-settled country. There is circumstantial evidence that the assassination was plotted in a place of public resort not far from the scene of the murder. Citizens rode by whilst Davis's body was still warm and before his slayers were fairly out of sight, yet, though liberal rewards have been offered for the detection and arrest of the criminals, no evidence has yet been obtained upon which an arrest could be based.

Pensions to Widows and Orphans of Officers Killed.
The successful close of the struggle to establish and maintain the internal-revenue laws of the United States is in my opinion a fitting occasion to renew the recommendation in my last report for the granting of pensions to persons disabled while engaged in enforcing said laws, and to the widows and orphans of officers killed in the discharge of their duty. The service in which these officers were engaged was particularly hazardous. No alternative being left except to meet force with force, they were armed by the government with breech-loading carbines to protect themselves against the assaults of those who resisted its authority. In this struggle thirty-one officers and employes have been killed and sixty-four wounded. . . .

With moonshining activity meeting a formidable foe, even the most determined of the illicit distillers must have felt pretty glum about the future of his industry. Revenooers were getting into places they had never been before. On horseback, by train and wagon they came into the most secluded hollows and ravines. They had even resorted to tricks of posing as timber buyers or cattle barons and sometimes with the gall of posing as big city sportsmen out for a day in the country. Even a cave or a cliff wasn't an absolutely safe place for makin' anymore. One moonshiner of that period felt the pressure of hard-pushing revenooers to the extent that he sent a letter to Commissioner Raum of the Office of Internal Revenue promising to abstain from moonshining practices in exchange for official protection. The story is taken from a book entitled *After the Moonshiners, by One of the Raiders*, a personal memoir written by George W. Atkinson, a revenue officer in the period of the late 1800's.* It is a story with an unusual ending for both the moonshiner and Internal Revenue —but let us afford the opportunity to the author, Mr. Atkinson, to tell the story. The battle which prompted the letter from the moonshiner to Commissioner Raum is shown first.

One of the severest battles ever fought between Government officers and moonshiners, occurred August 23d and 24th, 1878, in Overton county, Tennessee, nine miles north of Cookeville.

* Wheeling, W. Va.: n.p., 1881.

The United States forces, consisting of ten men, were commanded by Deputy Collector James M. Davis, the well known moonshine raider.* Campbell Morgan, next to Redmond of South Carolina, the most notorious moonshiner in America, led the opposition.

The following account of the engagement was furnished me by Capt. S. D. Mather, a Commissioner of the United States Circuit Court, who was a member of the raiding party:

"Just before sundown our party rode up to the residence of Mr. James Peek, an aged citizen of Overton county, for the purpose of procuring lodging. The old gentleman said he was not prepared to take care of so many persons and horses, and he and his son advised us to go to a Mr. Barnes, a mile beyond. We started, and after riding about half a mile, we met a man, who informed us that the chances were better for us to be entertained at Mr. Peek's than anywhere else in the neighborhood. We thereupon returned to Peek's. A portion of our party dismounted and immediately went to the house, myself among the number. Mr. Peek was at that time 102 years of age, having been born three months before the signing of the Declaration of Independence. I was engaged in conversation with Mr. P., while Capt. Davis and Deputy Marshal J. M. Phillips went out of the house, and back of the garden fence to find places to tie and feed our horses. Davis had a Winchester rifle in his hand, but Phillips had left his gun in the house. A partridge flew up into a tree immediately in front of them, and while Mr. Phillips was engaged trying to show Mr. Davis where the partridge was sitting, so he (Davis) could kill it, Mr. D. discovered six or eight armed men running down the hill-side, a short distance from them. Messrs. Davis and Phillips leaped over the fence into a corn field near the main road. While crossing the fence they were fired at, and one of the balls entered Mr. Phillips' breast, and passed entirely through his body, inflicting a painful and dangerous wound. Mr. Davis raised his gun and fired. At the first shot his rifle burst, and he had to rush to the house, for another gun. As Davis and Phillips were making their way to the house, a volley of thirty or forty shots was fired at them, but fortunately without effect. The other members of our posse now ran out and began firing at the enemy. I heard Mr. Phillips

---

* Killed in March, 1882, and the same James M. Davis referred to in the 1882 report of the Commissioner.

call out that he was shot, and I ran through a shower of balls to the gate to procure a gun, but seeing Mr. Phillips almost fainting from loss of blood, I assisted him to the house. By the time I had ripped his shirt off, and saw his wound was not necessarily fatal, I was going out of the house, and learned that the enemy had fallen back to the base of the hills, and our men were coming into the house. Charles Tippins was shot through the nose, and his face was covered with blood, and 'Pres.' Smith was shot twice through the arm and his shirt was a clot of blood. Tippins was knocked down by the force of the ball, but Smith stood up to the last, pouring hot shot into the ranks of the enemy. Mr. Rawls, mistaking the moonshiners for our men, ran over to them, and received a shot in his hat and a ball in the stock of his gun. There appeared to be forty or fifty of the enemy, all well armed and determined fighters.

"After the first attack was over, our wounded men were cared for in the best way we could provide. Darkness came on, and Messrs. Speers, Howe and myself stood guard during the night. The enemy only withdrew a short distance, and seemed to be getting ready through the night to renew the attack in the morning. Having only seven men left who were fit for duty, Deputy Collector Davis dispatched Lee L. Ayres and Charles Strain to the nearest point for reinforcements, and to report the situation to collector W. M. Woodcock, at Nashville. Mr. Peek's son, James, and Mr. Hurley, and Mr. Eldridge, who happened to be at the house when the fight began, preferred to remain with us, and I assure the reader that they rendered valuable aid.

"The next morning, a young son of John Peek went down the road to recover some horses which had strayed away, and he was fired upon by the moonshiners, who were stationed behind almost every tree on all the hill-sides. When he returned he undertook to water our horses, but was prevented from doing so by the men who were on guard all around the house and stable. We were now completely hemmed in and surrounded, by perhaps one hundred armed outlaws.

"Mr. Peek, son-in-law, daughter, and other members of the family, occupied an old house in the rear, while we were stationed in the front two-story log building, which was not yet completed, the upper story not having been chinked. This building, in its incomplete condition, was an excellent block-house, and not a bad fort.

"Firing was opened upon us early in the morning and was

kept up all day. Our ammunition being rather scarce, we shot sparingly. We had no water, and but little to eat. . . . Our wounded men needed attention, and fortunately, Dr. Martin, of Cookeville, came in. He dressed their wounds, and at once left. About sundown, it seemed as if there were a thousand men around and about us, judging from the bugles, the yells of the demon moonshiners, and the balls they were pouring into the walls of our block-house. The night that followed was almost pandemonium itself. Sunday morning dawned with armed men in sight of us in every direction.

"The first order issued by commander Morgan to the captives, was for no one to go to the spring for water. Mr. Peek's daughter, and one or two others of the family, however, disobeyed Morgan's orders, and went. Their buckets were taken from them, and they were given one minute in which to return to the house. Full tilt they came back, and, you may be sure, went out no more. The roads were barricaded with fences and large poles on top, which made the leaguerment complete. But it seemed that no one desired to pass, as the whole country had joined the moonshiners, or were in sympathy with them. . . . Firing was kept up about every ten minutes all through the day, but none of their shots hit us. About ten o'clock it began to rain, and we caught a small supply of water. During the fall of the rain, they fired at us almost continuously, possibly to keep their guns dry. Now and then we saw a chance to get in a shot, and promptly put it there.

"This was the condition of matters, when, late in the afternoon, some gentlemen came from Livingston, the county seat, having learned of our situation, to see if something could not be done to bring about an honorable peace. They had hardly explained their mission, when two of the moonshiners sent in a note asking permission to confer with the Government officers, whom they had been besieging for two days and nights. We consented to their coming in, and they did so promptly. They at once proposed to go, with the delegation from Livingston, to Campbell Morgan, the generalissimo of the besiegers, and, if possible, have the attacking party disperse. They went, and shortly after returned with a message from Morgan, to the effect, that if we would petition the President of the United States and the Federal Court, to pardon all their offenses up to date, they would let us go on our way; but under no other condition would they remove the embargo which, by superior force, they had placed upon us.

"We responded that we could not control the action of the

Federal Court, and would therefore promise nothing that we could not fully carry out; that we were citizens of the United States and of the State of Tennessee, and had rights, as such, which should be respected; that most of their force had come thirty or forty miles from home, to pursue and attack us; that we had plenty of ammunition, and that reinforcements were on the way to relieve us. We called upon the gentlemen then present, as magistrates and law-abiding citizens, to see that we were protected, and to exercise their authority in dispersing the mob that surrounded us.

"The delegation again went to Morgan, who stated to them that he had heard that Capt. Davis intended to kill him (Morgan) on sight, and that he had organized this forcible opposition only in self defence; that he knew Davis was a man of courage, and would not hesitate to kill any man in order to carry out his undertakings. He also said that if the Government had a warrant to serve on him, and would put it in the hands of some one other than Capt. Davis, he would promptly give himself up, and would do everything in his power to correct the evil ways of his neighborhood, and this should be his last resistance to United States authority.

"This last proposition was acceded to and Morgan and his men, some twenty-five in number, left their stations on the hill-sides, filed past our fort, and went their way. They all looked like determined men, and we know, to our sorrow, that they are fighters from the hills.

"By this time a number of peace-makers had come to the place, and with their friendly aid we departed immediately to Cookeville, and once again were free."

Narrator Atkinson continues with a description of the leader of the hostile moonshiners:

Campbell Morgan, well known through out the South as the chief of the Tennessee moonshiners, is a native of that State, and the son of a Presbyterian clergyman. In early life Campbell developed a wild and reckless nature, and soon passed beyond the control of his father. He spent the most of his time in the woods, hunting, fishing, and trapping—in all of which pursuits he excelled his associates. Being well educated, he became the recognized leader of the class of men with whom he associated. During the war he was a noted bushwhacker and guerilla, and proved a great annoyance to both armies in their operations in Tennessee. No efforts were spared, the while, to secure the arrest of Morgan and his gang, but all to no purpose.

Immediately after the close of hostilities, the Government levied a tax upon all spirits manufactured within the Republic. This afforded Morgan a fresh opportunity to continue hostile operations against the Government, and defy the laws of his country. He therefore began the illicit manufacture of whisky in the Cumberland mountains—sometimes in Tennessee and sometimes in Kentucky. Soon he became the head-centre of the moonshiners of all that section of country. Being a brave and daring man, the officers were not disposed to attack him, and for years he cut a broad and shameful swathe in the history of Southern Kentucky and Middle Tennessee.

Tiring, however, in holding out so long against the laws of his country, he wrote a letter to Commissioner Raum, of the Office of Internal Revenue at Washington, in which he proposed to give up his illicit operations—which, however, he maintained were legitimate and lawful—provided he was assured of protection in the future. To this impertinent communication General Raum replied as follows:

Treasury Department, Office of Internal Revenue, Washington, D.C., November 18th, 1878.
"CAMPBELL MORGAN, Esq., Gainsboro, Tenn.:

"Sir:—I am in receipt of your letter of the 9th inst., in which you give an account of the difficulty which occurred in April last, at the time of the seizure of your distillery.

"I must compliment you upon the ingenuity displayed in presenting yourself as an unoffending citizen, peaceably pursuing his avocations, and the officers of the United States as violators of the law. It is obvious, from your own admissions, that the internal revenue officers would not have visited your premises if you had not been engaged in violating the laws of the United States and defrauding it of its resources. By your act your distillery had become forfeited to the Government, and you had subjected yourself to the penalties of fine and imprisonment. Under these circumstances the officers were entirely justified in entering upon your premises.

"The use of the young men, 'who had just left the still house,' 'as breastworks,' was evidently done to deter you from resisting the officers by the use of fire arms. You state that, 'under these circumstances, a difficulty ensued.' I learn, from the report of the officers, that you forced the difficulty, and that they acted in self defense in the use of fire arms.

"To me it is a matter of extreme regret that it is necessary, in the enforcement of the laws of the United States, that officers should go around ready to defend their lives against assault and to meet force with force. In this free country of ours every citizen should have such a love of the Government and its laws as to cheerfully give obedience to their provisions, and not be found engaged in defrauding it of its revenues, or forcibly resisting, with fire arms, the officers engaged in the enforcement of the laws.

"The frauds upon the revenue by the illicit manufacture and sale of whisky have become so widespread, and the loss to the revenue so great, that the Government is determined to leave nothing undone to suppress these frauds, and bring the offenders to punishment, and you may rest assured that the efforts now being made to suppress these frauds will be continued and constantly increased until the desired result is attained.

"You say that you never intended to violate the spirit of the law, and you invite an investigation of your character for truth, honesty, sobriety, industry and peace. It is not necessary to discuss the question of your intentions. They are to be judged by your acts; and the establishing of an illicit distillery and operating it for years, as you admit, without paying tax upon the product, is conclusive evidence that you not only intended to violate the letter but the spirit of the law. Without having a knowledge of your character for truth, sobriety and industry, I deem it unnecessary to discuss it. I leave it to your sense of right whether a man can be considered honest who defrauds the Government of its revenue, or peaceful who, with arms in his hands, resists the enforcement of the law.

"There is no disposition to enforce the law in a vindictive spirit, but, on the contrary, I am very desirous of inspiring the people with respect for the law and a disposition to observe it. The difficulty in your case is that, not satisfied with resisting the officers some months ago, you assisted in besieging them for nearly two days and nights, in which affair three officers were wounded.

"I am glad to know that you have determined to abandon the business of violation of the law, but I am not advised of any reasons that would warrant a pardon in your case.

"Very Respectfully,

Green B. Raum, Commissioner."

Morgan was subsequently arrested, and, after paying the fine assessed against him, and serving out his required term of imprisonment, he accepted the position of a deputy United States marshal; and for upwards of two years, he has been engaged in arresting his former associates—in which business he has been remarkably successful. He and Capt. Davis are now sworn friends—while at one time they were deadly enemies —and they now frequently operate together in their efforts to suppress violations of law. Davis says Morgan is as true a man as he ever knew, and he would be willing to trust him in any emergency.

CHAPTER SIX

The Moonshiner at Work and at Play

The presence of effective federal forces and a policy of turning illicit distillers into legal distillers seemed to be working as the early 1880's began. A few of the most hardened moonshiners, or wildcatters as they were sometimes called, accustomed themselves to living with stamp taxes and being reminded occasionally of all the new laws which would make the penalty for illicit distilling even more severe than it had been. Still, the government storekeepers and gaugers who kept a sharp eye on their supply and activities were not a welcome sight to the reformed moonshiner, month after month. Talk abounded that the revenue offices and the agents were really Republican recruiting offices, and suppressing illicit whiskey making was only a part of the job.

Reluctant compliance with federal law continued among many of the ex-moonshiners, and still seizures continued to drop. After 1882, federal seizures dropped below five hundred annually, for the first time in bureau history. The downward spiral continued until 1886 when an upward movement of illicit activity appeared to be in the offing.

The whole whiskey issue seemed to be getting more confused by the day. Everybody was talking about it more and more, and nobody seemed to lack an outspoken opinion. The temperance societies, which had been quieted to some degree by the war, were being heard all across the land again. Some of their ideas even a half-literate moonshiner might understand. One of the many problems which they saw as catastrophic was the problem of the Negro drinker. Thousands of newly freed Negroes must not have the opportunity to be turned into drunken rapists, murderers, and assailants. That was one way to look at the matter, but then again nobody loved a good drink of white mule any more than a newly freed slave.

The prohibitionist sentiment was being felt by everybody except maybe the moonshiner so far back in the hills that he knew nothing of the issues of the day. The storm was gathering from a number of sources. The Prohibition Party, organized in 1868, would have a great deal to do with the future of the moonshiner, but few of either group were fully aware of such a fact just yet. Temperance societies attempted to close ranks and harden their attack on the entire liquor industry, both legal and illegal. Their loud voices cried out against the distilleries they labeled "hell's kettles," and no less a target of their wrath were the city saloons and tippling houses where evil men gathered. Liquor-license control, in addition, felt the weight of their influence, and the public support they had garnered was effective in suppressing liquor sales near churches and schools in several states. As the temperance societies and the prohibitionists continued the onslaught, the moonshiners stepped up their activities. Many fellow moonshiners who had gone legal now decided the best future lay in doing their "stillin' " unsupervised. While the North and South argued about the real reasons for prohibition, he would just start slipping further back into the mountains. Word had reached his ears that whiskey was getting scarce in some areas and that door-to-door salesmen were beginning to operate and that some people were even driving a long distance to drugstores for a "prescription."

The late 1800's was the beginning of what history would call the romantic era of the American moonshiner. Legal distilling companies were converting rapidly to the higher volume, more complex and costly column stills. Before long the moonshiner could have a near monopoly on pot distilling. After 1878, when the government allowed the legal industry a three-year bonding period for which whiskey could be held without tax, the legal distillers had overproduced. Their efforts to form pools and trusts to control output and prices had brought down the wrath of government in the form of the Sherman Anti-Trust Act to counter such monopolies. After this period and with the black mark of the Whiskey Ring fifteen years behind them, the legal industry seemed destined to operate in harmonious concert with the federal government with only occasional exceptions.

With the legal distillers under the close scrutiny of government, the Southern moonshiners had a whole new opportunity open to them, but few were so wise as to see the range of it. For the most part their new activities would be predicated on instinct and force of habit. Northern moonshining had dropped to practically nothing in the late 1880's, and there would certainly be no competition here even if the southern practitioner had been concerned about such. What little activity there was in the North centered around New York and New Jersey, chiefly involving moonshining of rum and occasional grain spirits. A revenue agent's job there was vastly different from trudging the hills and hollows of the rural and small-town South. An agent's climbing duties in New York or New Jersey would be over rooftops, smelling chimneys for the telltale aroma of distilling molasses—or watching suspicious movement around the sugar and molasses houses. If he saw no questionable comings and goings, he might pause at a series of alley doorways and listen for bungs being driven into recently filled barrels.

The revenooer well earned his pay of about a thousand dollars per year in the pursuit of the elusive and knowledgeable mountaineer. The moonshiner soon came to have a profound respect for his adversary, too, but it was only after the revenooer had proved himself. In the early years, the revenue agent assigned to areas unfamiliar to him was on occasion new to the ways of the mountains. He could only know the woodsman through experience, and learn he did. From the beginning to the present day the job would be a sort of guerrilla warfare, and the early revenue agent was not found wanting for very long.

There was much to learn, and no manuals of instruction were available. However, no agent was on the job for very long without knowing the work was physically hard and seething with danger.

In the earliest years of the revenooers' raiding duties, many of the illicit stills were housed in permanent or semipermanent stillhouses. Before the whiskey tax came into being in 1862, the stillhouse had been a permanent fixture, the same as the barn or any other building. Even after the advent of federal taxation many a determined distiller didn't bother to move it or to take out a distilling license. Some vowed from the beginning they would not move, dismantle, or discontinue operation of their still on anybody's terms even if a shootout happened to be the result. It was. Before many shootouts, the stillhouses were being relocated in concealed areas away from the house. In many instances they still remained permanent structures, for the moonshiner meant to stay in business, year around and in any kind of weather. The stillhouse did change somewhat in design, however; the newer ones had "portholes" through which a moonshiner could safely look out and, if need be, push his rifle through and aim it accurately. As the pressure mounted and bullets kept knocking the chink and daub from between the logs, the permanent stillhouse declined in functional application. Future stillhouses would be semipermanent in deep-woods locations or just a simple roof over a secluded work area. Many moonshiners used no structure at all and resorted to the use of caves or cliff overhangs. The location needed to be near a stream of cool water, and this knowledge did help the revenooer considerably. The revenooer always felt at an advantage when raiding a moonshining operation in a cave. For one thing, after he found the moonshiner, he had him cornered, and secondly the fire or lanterns were always nearer the offenders, putting them in the light and the revenooer in darkness. Such an advantageous situation made a gun fight less likely, for the moonshiner realized the revenooer already had the drop on him.

The revenue agent soon became a proficient detective. By watching the small mountain streams as he walked in the woodland, a revenooer could sometimes spot bits of cornmeal or other residue floating down the water. Such tell-tale evidence of waste disposal could often lead him to the location of the still. The mere taste of the water would sometimes tell him if mash (ingredients to be distilled) had overflown. After the revenooer had really become expert at his job and trained his nose, he could sometimes smell a distilling location a considerable distance away.

The moonshiner resented being pushed into the mountains to operate, for more than reasons of pride. His distilling could benefit him in many ways. The leftover mash, after distilling, made excellent feed for his swine, and it angered him to be so far back in the mountains that it could not be so used and ended up wasted in a gully or went floating down a mountain branch, useless and maybe contributory to his seizure.

The revenooer couldn't always take credit for locating a still. Often, the moonshiner had an enemy or competitor who would do him in. This practice became especially widespread when the federal government started paying witness fees and travel expenses to court. Many a hungry or greedy mountaineer risked such an adventure for the $1.50 and five cents per mile his gamble might pay him. The moonshiner hated this practice and sometimes discouraged it by the assassination of such a cooperative citizen. The moonshiners were never successful in stopping this practice of informing, but they kept it to a minimum by threats, occasional acts of violence, and coercion. Sometimes one moonshiner would report another. On one such occasion a moonshiner wrote to a revenue officer to come and see him "for information I have of interest." When the revenue officer arrived on the scene, a third party passed on the word that the reporting moonshiner had killed his competitor and there was no need of the revenooer to be bothered. Many citizens in heavy moonshining territory remained on the side of the moonshiner. Some did so from fear, and others genuinely believed in the right of the moonshiner to practice his trade. The frustration to the revenue agents in areas of staunch support became maddening at times. On many raids after painstakingly planning and preparation, someone in the community would spot them and start the "horn blowing." The horn blowing was the mountaineer's early-warning system and consisted of the following plan: Upon seeing suspected revenooers enter a village or remote mountain area, the first sympathetic observer to see them would sound a horn (usually a horn of an animal, or gourd, fashioned for such use, or for dog calling, etc.). Before the melody of the first horn had echoed back from the mountains, the next horn blower had passed on the warning. This continued across every ridge for miles, and as a result the revenooer could expect one of two things upon his arrival at the scene; the moonshiners would all be gone or he would find himself staring down the barrel of a loaded gun.

Some of the moonshiners of this period were indeed vicious men who had not the least hesitancy in gunning down any man who stood in the way of their freedom of makin'. The reputations of such men for fearlessness sometimes traveled before them, exceeding the opinion of their pursuers. Witness this comment from the memoirs of George W. Atkinson, revenue agent of the period:

> Redmond is the best known, and the most dreaded of all the moonshiners of the south. He is to-day, perhaps regarded as the most notorious character in America. Just how he became so distinguished is a mystery to those who know him best. In point of fact Redmond is not specially dangerous, nor is he, in a true sense, either brave or daring.
>
> Redmond was born in the northern part of South Carolina, not far from the base of the Great Smoky mountains, and is at this time about thirty-seven years of age. He is almost entirely

uneducated, but has a good deal of the native cunning and shrewdness so common among moonshiners. Bishop Simpson claims that grand mountains inspire the persons who live near them, or among them, with grand ideas; that such people inherently possess minds capable of greater power, and certainly broader sweeps of imagination, than any other people. The physical climbing of mountains, which they are so often required to do, imbues them with the thoughts of intellectual development—a climbing up, as it were, from the valley of ignorance to the heights of knowledge.

Redmond, at best, is a very ordinary man. He is five feet ten inches tall; is of light build; has blue eyes, and rather light colored hair. For a number of years he has been engaged in manufacturing moonshine whisky in Southern North Carolina, where he now resides, and until within a few weeks past, has successfully evaded the vigilance of the officers. Becoming tired of moonshining, he gave it up for a while, and devoted his time to farming a little tract of land which he owns in Ashe county, North Carolina. But he did not continue long in this legitimate pursuit, and again went back to moonshining. The officers succeeded in locating his distillery, and one dark night crept up on Mr. Redmond, destroyed his establishment and arrested him. He is now in prison at Greensboro, North Carolina. He will shortly be tried, and, no doubt, justly punished.

Some two or three years since, a pamphlet, purporting to give a correct narrative of Redmond's life and adventures, was given to the public, and had a wide sale. The writer of that work, made Redmond one of the most distinguished characters, for daring and adventure, of the nineteenth century. From personal knowledge of my own, and from facts derived from United States officers in the two Carolinas, I pronounce the whole story a fabrication and a myth.

Redmond has killed two men, and only two, in his entire career; and when the Federal authorities get through with him, I am informed he will be tried in the State courts for murder. Generally, men's crimes come home to them in the end. Like all outlaws, Redmond has run out his career of crime, and now he is required to pay the penalties of his infraction of the laws.

From the pamphlet above referred to, I quote a few paragraphs, narrating one of Redmond's adventures. It is perhaps, untrue, as applied to Redmond, but it graphically pictures scenes which I myself have once or twice witnessed. . . .

"One fine morning, I left our stronghold in the Smoky

mountains, driving a stout pair of mules, which were attached to a canvas covered wagon, in the body of which, hidden under a pile of corn husks, were five barrels of the precious fluid. My destination was Asheville, where I could find a customer for the liquor. The road was an ordinary mountain trail, and I drove all day without meeting any one. The sun was just sinking behind the mountains, when three men, whom I immediately recognized as deputy-marshals, same suddenly upon me at a cross-road. I was disguised with a beard and butternut clothes so effectually that my dearest friend would not have recognized me; and although my heart throbbed a little faster as the three horsemen approached, I was outwardly calm and collected, and regarded them curiously as they drew nearer. Their uniform was concealed under heavy cloaks; but their holsters contained pistols, and they had Winchester repeating rifles thrown over their shoulders. My wagon had nothing suspicious about it. The fly was up, and the shucks looked very innocent. When they reached me they drew their horses to one side, and the leader of the party, whose name was Crowder, accosted me as follows:

" 'Howdy, neighbor?'

" 'Howdy, gentlemen?' I replied, touching my hat, 'powerful fine weather we'uns are hevin!'

" 'Yes,' said one of the marshals.

"I reined up my mules, and Crowder again took up the conversation.

" 'Can you tell me,' he said, 'where we can get some whisky? We are strangers in this section, and are dry as herrings.'

" 'Gentlemen,' I replied, still imitating the uncouth twang of the crackers, 'whisky is mitey hard to git. Thar's so meny uv these hyar dep'ty marshals 'round that we'uns are 'fraid to tech the pesky stuff.'

"At this they all laughed, and Crowder continued:

" 'I believe the marshals do create considerable disturbance among you occasionally, but we don't want to buy much—just enough to fill our flasks.'

" 'Well, now, gentlemen,' I said, with a cunning leer, 'you can't prove it by me that you'uns haint marshals!'

"They laughed again, louder than before, and one of the marshals denied that they were revenue officers.

" 'You know all about these illicit distilleries,' said Crowder, 'and I believe you've got blockade liquor hidden under those shucks.'

" 'Well, now, gentlemen,' I said, with a look of surprise, 'you'uns hev hit the nail right on the head. I heve got a leetle moonshine hyar, and I run a pow'rful risk in conveyin' hit; but hit's only a few gallon that I use for my stomach's sake. I more'n believe that you are rev'nue officers; but you seem tolerbul clever, and if you'uns will promise not to say anythin' about it, I'll let you heve a little.'

"This frank confession of mine rather staggered them, but I saw that it threw them off the scent, and still laughing, they produced their flasks. I had a jug containing about three gallons under the wagon seat, and taking this out I filled their bottles and handed them back. Crowder offered to pay for the liquor, but with assumed cunning I answered him that the acceptance of money for the liquor would lay me liable to arrest. At their invitation I drank with them, and then whipping up my mules, drove on, having completely hoodwinked them by this shrewd trick. I sold my liquor in Asheville, made some necessary purchases and reached the mountain again without further adventure. Afterwards I made many similar trips, and always with success."

Few of the moonshiners were getting rich in this era for it was not yet the period when easy transportation could enhance the productivity of the most progressive moonshiner. Quality of moonshine whiskey was excellent, but even so, two dollars to three dollars per gallon was about the top retail price at the still and even lower if a moonshiner was in need of some ready cash. Youngsters weren't immune from illicit activity, and many of them helped at the still or helped to gather and transport the makin's needed for continuous running. An especially bright boy might carry his opportunity further and mix some "high wines" with a dose of fresh spring water and peddle the white-mule relaxer at a community picnic.

The moonshiner had his everyday problems though, just like any other businessman. Sometimes, innocent adventurers would stumble by his still and see the whole operation. He had a solution for that problem too. Such persons would be required to perform some work for a few moments, any kind of task to make them legally a party to the operation. Their assignment might be to cut green wood for the still furnace or help unload grain. The idea in making the accidental visitor a party to the work was to insure his silence. If he reported the moonshiner, the moonshiner could swear honestly that the "reporter" was a party to the illicit act.

Going to the still on a Monday morning to begin the day's work often held some discovery that was downright discouraging. It was not an unusual sight to see the mash boxes empty or turned over and the whole work area in disarray. Occasionally, the guilty offender was still on the scene—in the person of a drunken bear. One moonshiner of the period recalled such an incident and added a few facts which will be strictly up to the reader to believe or not: On a warm day in September near the southern Tennessee border, a moonshiner approached his still on a Sunday morning. He would be missed at the Primitive Baptist church for the service, but the mash was ready to run—it was that simple. He was in the midst of mash barrels and the area of the still before he noticed three bears completely relaxed, stomachs bulging and propped against three separate trees in a human sitting position. Being considerably frightened and outnumbered three to one, the moonshiner started to climb the nearest tree. The bears, seeing his attempt to evade the party, staggered to their feet. After a few moments of drunken disorientation, the bears converged on the poor moonshiner, who had managed to shinny only a short distance up the tree. When the moonshiner was pulled to the ground, terrified, a grand idea born of fright occurred to him. He couldn't fight the bears, but there was another alternative to save his life— he would make love to them. After scratching the belly of all three and rendering other body manipulations which put all three bears in a reclining position with a toothy grin of complete relaxation, the moonshiner plotted his escape. In a quick dash for freedom, the moonshiner cleared the first quarter mile of distance but felt his hair stand on end from the ferocity of the growls at his heels. Turning just long enough to look back, he witnessed the three bears panting behind him and running on their hind legs—not with their fangs flaring but motioning frantically with front paws cupped, come back! come back! come back!

The moonshining clans also had their Judases among them. The betrayal would usually come when the revenooers were getting close to a stilling operation and the betrayer was reasonably sure the raid would succeed. His motive would be immunity from prosecution or a light sentence and the witness fee his action would profit him—if he lived through it all. The same arrangement could, and often was, used for a ruse or a money-making venture. It was not unusual for one moonshiner to make a purchase from another moonshiner and finance the transaction by false witnessing and mileage fees. The arrangement would work like this: Moonshiner A would buy a cow from Moonshiner B with the understanding that payment would be made by X number of court appearances as a witness against several fabricated distilling operations (hatched up between the two of them). The addition of travel expenses figured in sometimes exceeded the purchase price of the cow, and the leftover amount could be used for more distilling equipment.

Fabricated evidence and habitual tale tellers became a real problem for the courts and revenue agents, but experience allowed the revenue agents to become more proficient in judging the validity of a report. Threats of prosecution against false reporting, by the revenooers and the courts too, no doubt had a bearing on keeping the opportunist in line.

A federal judge not accustomed to prosecuting moonshiners was obliged to preside over a series of trials that promised to be challenging if not downright dangerous. The first week of the trials had gone very well with a minimum of difficulty, and the judge seemed to feel a great deal of pride in his disposition of the matters before him—in fact he was beginning to have a real "feel" for the little North Carolina town and the people of the area. Musing over his current situation, the judge took a Sunday morning walk from his hotel, and found himself caught in a shower while walking down a country road. The trees offered him shelter until the shower passed, but returning down the road back toward the hotel, his shoes became saturated with mud. As he crossed a wooden bridge, he stamped each foot a few times to dislodge the mud and walked on. At the end of the bridge he was met by an overall-clad hillbilly, laden down with gallon-sized demijohns. "Can you carry all seven gallons, boss, or you want me to unhitch the mule?" the stranger from under the bridge asked politely. The judge remained silent in confusion, and the moonshiner reiterated: "I heer'd you right didn't I, boss? You did stomp seven times, didn't ja?"

A stomp on a bridge was only one of many ways to make a purchase of mountain dew. Every hill and hollow in moonshining country had an outlet. The "hollowing tree" was always a well-known spot. This retail outlet worked by a sign on a certain tree, saying, "Leave $2.00 and come back in 15 minutes." In fifteen minutes the two dollars would be gone, and the jug would be filled, with neither party speaking to the other. Sometimes a traveler would see a four-by-four shack along the road with a boy or older woman lounging therein, apparently idle. Upon being approached, a conversation with the proprietor might go something like this:

"Howdy. I was wonderin' if you might know where I could get some good quality squeezin's hereabouts?"

"Don't know ifin I can help you none. Good likker is a mighty scarce item, mighty scarce. You strangers hereabouts?"

"Yep, we're traveling through to Nashville. Sure would appreciate somethin' to wet our whistles."

"You're right sure you hain't revenooers?"

"No'am, ain't no chance of that." (Silence, while the eyes of the would-be purchasers are studied intently.)

"Well I hain't got none, but I got an idee whur there is some. You give me your money and wait here awhile."

The roadside shack would be vacated for half an hour, and the "order" would come down out of the woods to the rear of the shack. No moonshiner ever made such a claim, but it is possible the first drive-in in America might have originated in moonshining country.

The town or city user of mountain dew might have his delivered by buying a bushel of peaches. After receipt of the basket, three dozen peaches would be taken off the top to reveal four jugs filled to the top and plugged with corncobs. Nor were salesmen lacking in those days. A stranger might be called out on his porch at night by a voice which carried a strange inflection: "Is your stommik in good order today, brother?" Or, "Ye reckon the makin' will be good in the dark of the moon?" Such offhand questioning made the point without waste of words, and the sale was made or declined. City sales were made through bellhops at the hotels or on the street corners. A prospective buyer might be approached by a moonshiner/bootlegger with the following question: "Would ye like to take some mountain mineral water back home to yur ailin' grandpappy?" If a stranger didn't get it that way, a discreet inquiry to a livery-stable operator or a hardware store would get results. If the town had a saloon or tippling house, the stranger could usually get moonshine or legal whiskey, whichever he preferred, from at least one such establishment along his journey. If the town had no such place, he could bet with certainty a good drink was just a stone's throw away—all he had to do was find it.

There was great rejoicing among the moonshiners during those periods when federal courts were in session—great rejoicing we should say among those moonshiners who had no "invitation" to be in attendance. At this period it was almost a sure bet most of the revenue agents would be in attendance, leaving the moonshiner free to go about his work or rebuild a recently destroyed distilling operation. Such rebuilding added the impetus to use more ingenuity in construction. One way to conceal an illicit operation, if one's cabin happened to be near a cave, was to run stove pipes from the still in the cave, up through the ground under the cabin floor. Continuing up through the cabin and out the roof allowed for the expulsion of innocent-looking smoke.

Not every moonshiner of the period was mean by nature. Some, on occasion, would go to great lengths to avoid trouble. One moonshiner had the word spread by confederates that he had been killed. Sure enough, when revenue agents went to his cabin, blood appeared all over the cabin floor (where the moonshiner had slaughtered a chicken and used the blood to accomplish that very appearance). It's a reasonable guess that the conniving moonshiner enjoyed a few months of stillin', for nobody would be looking for a dead man.

Neither was the triangle of love absent from the life of the moonshiner. On one occasion, a rural schoolhouse dance was the opening scene of the final hours of freedom for a young, handsome moonshiner. The moonshiner had made the tragic mistake of dancing too much with a buxom young mountain girl who was not his steady girl friend. The steady girl friend fumed all night after the dance was over and took her action next day by reporting the young man to the revenooers. She didn't stop there, however, but personally led the federal men to his still. It can be assumed she waited for his release from prison, hopeful that in the future he would toe the line.

One of the tragedies that befell both the revenooer and the moonshiner was the terrible suffering both on occasion were called upon to bear. In gunfights, of which there were many, the wounded were usually miles from the nearest doctor. There was great bravery and courage among the men of both groups, and a strange affinity between them has existed from that day down to the present, as every ATF special investigator will testify. A battle between opposing forces was not lacking on occasion for acts of chivalry and honor. In the heat of battle, many a seriously wounded investigator has asked for and received the privilege of withdrawal. Others were not so lucky. Many moonshiners had no scruples at all, and any display of honor was foreign to their nature. Anonymous letters were often sent to revenue men by moonshiners offering surrender or cooperation. When the officer arrived at the scene, an ambush was his reward.

The revenue man was more often than not a fine and daring individual for whom even the most outrageous moonshiner had a professional respect; some grew in reputation as to strike fear in the breasts of their adversary. Such a man of the period was James M. Davis, and while the graphic picture of him is painted in the lines below by a fellow officer, it is doubtful the moonshiners who knew of him or who had felt his wrath would find much of the résumé to be disputable insofar as his professional reputation was concerned.

> James M. Davis, the distinguished revenue officer, raider, and scout, is a native of Tennessee, and is, at this writing, in the thirty-third year of his age. He is six feet two and one-half inches tall; is large boned, and muscular, and tips the beam at two hundred and ten pounds avoirdupois. Although of great courage, and physical strength and endurance, he is one of the kindest hearted and most gentle natured of men. The individuals against whom he has operated for violations of law, quake at the bare mention of his name; and yet, when he has made an arrest, he never fails to win the affection of the prisoner. He has arrested upwards of three thousand violators of the law, and I am credibly informed there is scarcely one of this vast number of wrong doers, who would not divide his last dime and morsel with Davis; and, if necessary, would even shed his blood in his defence.
>
> Capt. Davis has all of the peculiarities of the woodsmen of the South. He looks like a back-woods-man, and he possesses much of the native shrewdness, activity and daring of the Indians. He lives much in the woods, and is intimate with nearly all the by-paths and deep recesses of the Cumberland mountains. Though comparatively uneducated, he remedies

this disadvantage by having a remarkably retentive memory and keen perceptive faculties. He is a correct judge of human nature, and possesses every trait necessary to a man who exhibits quick decision, and prompt action. When entering on a man's trail, he acquaints himself with all that man's habits and movement, and all this time never allows his intentions to be discovered, until he catches his quarry, which he does generally, napping, and then he coolly takes him in.

Capt. Davis is, therefore, well up in all the requirements and acquirements of a detective and scout. To begin with, his physical strength and power of endurance are wonderful. He can tie any ordinary man once he gets his hands upon him. He has been known to travel, afoot and on horseback, four days and nights, without rest, refreshment, or sleep. He is a superior woodsman and rarely loses his way, though often in strange localities and imbedded deeply in dense woods and high mountains. He is an expert marksman, estimates distances correctly, and when he pulls the trigger of his Henry rifle, something is sure to bite the dust. He is a natural born leader and commander of men. Had he been educated, and taught the military art, he would, no doubt, have proved himself a chieftain, of no ordinary rank.

Neither was the revenooers work all shoot, kill, climb, search, and destroy. Situations developed whereby his social reform efforts could be put to good use. One opportunity involved a still raid during which a woman moonshiner was captured. Revenue men learned from the woman that she was stillin' in order to pay the lawyer his fees for defending her husband. The husband had been caught for makin' and sent to prison, and the investigators were convinced the woman was sincerely raising money the only way she knew how. They could not refrain from destroying her still, but they did promise to talk to the judge about her situation and press the lawyer in question for a reduction or a delay in payment of her husband's fee.

Neither was the moonshiner without his more human side. There were times when he was grateful for being detoured from his illegal business and thanked the investigators accordingly. Such men were not in the majority, but they did exist. The more determined ones would live on and propagate a new generation of illegal distillers.

On occasions of celebration, some of the moonshiners could

be jovial. One of their favorite methods of celebration was a "pine knot" feast at the still. This affair was held at the conclusion of a long and successful run (free of arrest or bad luck) when the output was heavy and profits looked generous. The moonshiner's friends, family, and still helpers would carry food into the mountains and sit around the still to feast. Pine knots would be lighted and suspended from trees or plunged into the ground between forked sticks, to provide illumination. Needless to say, before such an event was enjoyed, the absence of revenooers in the area would be ascertained and the horn blowers put on special guard.

The moonshiner also liked mountain-music sessions, and none could go on or be properly performed without a contribution of at least some of his squeezin's. Coon hunting and bee-tree cutting also were favorite pastimes. The moonshiner's love for his hounds is legendary and he liked "fox and the goose" games, "gander pullings," "coon baitin'," hunting and trapping.*

The old pun "she was a moonshiner's daughter but he loved her still," brings to mind another colorful aspect of the moonshiner's social life and customs. Nearly every moonshiner took fierce pride in his daughters (this was not overtly demonstrated, but it was understood). Especially was this so if she was his willing helper and had become expertly knowledgeable in his occupation. If she happened to be really beautiful, she was the queen not only to her father but the grand duchess of the whole moonshining community. The marriage of such a girl (sometimes within the

---

* The Fox and the Goose" was a game played with a marked board and corn grains, and was somewhat similar to checkers; except that one player was the fox and the other the goose. The fox had to catch the goose to win the game.

"Gander Pulling" was a rather cruel sport of the mountains. A gander (male goose) was hung by the feet to a high tree limb and his neck greased. Ringmasters then lined up participating riders who would go in a gallop under the tree, all the while making a lunge at the greased neck of the gander. The gander's neck was hard to break at best, but thoroughly greased, it took repeated effort. At the expense of being called an amateur psychologist, this sport, though cruel by standards of today, did serve a purpose. It was one of the many ways a mean mountain man vented his hostility. Without sports of this kind and many others like it, that hostility was sure to find its outlet toward another human being.

"Coon Baitin' " was simply the capturing and training of a raccoon to do astounding tricks. A squirrel was also used on occasion.

clan of another moonshining community) was a colorful event that would be memorable even by the standards of today. It began in the following manner: Six bridesmaids gathered at the home of the bride where they awaited the arrival of the groom's escort. Also waiting was the entire complement of citizenry within possible reach. On horseback, the groom and his escort of six youths departed from his home in time to reach their destination by noon. The cavalcade was led by a young man carrying a flag of red, white, and blue handkerchiefs, and the pace they set was limited only by the speed of the horses and not the nature of the road.

Circling the home of the bride thrice, they dismounted and entered the living room where a long table was set for the wedding dinner or infare. Behind this table were aligned fourteen chairs, and in the seven on the right-hand side sat the bride and her attendants. The groom and his escort marched in and took the other seven chairs.

At each end of the table stood a miniature cedar, emblematic of long life and happiness for the bridal couple. The bride wore something white and something blue, something old and something new.

The bearded old hardshell preacher faced the party across the table and when the charge and ceremony had ended, and the bride had sworn her obedience to her husband, the bridal party and the guests came forward in single file to give expression to the formal "I wish you'uns much joy and happiness." Then came the infare, for which the table was loaded with every edible known to the hill country, and the guests ate in relays throughout most of the afternoon.

Among the necessities for the infare were "busses," "ginger cakes," "kisses," "bear-claws," "stack cakes" with apple-butter icing, "burr flour bread," and "matrimony cakes," these being edibles of various shapes and sizes, rarely used save for the nuptial ceremonies. The infare over, the room was cleared for the square dance, and until dawn the string band played the Figure Eight, Building the Star, the Irishman's Trot, Ladies' Do-Si-Do, Cross-Eyed Snap, and the Virginia Reel. The intricacies of these dances, which were executed with a beautiful skill, must have appeared to border on the marvelous in the eyes of the uninitiated observer.

The string band consisted of a fiddle, banjo, and sometimes a guitar, dulcimer, and autoharp. The musical repertoire included "Money Musk," "The Fisherman's Hornpipe," "Old Dan Tucker," "Turkey in the Straw," "Sourwood Mountain," "Little Brown Jug," "Chicken in the Breadtray" and numerous other mountain ballads.

With the coming of dawn the dance was halted, and the wedding party departed for the home of the groom, riding behind the flag. When arriving within "a whoop an' a holler" of the groom's home, shots were fired by the groom's escort and then came the reverberating notes of the Bride's Salute. This was a call of welcome by the parents of the groom, blown through the tube of a gourd or animal horn. The bride and groom were left alone after a final serenade and allowed to retire upstairs and consummate their marriage. The coming of night, however, demanded presence of all the wedding party for the final all-night dance at the home of the groom. On the dawning of the next day the celebration was over, and everyone returned to his home.

The cunning of the moonshiner is legend. Any trick ever conceived in the mind of man was probably tried by him time and again. After the days of revenooer penetration into the southland, the moonshiner did indeed work by the light of the moon on occasion. This still failed to stop the revenooer, though the going was difficult in darkness and through treacherous, wooded territory not familiar to the revenue men. The moonshiner fought back by sending out a man with a decoy torch, when evidence of the raiders in his area was suspected. The decoy torch was a lighted pine knot or other improvised torch, which would be planted high on a ridge far from the actual scene of the distilling activity, to draw the revenooers away from the real location. Time could thus be gained to finish a run, and then a movement could be made to another secluded location. The decoy was sometimes not so harmless. A torch or a fabricated distilling operation was sometimes placed on the side of a deep ravine, opposite the direction from which the agents would be approaching. The idea was to lure the revenooers over the edge of the cliff before they realized what was happening to them. On these occasions a revenue officer might be saved by the instinct of a trusted horse and not his own awareness of danger.

Trickery was used in the courtroom as well as in the mountains. Let us return into history almost a hundred years to a courtroom in Nashville, Tennessee, and listen to the comments of a man who came to know moonshiners well. This was the period in moonshining history when the government sought to eliminate the problem in certain states by a blanket pardon, if the moonshiner promised to give up his illegal occupation. The narrator is George W. Atkinson:

> Raiding moonshiners enables one to meet with all of Dickens' characters, and with a great many more that observant writer overlooked. They embrace all classes of men and women, and when you get back into the mountains, they are seemingly a race peculiar to themselves. Court days are the occasions when they usually congregate. I have seen as many as eight hundred of these rough mountaineers in attendance upon the United States Court at one time. This, however, is an unusually large number to find at one court, and would not have occurred in this instance had it not been for an offer of pardon by the Attorney General of the United States, extended to all violators of revenue laws in certain States, up to that particular time. The idea of being forgiven for past crimes upon the mere promise of good behavior in the future, was too good an opportunity to be lost, hence the multiude that thronged the United States court room at Nashville, Tenn., in the spring of 1879, who came to have their moonshine sins forgiven.
>
> The average moonshiner dresses in homespun, has long hair, has meal and still-beer on his clothing, and rarely, if ever, cleans himself up or tries to look neat and comely. The witnesses are usually of the same class; and when a hundred or two of these odd looking characters fill up a court room, waiting for their cases to be called, they present an unsightly, not to say ludicrous, appearance.
>
> While these parties are roughly clad, are uncultured, and know but little of the ways of the world, many of them possess an unusual amount of native good sense, and appear in court as their own counsellors, managing their own cases shrewdly, and often successfully. I call to mind the case of a Baptist preacher who was brought into court on the charge of illicit distilling, and for bartering "the ardent" also.
>
> The old gentleman appeared greatly surprised that a minister of the gospel should be arrested and dragged into court, for no other offence than *making a little liquor for medicine*. He was a man of considerable property, and knowing himself to be guilty, and fearing that the court might convict him, he

brought $700 along with him, but was shrewd enough to let no one about the court house know he had that much money. When he reached the city of L——, where the United States Court was in session, he inquired of the marshal if he knew of a prominent Baptist layman to whom he could be introduced. The marshal responded in the affirmative and took his *reverence* around and gave him the desired introduction. The sequel showed that at this interview our ministerial brother asked the other, the layman, to take care of the $700 until he would call for it—being careful, business like, to take a receipt for the money. Then the old psalm singer went into court and took his seat among the lawyers at the bar. When his case was called, the old man arose to his feet, with the ejaculation, "Your honor, I am the man." His manner and appearance attracted general attention. Feeling in his pockets for his spectacles, and finding he had left them at home, after looking around the court room, he turned to the judge and exclaimed: "Jedge, I see you are a man about my age, will you be kind enough to loan me your specks for a few minutes." The effrontery of the old parson created general merriment, and while the court and bar were enjoying a hearty laugh, the judge sent his spectacles to the old moonshiner by a bailiff. Holding up the glasses and while rubbing them vigorously with a faded cotton handkerchief, he proceeded to remark: "Jedge, them's might nice lookin' specks. They are yaller and look as though they mout be gold. Are they gold or brass, jedge?" Here the excitement was intense, and all in the court room were laughing. But the parson was not the least disturbed. After adjusting the glasses properly, he picked up a book and began to scan its pages. His uncouth actions and the sublimity of effrontery which he displayed, brought down the house. Again he turned to the judge, and remarked "Jedge, these is fine specks, but they are a little too young for me; and I'm sure I wouldn't thought so, seein' as how you are so gray headed; but gray hairs is not allers a sign of age. There's my old woman, she's whiter headed nor you are, jedge, and she's ten years younger nor me, so you see that's no sign. [Renewed laughter, and cries of "order," by the judge.] Now, jedge, if you will let me see what you say agin me in your warrant, I'll tell you what I've got to say about it." [Applause.]

The district attorney produced the indictment, and the old parson began reading it aloud, and commenting upon it as he proceeded. After he had read it all through, he threw it upon the table in front of him, and made the following statement to the court: "Jedge, that paper says I carried on the business of a distiller, and the business of a retail liquor dealer, when I tell your honor that I did no such thing. My business is farmin' duren the week days, and preachin' on Sundays, and now I would like for you to tell me, when I have spent all my time as I've been tellen you, how I could carry on them two other kinds of business what that paper says I do. [Laughter.] If I do all that, jedge, I must be an unusual kind of man, mustn't I? [Laughter.] Now, I tell you what I have done—no more, no less—and I am tellen of the truth, too. I just made two runs last fall and one run of peppermint* in Jannywary, and in them three runs I didn't make over thirty gallon in all, and it was for medicine, too. One of the gals in the neighborhood was sick with the breast complaint, and another one was down with the yaller janders, and I wouldn't of made the runs I tell you about if it hadn't been on their account. Now, them's the facts, as God is my jedge." [Applause.] There the old man rested his case.

The judge asked the old parson if he were to be lenient with him for this, his first offense, whether he would be guilty of anything of the kind in the future. The minister responded in the negative. The judge then asked him if he could pay a fine of $100 and the costs of the suit? The old parson, after humming and hawing a while, said he would go down street and see *brother* W—— (the party with whom he had left his $700), and perhaps he could raise the money. So out he went, and in a few minutes was back in court, paid the $100, and was discharged from custody.

There were several reasons why the moonshiner with the more voluminous output preferred to work near the various state lines. First of all, if he was being pressed too actively, he could simply move across and continue in business. An agent in hot pursuit of a moonshiner didn't have to stop at a state line—for he was, after all, a federal officer—but normally the agent worked in a certain district, and the moonshiner tried to take advantage of this situation. The other and more important reason was the fact that his distillate could be better marketed if he had a multistate territory. Moonshine operations were getting bigger in the very late 1800's, and the illicit distiller who hoped to grow with the times had to start marketing over a wider range of territory. Many Southern states at this period were in a state of transition over the

* This was a flavored drink used for medicine.

whiskey issue, and all sorts of opportunities opened up for the more businesslike moonshiner. Prohibition of manufacture by the legal distillers was being asked by the voting citizenry, and the legal liquor industry was in for hard times. Manufacture had been stopped in several instances in the southland, and state-wide prohibition seemed the tide of the future in most of the moonshining states.

In 1894 the whiskey tax jumped to $1.10 per gallon. More legal distillers became illegal distillers and not all of them by choice. Part of the new laws of that age forbade the manufacture of spirits outside of towns, and many legal distillers closed their doors and witnessed the decline of their industry. Temperance forces of local and national influence kept up the pressure, and the moonshiner went about his business sensing a brighter future than he had ever known before. Some states tried a new system that had a name that sounded foreign to the moonshiner— dispensaries. This—a method reluctantly agreed to by some in state government and tolerated by most of the citizenry—was a system of state-regulated liquor stores, selling intoxicants to be consumed off the premises. The movement was really an effort to head off state prohibition, but nobody seemed to be happy with it, least of all the saloon keepers. They were ready for any eventuality, however, and if running a blind tiger loomed in their future, they knew just the mountain spot from which just such an establishment could be supplied.

Everybody seemed to be anticipating the coming storm, and Internal Revenue records reveal how many men were making preparations in case the country dried up or came under strict control. In 1894, federal still seizures went over a thousand per year, and by 1895 they had reached almost two thousand annually. In 1897 and 1898 seizures were getting dangerously close to 2,500 per year. It didn't take a smart man to figure just where the odds lay. The country was going dry, and the whiskey tax was going up. A farm hand could be employed for seventy-five cents per day— almost half the amount of the tax on a single gallon of spirits. The same farm hand could get his drink tax free and earn a couple of dollars besides—if he was willing to try a new enterprise. And he was. The Woman's Christian Temperance Union, the Anti-Saloon League, the National Temperance Society, the Total Abstinence Brotherhood, and the whole Prohibition Party could wave their banners from West Virginia to Georgia and the Atlantic coast to Texas, but the moonshiner would be too busy to see. The moonshiners didn't have a unified organization of their own but most of them liked the "talkin'" of an organization they would historically support—the Ku Klux Klan. And from post-Civil War years until the late twentieth century, illicit whiskey manufacture would be one source of Klan fund raising.

CHAPTER SEVEN

Moonshining
Methods
and
Equipment

We have seen the evolution of the distilling art from antiquity, the movement of that art to America, and the history and events which preceded the man known as the moonshiner. We have also seen him in action, in his native habitat and looking over his shoulder at his pursuers. But what made the moonshiner as he was up until the beginning of the twentieth century? We can only sort from history the arguments used by the man himself.

In the beginning, the reason for his illicit activities was first and foremost to evade the payment of tax. In his mind no government had the right or the authority to place a tax on the needs of a man or the fruits of his labor. Nor did that same government have a right to sweep away an honorable family heritage.

It is true that inherent in the moonshiner's background is a long history of the distilling art. His ancestors were probably among the first practitioners of it, in this country as well as England, and worked their trade from their own corn patches and rye fields as the new country developed and spread westward. They provided for their own family needs and counted as their cash crop the squeezin's derived from a surplus of grain—a crop that, unlike grain itself, could be easily shipped long distances. Family or commercial gristmills probably could not have survived without the subsidy of work done for stillin'.

Good reputations for quality makin' and family recipes requiring years of experimentation and trial-and-error effort were matters of pride not easily given up. Many moonshiners felt they could not bend to the requirements of the law because of their economic situation. Much of the land in moonshining country was poor, barren, and steep. Few vast grazing lands or flat, fertile grain fields abounded, by which wheat or other crops could be raised in quantity. Small mountain corn patches could provide a living only if turned into liquid form and sold at greatly increased prices. Twenty bushels of corn might bring ten dollars; turned into corn liquor, it would bring seventy-five dollars. Some of the mountainous areas were accessible only by horseback or mule, and a few days' output of squeezin's would support a family for a month, whereas the corn from which it was derived certainly would not, even if the problem of transportation to market could have been overcome.

There were other legitimate factors in the mind of the mountain moonshiner and his counterpart beginning to practice in or near the growing cities. In the South, such practitioners would never accept the role of national government administration. In their own minds the "givernment" could do as it pleased, and they would do as they pleased. Hadn't they or their people fought to make theirs a free land? Hadn't their people pushed westward, felling the trees and clearing the wilderness and dying by the arrow and tomahawk? Hadn't they been a part of the Spirit of '76? Where now was the freedom they had earned?

Nationally, the moonshiner would be different in many other ways from most of his community fellows. Little community spirit and belonging seemed worthwhile or even necessary to him. He was not interested in the growth and improvement of his nation and couldn't care less that each year brought economic and cultural progress. He desired only to be left alone to operate as his ancestors had done. He was little interested in education for himself or his children, aside from teaching them the art of stillin'. But he was not to be considered a stupid individual, and as we have already seen, many of his number could be considered downright bright. He was never lacking in common sense and oftimes mechanical knowledge. Many moonshiners were capable of making their own still equipment and some ingenious accessory devices. For those who were not so gifted, nearly every community had its own blacksmith or tinsmith who could turn out the components of the still and take his pay in squeezin's for consumption or resale.

If a further understanding of this man of legend is to be attempted, a closer look at his still and what comes from it will prove valuable.

The product of the moonshiner is distilled alcohol, made drinkable, intoxicating, and as full-bodied and palatable as possible. Such drinking alcohol has been made and can be made from a variety of products from milk to strawberries. For the most part, however, moonshine has been made from grain—corn or rye (often a mixture)—and the moonshine brandies usually from apples, apple cider or peaches. The moonshiner's task is to take these base ingredients, prepare them properly, and with his skill, know-how, and sense of timing distill a beverage that meets the test of his own lips and that of his customer's. The late 1800's was the age when quality moonshine was on a par with the legal distillate, and sometimes excelled it. Many of the early moonshiners in fact had been owners or employees of the legal distilling companies. Illegal distilling had to be done without scientific instruments, sophisticated equipment, or the exact knowledge of a chemist, and the task was performed under adverse conditions. As unbelievable as it may appear, the mountain moonshiner's still had not changed drastically from the ancient still of Tahiti (Chapter One, Figure 3). Essentially, the principles and mechanics are the same, with some latter-day improvements. These few improvements will be discussed in later chapters as the art and the equipment evolves.

One important note should not escape attention at this juncture: No moonshiner, in any one locality or in any one state, operated necessarily in the same manner as another. Methods and procedure varied widely from area to area and state to state, and there were great differences in still design, workmanship, and capacity. Formulations and proportions of ingredients also varied with individual moonshiners.

When formulas and methods seem to be at variance with scientific distilling practices, it should not be assumed that the moonshiner knew nothing of what he was doing; on the contrary, he had been practicing his craft successfully for a long time, and had many satisfied customers to prove it.

Figure 8 illustrates a 120-gallon pot still, a commonplace unit of the 1880–1900 era. Construction would have been of copper throughout, a metal still recognized as the best material for a quality distillate. Copper was easily worked or shaped, and it offered the properties of good heat conduction and left less residue in the distillate than other metals. The absence of metallic residue was important in maintaining taste quality and purity of the drink. The components of the still illustrated are as follows: the copper shell of the still; the still cap (removable); the cap arm or extension; the worm or coil; the worm barrel or box; running water surrounding the coil; the still spout or cock; and the stone furnace and supporting base.

Labels in figure:
MOVABLE CAP
WATER SOURCE (FOR COOLING)
CAP ARM
BOILING MASH
OVERFLOW WATER
STILL
WORM BOX
WORM
WORM COCK
FURNACE AND BASE
STILL FIRE

Figure 8   Drawing of a 120-gallon pot still with operating components.

Lyndall Mason

Let us review the exact methods of a Virginia moonshiner practicing his craft for over forty years, between 1900 and 1941. Still
living, he is an invalid, but his mind is sharp at eighty-seven. His
formula was passed down to him by his father with whom he
worked at the still from the age of ten.

Before the still is fired and put into action, it will be helpful
to pause and review the preparation of the mash (ingredients to
be distilled). For the demonstration, ten mash barrels, or boxes
of 120 gallons capacity each, have been placed to the side of the
still. Into each barrel is poured one bushel of corn, previously
ground into meal. The still has been filled with water and a
fire built underneath to heat water. (The still is uncapped, being
used only to heat scalding water.) When the water is scalding
hot, a sufficient quantity is poured into the mash boxes over the
corn meal to "scald it down." This is stirred into a thick mush.
Hot water has now started to gelatinize the starch, which is the
first action of the mash. This mixture cooks for one hour, and
then one gallon of ground rye and three-fourths gallon of malt is
added to the top of the mush. After one hour, malt and rye are
stirred down into the mush approximately six inches in depth

and one gallon of warm water added. Slow mixing of rye and malt with the mush prevents overcooking the malt, which would kill it (destroy its full effectiveness). The malt is the substance which will break down the starch and convert it to sugar, from which the alcoholic distillate will be derived. After another hour of soaking, all ingredients in the mash box will be stirred thoroughly. The mash will now tend to thin out as conversion action starts. Cake yeast (approximately one-third pound) is now broken up and dissolved in a pan of water. When the temperature in the mash boxes is down to 90—100 degrees (referred to as "body heat" temperature by the moonshiner), the dissolving yeast is added into each mash box. (Keep in mind the same operations have been performed in all the mash boxes.) After the yeast has been stirred in, a "cap" of malt one-half-inch thick is added to the top of all mash in the boxes (this was optional with different moonshiners). This cap is thought to keep in a greater degree of heat and obtain maximum yeast effect. The yeast will act as the fermenting agent. The yeast is a budding fungus or unicellular vegetable organism containing enzymes which act upon sugar. The entire mixture of all the ingredients in the mash boxes is known as wort or mash. The beginning of fermentation causes agitation within the wort, and such action is noted by bubbling and gaseous action in the mash barrels. Bubbles are called "snowballs" by some moonshiners. Emerging carbon-dioxide gas and low-proof alcohol combine with other ingredients to produce what is called "distillers' beer"—or more commonly among moonshiners, simply "still beer." This rises to the top of the mash barrels as the solids are broken up and sink to the bottom. Moonshiners as a rule have no scientific way to check the percentage of alcoholic content in the still beer, but rely on taste and the appearance of the bubbling of the agitated mix. Near the last stage, the mix clears up and appears like milky water. They believe the still beer (depending on weather conditions, proportions of mix, coarseness of meal and rye, and its quality) to have an alcoholic content of from 6 to 12 percent alcohol. It is most probably 5 percent to 7 percent.

The fermentation period varies greatly according to weather temperatures. In hot weather fermentation occurs more rapidly. Generally, fermentation in hot weather is complete in four to six days. Chilly or cold weather can retard completion of fermentation by days.

After fermentation is completed—a fact gauged by our moonshiner's finger pulled through the surface of the still beer to make a clear channel and an observation of the time rate at which the channel closes up; by his taste, nose, feel of temperature, and observation of disappearing bubbles—the still can be fired and a sufficient quantity of wood laid by for the complete run of all the still beer in the mash boxes. The moonshiner watches his timing carefully. He knows that to run the still beer before it has stopped working or to let it sit too long after it has stopped working will hinder or spoil the entire run.

The still is filled to a few inches below the cap, then the still fire must be prepared. There is no rest until the last mash barrel is empty. Approximately two days and nights are required to accomplish all the tasks that lie ahead. With good luck and a still that "holds her cap," one hundred and twenty gallons of grain whiskey will be the result.

As the still fire begins to do its job, the mash in the still rises in temperature. Approaching is one of the most critical phases of the operation. The mash is stirred continuously in the still before capping, to prevent scorching. Temperature control is of upmost importance. The still cap, which is the gathering place of steam vapor, is set in place on top of the still just as the mash starts to steam or generate vapor. As the temperature in the still rises further and the mash starts to boil, steam and solid matter make their appearance around the base of the still cap. Temperature is still the critical element. The fact that alcohol and water have different boiling points is the basic principle of distilling. Alcohol boils at 172 degrees F. and water at 212 degrees. Temperature then has to be maintained at a correct level to cause water and alcohol to separate and obtain ethyl alcohol and the other constituents which are needed to give the distillate its character, body, and aroma. These minor constituents, called congeners, include higher alcohols, aldehydes, esters, volatile acids, and other organic compounds whose contribution to the distilled beverage is out of proportion to their quantities but extremely vital to the well-blended alcoholic drink.

The still begins to show signs of working, and the still cap is sealed on by clay or thick rye paste cemented about the base. This operation prevents further leakage around the still cap and allows vapor pressure to build up in the still cap and to be pushed through the cap arm on its way to the copper worm. The moonshiner weights down the still cap, after tapping it with a stick to determine the pressure buildup taking place. He is skilled at this and can tell, by the sound his tapping makes, the degree of pressure build-up or reduction. This operation is called "whoppin' the cap." Weighting the cap down helps to prevent "blowing the cap" and losing the run—or, worse yet, getting a dangerous scalding. On much bigger stills pictured elsewhere in the book, the still cap is chained down.

A veteran moonshiner can hear the creeping vapor as it starts through the still, and he waits for the first sign of passage through the worm, called the "foreshot." The worm, a simple condenser, is a coil of small diameter pipe (usually copper or pewter) submerged in cool water, which runs continuously with a fresh supply. The vapor enters the worm, and as it is forced through the cool worm coil, it is changed into liquid form. This first emission contains undesirable solid matter and water. Soon a trickle begins and then a steady stream, the thickness of a thin pencil. The liquid distillate that comes from the still is called "singlin's" or "low wines." The temperature is still an important factor; if the heat is reduced too much, the flow will slow down or cease; increased too much, the worm will "run hot," and the distillate will have a "scorched" taste, foam over, and be flooded with solid matter. Even with the best of luck, variations in the run occur. Best functional control of the still seems apparent from shortly after beginning to about midrun. Higher percentage alcohol with less water and foreign matter comes through the worm at this point. The last of the run is called "backin's," "tailin's," or "faints."

When the last of the still beer has been consumed and the last of the low wines has been run, the still is washed out, in preparation for the job of "doublin'." This operation consists simply of running the low wines back through the still for a second distillation. This accomplishes two things: Impurities from the first run of singlin's can be reduced considerably, and harsh or raw effects curbed; secondly, the alcoholic content or "proof" can be raised considerably. This second distillate is called "high wines," and the best of the run will be from 140 to 160 proof. (The proof number is exactly double the amount of alcohol by liquid measure. For example, a pint of whiskey labeled 100 proof is 50 percent water and 50 percent alcohol.) The moonshiner will try to average the alcoholic content of his "moon" to about 100 proof. This operation is called "drappin' the bead." He will mix high wines with low wines for the average he wants.

If the moonshiner wants to make "sour mash" moonshine, he will follow this procedure: As each mash barrel or box is emptied of the original fermented mash, he will add the correct proportion of grain to that same empty mash box. When the mash in the still had been exhausted or "spent," he will catch the hot "slop" from the still drain cock and scald down the fresh mixture with the hot slop, rather than with hot water as in mixing the original mash. This sour-mash procedure is called "sloppin' back." After he scalds down with hot slop, the new batch will have added to it, after sufficient cooling, additional water, fresh yeast, malt, and rye (optional). The only difference in moonshine sour mash and the original "sweet mash" is that the sweet mash uses fresh water for scalding down, whereas sour mash is scalded down with hot slop and a lesser quantity of fresh yeast, malt, etc.

Some purchasers of moon like the sour-mash method the best, and others prefer the sweet mash. Made by the moonshine method, it takes a genuine connoisseur to know the difference.

The repeated use of the same mash for several runs was not practiced by the old moonshiners of the 1800–1900 period. This factor would be subject to change as the twentieth century rolled onward.

Few mountain moonshiners have any scientific method of checking proof consistency or other precise methods of quality control. Occasionally, a simple thermometer may be used for temperature checking, but the presence of a hydrometer or other scientific equipment is rare. This was especially so in early days. The moonshiner claimed that his eye and his experience told him when the "proof was right." After the foreshot had cleared the worm, he claimed he could read the bead. This bead was his indicator of alcoholic strength. The first bead to be evident from the singlin's he called "frog eyes" because of the larger than usual bubbles or beads. He analyzed the proof content by expertly shaking a jar of his distillate and watching the way the bead "sat." The collection of beads, or bubbles, first circles in the middle surface of the liquid, then spins off to the wall of the fruit jar and bursts or disseminates. Before dissemination, if the bead sat half in the liquid and half out, proof is 100. Bead sitting higher or lower gives plus or minus variations.

If this method is not used, there are two others most often practiced by the moonshiner. The first and simplest is the practice of tossing a cupful of distillate into the fire under the still to see if it would flame up. Near the end of a run, the alcoholic content of the distillate drops, and when it reaches the point where it will not burn, the moonshiner knows the rest of the run will be worthless. Anything that will burn, he considers usable. This second method dates back to the origin of the term "proof." By this method a moonshiner mixed his distillate with a portion of gunpowder and set fire to it. If the spirits burned off and ignited the powder, it was said to be "proof spirit." If the alcohol content is less than 49.3 percent by weight, the water left after the flame consumption of the alcohol is sufficient to prohibit burning of the powder. Fifty percent of absolute alcohol will fire the mixture and give proof spirit. Some moonshiners claim the ability to read proof or overproof by the color of the burning glow of the flame.

The run completed, the illicit alcohol is bottled in crocks, casks, one-gallon jugs, or whatever may be available.

Well into the early 1900's many moonshiners still made their own malt and yeast (especially if they were remote from sources of supply). Before this period, they had less choice in the matter. Malt was made by taking corn or barley grain and placing a small quantity in a cloth sack, which was submerged in water until it was ready to sprout. When sprouting began, the grain was spread out in a warm place (usually a barn loft or house attic) and allowed to dry and sprout further. It was then ground up and ready for use in the still.

The moonshiner could make his own yeast if he was not near enough to the source of a commercial supply. One of the early formulas for homemade yeast is as follows:

> Put six medium size potatoes to boil in two quarts of water in a granite saucepan. A tablespoon of dried hop blooms, tied in a bit of cheesecloth, should be dropped in the saucepan at the same time. After potatoes are thoroughly soft, squeeze the hop bag against the side of the vessel with a silver fork to get all the strength of the hops (a steel fork will darken the yeast).
>
> Lift the potatoes out of the water and mash them through a colander into an earthen bowl or a graniteware vessel. Measure the water in which potatoes were boiled, and add enough

from a boiling kettle to make up the two quarts of liquid. Pour liquid over potatoes, add one-half cup of sugar and one-third of a cup of salt, and stir well. Let cool to lukewarm, and then add one cup of good yeast, or half a yeast cake broken in the liquid.

Now set the bowl in a sheltered place, out of all drafts, and where the contents will keep about the same temperature for five or six hours. Put into glass jars, and only fill jars half full. When perfectly cold the tops may be screwed on, but not before. Keep in a cold place, and use as needed. Always shake jar well before pouring out any of the yeast.

Of course this formula depended on the addition of seed yeast to the homemade variety.

Commercially prepared yeast was available in quantity around the period of the Civil War. After the 1860's yeast cakes were available even in mountain villages. Prior to Civil War times, imported yeast was available but not in the more remote areas of the country. In 1796 Felton Mathew, in France, had patented a process to produce dry, pressed yeast which could be stored in airtight vessels and sold commercially.

Predating these periods, yeast was made by a simple process in existence as far back as recorded history. Yeast making by this method involved the scraping of the white "frost" (or must) from grapes and kneading it with the ground grain millet. This combination was then kneaded with ground wheat, dried, and made into cakes.

There was still another method of yeast making, used by the Indians of Mexico and areas later to become part of the United States. This yeast making consisted simply of chewing the corn or other plant on which fermentative action was desired, and letting the saliva of the mouth supply the yeast cells needed.

Yet another method of yeast making was used by a select few who considered the art of distilling the highest and most challenging calling to which they could aspire. This method was for years a most carefully guarded secret. The moonshiner would take a small crock, fill it half full of a mixture of honey and water, and then carry it to a special place of his own choosing—usually deep in the woods by a spring—and set it high on a rock, to prevent wild-animal invasion, and completely exposed to the elements. This exposure to the elements allowed the yeast enzymes of the air to combine with the honey mixture and grow to a purity that would make his yeast and moonshine superior to all others.

The coil or worm, acting as the condensing device of the still, could be fashioned from pewter or copper by the skilled moonshiner. The size of the coil, the number of turns required, and the diameter of each turn depended on the size of the still on which it was to function and the mechanical ideas of the individual moonshiner. The 120 gallon still in Figure 8 would function properly on five to eight turns of fashioned pipe, one inch to one and one-half inches in diameter and having coils eighteen to twenty-four inches in circumference. After the pipe was procured, the moonshiner could make his own worm by filling a straight length of pipe with sand, salt, or resin and then bending it around a circular post or tree stump. Each end of the pipe would be plugged until the desired shape was obtained, then unplugged and the filler material dumped out. (The filler material prevented the pipe from crimping in the wrong places, thereby obstructing the passage area of the worm.)

Other equipment on hand would be a horse blanket or sack of charcoal for filtering or leaching the distillate. Fusel oil and other undesirable by-products could be reduced by this filtering. Charred wooden barrels were used for aging by the moonshiner who was more interested in quality than quick profit. If charred barrels were not available, the moonshiner might drop a few small pieces of charcoal into the jug, jar, or cask, much as spices are added to a jar of homemade pickles.

There was yet another strange object which could be found around the distilling sites of the deep South. The object was the moonshiner's "mogo." The mogo was a sort of voodoo charm. The believers use two of them—one to wear about the neck and the other to bury in the still yard or site. The practice is believed to have originated with slaves and others coming from Africa and the isles of the Caribbean in early colonial days. The buried mogo was supposed to bring good luck and good output from the still and protect it from natural or man-made disaster. The charm about the neck was for the protection of the wearer from like causes. In early times, particularly among the illiterate and superstition-prone, an aura of spirituality pervaded the distilling location at all times. The Dark Age concept of alcohol as a liquid of the gods lingered on, so that men felt something magic took place at the distilling site.

In addition to the equipment heretofore described, the moonshiner would have his rifle, cocked and ready for any unwelcome intruder. The moonshiner was serious about his business, and death awaited any man who thought otherwise—especially any revenue agent representing the U.S. government.

CHAPTER EIGHT

Moonshining Before and During Prohibition

By 1899, federal still seizures were bouncing between the 2,000 and 2,500 mark annually. Revenue agents reported to their superiors the suspicion that moonshiners were spreading out into new territories and making preparations for long-term operations. Some of the locations chosen had heretofore been too undesirable or inaccessible even for the moonshiner. Along the southeastern coastal area, the moonshiner was beginning to operate in inlets and sounds. In the inland and mountainous area, he was getting more remotely located and geared for heavier production. Something more than the mere rise in prohibition sentiment was causing these drastic changes. There was money to be made and less danger in these outlying areas. The price of moonshine whiskey was going up, and judges and juries were letting convicted moonshiners off with light sentences. Few moonshiners, even when caught and convicted, left off illicit activity for very long after again being free.

Legal distillers of the South, who might have preferred to operate legitimately, were being forced to go illegal to meet the competition of moonshining activity. Commercial grain sales for legal distilling dropped drastically, and some large and influential industries climbed onto the bandwagon against liquor.

The big surge in illicit sales did not occur as quickly as the moonshiner and ex-legal distiller might have expected. Temperance pressure, church influence, and political prohibitionist sentiment was genuine and effective (and the moonshiner's vote in that direction couldn't hurt him any). Churches were beginning to preach total abstinence. It seemed as though a good part of the citizenry was dead serious about the evils of drinking, and had taken upon itself the obligation to stop it individually and collectively.

In the South the motive for prohibition was not predicated on moral and social grounds alone. Southern Democrats still felt

Figure 9   Moonshiners and their captors in the early 1900's. Agent on right prepares to axe the still while agent on left holds pistol at readiness. Wife of one moonshiner stands by helplessly.

Library of Congress

that Internal Revenue policing and control was tied too closely to the Republican appointments of the 1860's and that such revenue offices and officers still smelled of foreign element and Republican political sentiment. With this belief to back them up, the prohibitionist forces and the Democrats formed a somewhat strange alliance in seeking to do away with liquor or at least federal control of the product.

During 1900, federal still seizures dropped very slightly under the annual figure of two thousand. In the period of 1901–1903, seizures dropped still further to an average of just under 1,500 annually. It did indeed appear that John Barleycorn might be going out of style. Total of all distilled spirits in the United States stood at 148,206,875 gallons annually, an all-time low for the period. Legal distilleries declined still further, and new laws further tightened restrictions on the retailer and buyer. Many states of the South henceforth forbade the sale of intoxicants in unincorporated towns. Legal distillers in rural areas were prohibited from distilling for reasons of inadequate police protection outside of towns; and still further state laws prohibited legal distilling operations in towns of less than one thousand population. These moves anticipated potential trouble from marauders who could not be dealt with quickly and adequately. Even more importantly it placated voters with prohibition sentiment. A series of antijug laws was passed to prevent liquor from moving out of "wet" states into "dry" states.

Whole new territories were now being opened to moonshining infiltration: the small towns with no retail sales outlet, counties and states that were for all practical purposes as dry as the proverbial bone. The antijug laws were in themselves a sales aid for the moonshiner, providing him with a territory free of legal liquor. The low in federal still seizures, a thousand annually in 1904 and 1905, now started a significant upswing. Nobody could deny that prohibitionist sentiment was gaining ground fast. In 1906 thirty states had local-option provisions, whereby the liquor issue, in theory, could be dictated by the will of the people. Local-option elections brought the freed Negro back into politics in a big way, and the North-South argument of Southern reasoning for prohibition continued to flare as a minor side issue.

By 1908, annual still seizures had gone well over a thousand, but revenue men fought hard to keep illicit activity under control. New efforts by the commissioner of Internal Revenue sought to tighten government control. A closer working alliance between revenue officers, United States marshals, deputy marshals, United States commissioners, and district attorneys was pursued, with encouraging results. The moonshiner/bootlegger wouldn't behave for long, however, and he was learning new tricks every day. Supplementing the legal spirits the drugstore could dispense in dry areas, he was shipping in illicit spirits by express and by mail in addition to the more time honored and conventional methods of delivery. The production of moonshine distillate was now starting the expected climb, and new areas were being heard from. The States of Florida and Louisiana were now hitting the charts of still-seizure records. Even Alaska was making moonshine, a distillate called hooch, and the overburdened commissioner must have really scratched his head at the mere thought of policing that vast area. Little illicit distilling was taking place on the Pacific coast, but the Hawaiian Islands had gotten into the act by making a moonshine distillate from the ti root. Illicit distilling in the North was under control; it was still centered in New York, New Jersey, and New England, but there were occasional seizures in the Midwest.

By 1910 federal still seizures reached almost two thousand annually, again double what they had been only five years previously. The number of agents sent into the trouble areas was increased sharply to counter a situation obviously getting out of control. Some states that had heretofore not been so concerned about the moonshiner/bootlegger took a new look. Texas, in this same year, made it a felony to transport liquor into no-license territory. Individual state efforts to protect their own dry territory by their own power alone ran into legal difficulty. The federal government alone had jurisdiction over interstate commerce. However, in 1847 The Supreme Court, in a series called the License Cases, had ruled that state legislation could prohibit the sale of liquor without a license, even if still in the original barrel brought in from another state. The Original Package case in 1890 practically reversed the 1847 rule by holding that a state could not prohibit a liquor dealer from importing liquor from another state for resale in original packages. This had the effect of making state prohibition ineffective, and Congress immediately passed the Wilson Act, to take from intoxicating liquor its interstate character. This would be done by the stipulation that spirits transported into a state would, upon arrival in such states, be covered by the laws of that state and be under the police power of that state to the same degree as if such spirits had been produced there.

The act presented serious constitutional difficulties, but the Supreme Court upheld it in *In re Raher* in 1891. However, in a later case (*Rhodes vs. Iowa*) the Supreme Court construed "arrival" to mean delivery to the consignee and not simply arrival within the boundary of the state. This allowed the traveling bootlegger/moonshiner/salesman to evade the intent of state prohibition and, in addition, to continue his mail-order business with a great deal of ease and comfort.

Figure 10   Scrap heap of axed stills prior to World War I. Parts of worm coils lay chopped into short sections, at bottom of photo.

Library of Congress

State prohibition laws were increasing in effectiveness, sufficiently to force the prices of illicit products even more sharply upward. Never before, with the exception of the Civil War period, had white lightnin' been so much in demand or fetched such a good price and willing public. By 1911, still seizures jumped to almost 2,500 annually. The commissioner could look at the prohibition situation in every Southern state and all but forecast the result: States and localities that enforced their prohibition laws with muscle, had the fastest growing moonshining areas. But it didn't always work that way, and some moonshining areas just seemed to be growing in the midst of areas where a legal drink could be had.

In the fiscal year of 1912, Congress cut the appropriation for illicit still seizures and other alcohol-tax violations. This was done on the assumption that strict prohibition measures by the individual states would soon have the matter of the liquor problem under control. They appeared to look upon the increase in illicit distilling as merely a temporary problem, and if it wasn't, here again the states and localities with their own enforcement agencies should take on part of the burden of the problem. Local police and sheriffs, however, were for the most part ineffective. They had not the number of personnel required to meet the increase in activity, nor did some of them have the desire to eliminate it. Some areas, with enthusiastic support by law-enforcement officers and the citizenry, did effect a downward spiral in moonshining activities, by pursuing the moonshiners with the same fervor they applied to the prohibition laws. Such was not the rule, however, and if the facts could have been known, it is probable that for every illicit still seized four more were running successfully. This kind of speculation would put the number of stills in operation at approximately ten thousand annually. The following excerpt from the 1912 commissioner's report, presents even more graphically the problem of the times:

> Illicit distilling and "bootlegging" continue without sign of abatement. During the past fiscal year practically the same number of illicit plants were seized and destroyed as during the previous fiscal year. Two thousand four hundred and sixty-five were seized and captured during the year just closed, as against 2,488 the previous year. During the past year, however, on account of the very severe winter weather during January, February, and a part of March, 1912, the work of raiding had to be to a large extent discontinued, and at certain times during the year a portion of the raiding officers had to be detailed for other work which appeared at the time to be of greater importance. But for those facts the number of distilleries seized and destroyed during the past year would have considerably exceeded the record number of the year previous, and as it was, as above stated, the number almost equaled it. In some sections where public sentiment seems to be crystallizing against this species of fraud a considerable decrease in the activity of the "moonshiners" is reported. This, however, seems to be compensated for by the increased activity reported in other sections. It appears that in some sections of the country, where local officers make some effort to enforce local prohib-

itory laws, there is a correspondingly greater demand for illicit whisky, and as the price goes up more persons are willing to run the risk in violating the law. While most of the plants captured are comparatively small, when it is taken into consideration that there are great numbers of plants which are running which we do not succeed in locating and destroying, the tax on the entire amount of spirits aggregates a large amount of revenue, that is lost to the Government, and represents a tremendous disturbing element and a great amount of lawlessness in communities many of which are otherwise law-abiding and respecting. . . . The force engaged in raiding could, with propriety, be greatly increased, and if illicit distilling is to be eradicated it will be necessary to maintain, in sections in which it is prevalent, a much larger force than the present appropriation will permit.

In 1913, as in most years since 1862, the commissioner of Internal Revenue voiced the old charge of failure on the part of state and local authorities, and their citizenry, to cooperate in the task of suppressing moonshining. The courts, the juries, the enforcement officers, and the majority of the citizens either approved of the illicit activity or were at least tolerant of it. But now Congress took some action and passed (over President William Howard Taft's veto) the Webb-Kenyon Act, to tighten control over the liquor traffic. The act removed from liquors their interstate character and forbade the transportation of any intoxicating liquor into a state, *by any persons*, and banned the receipt, possession, or selling of liquor *in original packaging or otherwise*, in violation of any state law.

Prohibitionists forces might well have rejoiced at the passage of the Webb-Kenyon Act, but their elation would have been dampened by a glimpse at the commissioner's annual report for 1914. Federal still seizures were heading fast for the three thousand annual figure. In 1915 seizure statistics were indicating a figure just short of four thousand. Other bad news was in the offing for this critical year: Two federal agents and other subordinate officers had been caught conniving with moonshiners to defraud the government of the whiskey-tax revenue. Other frauds against the government, by its own personnel, began to surface gradually. Government warehousemen and gaugers started the manipulation practice of slipping out small quantities of whiskey for resale or otherwise covering up for missing stocks, which on paper remained in government hands. This practice became known as "equalizing" and added one more avenue of illegal activity. The temptations were too great and the profits too enticing to pass up.

In 1914, the Congress had foreseen the coming of national prohibition and possible war. The tax revenue which had for so long been provided by distilled spirits and fermented beverages now would be supplemented by revenue derived from the income-tax law under the Sixteenth Amendment. The income tax in years to come would be a powerful tool against the moonshiner, but that time had not arrived just yet.

Moonshining activity appeared to take a drastic nose-dive in 1917. Federal seizure records indicated only 2,232 seizures for that entire year. Though the apparent drop looked encouraging on paper, it reflected a distorted picture. During this year, the federal government dropped any payment to informers ("reporters") or possemen. There had been too many violent deaths among such helpful citizens, too many frauds on the government, leading to useless raids and witch hunts. It meant, however, that agents would have to rely on voluntary information, devoid of reward fees, for help in tracking down the moonshiner and the site of his still.

In 1917, about the time America was entering World War I, Congress passed the Lever Food and Fuel Act, which prohibited the manufacture of distilled spirits for beverage purpose from grains, cereals, fruit, and food products. A tax increase to $3.20 per gallon on all existing stocks was also made applicable. The tax was up again, and distilling fell sharply in compliance with national law. Only 236 distilling companies (seventy-two grain, twenty-seven molasses, 137 fruit) were in operation in the United States in 1918. The act of 1917 was supplemented by the War Prohibition Act of November 21, 1918, which prohibited the manufacture of *fermented* malt liquors and wines from grains, cereals, fruit, and food products after May 1, 1919. This same act prohibited the *sale* of distilled spirits, malt liquors, and wine for beverage purposes after June 30, 1919. All of these acts were later consolidated in Title I of the National Prohibition Act which became effective October 28, 1919.

This wartime prohibition, which reached into the ranks of the military, forbade the sale of liquor at military stations or to members of the military forces in uniform, in or near military camps.

On January 16, 1919, the Eighteenth Amendment was ratified by the thirty-sixth state as required, to become effective one year thereafter. This one-year stay of execution allowed legal distillers to dispose of the products on hand, which at the time amounted to between 58 and 60 million gallons. The Volstead Act, enacted to give the government ample enforcement powers, was passed over the veto of President Woodrow Wilson, and became law on October 28, 1919. The Volstead Act also set the percentage of alcoholic content allowable for sale at .05 percent by volume.

The Volstead Act placed upon the commissioner of Internal Revenue the primary responsibility for the investigation and enforcement of the prohibitory terms of the law. The actual prosecution in the courts was still to be conducted by the Department of Justice. Under the new law, the commissioner was granted authority to issue permits for the manufacture, sale and transportation of alcoholic liquors for religious, industrial, and medicinal purposes as recognized by law. The spirits so designated would continue to be subject to the existing excise taxes of $6.40 per proof gallon. With the passage of the required one-year waiting period after ratification, constitutional prohibition was a thing of reality, and the United States was legally dry on January 16, 1920.

After the effective date in January of 1920, the Prohibition Unit of the Bureau of Internal Revenue, which had been organized in December of 1919, was divided into two branches. One branch was responsible for the enforcement of the penal and regulatory provisions of the act, while the other supervised the administrative aspects of the law covering traffic in nonbeverage liquors. A federal prohibition director for one branch was appointed for each state and was assigned an inspection and clerical force under his command. The other branch was to operate in the states as units in nine national districts (this was later increased to twelve). The moonshiners in existence and those to come would now, if concerned about propriety, refer to their adversary as prohibition agents. It is doubtful if the old timer ever knew the difference—he was still facing a revenooer.

There is every evidence to suppose that the old timer as well as the city syndicate man was cocked and ready for prohibition. Wartime controls and all the Congressional law-making pertaining to foodstuffs didn't cause a serious ripple in the established moonshiner's output. It was still the age when the moonshiner had his own source of supplies and in many cases raised them. If he didn't have enough grain, there were plenty of moonshine buyers who would gladly continue the old barter method: four bushels of corn for one gallon of moon. Moonshine brandy posed no problem either; the typical moonshiner lived in the heart of peach and apple country, and ten times the amount of moon brandy he could turn out wouldn't consume half the available supply. During the very year of wartime prohibition, federal still seizures had jumped to almost six thousand. In two years, still seizures in Georgia jumped from 741 to 2,089; North Carolina stills from 753 to 3,104; Virginia stills from 324 to 2,165. While these figures are revealing, they by no means tell the true story of just how many stills were actually in operation throughout the whole country in the very beginning days of prohibition. States that in the past had known only occasional still seizures now started to show increasing numbers of violations. Such states include California, Colorado, Connecticut, Illinois, Indiana, Maryland, Massachusetts, Michigan, Minnesota, Missouri, Nebraska, New Hampshire, New Mexico, North and South Dakota, Ohio, Oklahoma, Oregon, Texas, Wisconsin, and Pennsylvania.

Long before national prohibition became law, speculators, crime syndicates, and opportunists of every design had anticipated by years the problems and opportunities which lay ahead. Vast shipments of spirits left the country for future illicit return. Arrangements were made with foreign sources for the illegal importation of foreign-made spirits. What had been the legal industry now turned into the illegal industry; illicit manufacturing of spirits increased by tremendous strides in large metropolitan areas. Practice of counterfeiting foreign and domestic labels to be placed on a substandard product became widespread; a thirsty public never questionad a label, so long as the drink was wet and intoxicating.

A new gimmick—diverting commercial alcohol from its legitimate destination—proved a policing nightmare. Captive outlets sold only enough industrial alcohol to appear legitimate—the rest went for beverage making. Denatured alcohol, already subject to government control, was treated by various methods to make it unfit for human consumption. Illegal distillers countered by re-distilling it or boiling off contamination properties, making it again drinkable. Expert technicians in the field of distilling were brought in from foreign countries by syndicates and racketeers to supplement the available talent needed to foil the government. No expense was spared to erect distilling plants that equaled in quality and output what the legitimate industry could offer.

Internal Revenue stamps were counterfeited by the syndicates to allow sales of spirits, supposedly manufactured under government authority. Withdrawal of legal liquor from government controlled warehouses by the use of falsified permits worked well for a while, but as prohibition agents became more successful and better organized, this avenue of activity became less rewarding. With government heat on the denatured-alcohol racket, counterfeiting, and illegal warehouse removal, racketeers pressed harder for imported stock from abroad. Time would be needed to get numerous distilleries in functioning order, and the void had to be filled.

Increased smuggling resulted, and vast numbers of ships under many foreign flags sailed to the limits of United States territorial waters. At this time the Coast Guard was ill prepared to patrol the vast coastal areas of the United States. Border patrol along the Canadian and Mexican frontiers was another big hole to plug.

A tally, with the rendering of the 1922 commissioner's report, showed that since the beginning of constitutional prohibition in January of 1920, 54,381 stills had been seized and 83,946 persons arrested. Prohibition had made its formal debut.

In the very beginning of prohibition came a milestone in the history of moonshining that was to change the method and the product of moonshine distilling from that period forward. This was the use of pure sugar as a voluminous addition to fermenting mash, or as time evolved, to the use of sugar as the dominant base substance for illicit distilling. There is some evidence to support the employment of this revolutionary step, at least on a small or experimental scale, as far back as 1910. Some moonshiners yet living, and especially those who worked their trade in several states, support this theory. If the practice did predate World War I, it is likely that the idea came from a chemist or distilling technician who deserted the ranks of the legal industry, or at least offered technical advice to the illicit industry. Of course, some moonshiners for years had used pure honey in distilling, as did many distillers of antiquity. It is safe to say, however, that the massive use of pure sugar had its beginning in the prohibition era and was for a while practiced mostly in the metropolitan areas. This was one step in moonshine distilling that spread first among city moonshiners and then filtered down into the hill country.

There was a commanding reason for the use of sugar on a mammoth scale—it saved time. The grains composing the mash for distillation contain starch, which must be converted to sugar, before it can be utilized by the yeast to produce ethyl alcohol. The addition of pure sugar (with no need of further conversion except for yeast action and distilling) therefore cuts the conversion time of a volume of mash. Instead of taking the four to five days needed for old-fashioned grain fermentation, a mixture of sugar mash is ready to run in seventy-two hours. Moreover, the gallonage of distilled alcohol derived from such a mixture could be double that of pure grain whiskey.

This quick fermentation and double output was a real bonus to the prohibition moonshiner/bootlegger. In lieu of a supply from a once legal industry, the demand for whiskey was monumental, and time was of the essence. As fast as the distillate could be produced, a customer was waiting. It mattered little to the seller if the drinker developed a quick headache or new heights in a king-sized hangover. Illicit distilleries, as modern and efficient as anything in the legal industry, continued to be erected in or near the larger cities. Money was no object, and if such a distilling setup cost $50,000, as many were reputed to have cost, even with a short term of operation a handsome return was sure.

There were those who were just as determined that such stills would never operate, and they were dying in the performance of the task. Some prohibition agents were killed during still raids, others in the attempt to execute search warrants. One agent in the first year of prohibition was shot down by a local law officer who was refused a drink of seized liquor. Killing of agents from ambush was an old trick that now moved out of the hill country into the cities. One agent in 1922 was pushed from his automobile by liquor transporters, and others were dying by gunfire in arrest attempts. The slaughter had just begun.

Federal still seizures for 1923 and 1924 were 51,368, and

107,991 persons had been arrested for violations in the same two-year period. The commissioner's chart of still seizures throughout the United States lighted up like a Christmas tree. In number of violations the leading states were ranked as follows: Georgia (6,155 seizures), Tennessee (4,232), Virginia (3,919), North Carolina (3,287), Alabama (2,767), Kentucky (1,599), Texas (1,240), Massachusetts (1,226), Florida (1,107), South Carolina (1,077), California (976), Indiana (957), New Jersey (879), West Virginia (683), Ohio (656), and Missouri (649). Numerous other states were close behind. No state was missing in the records of still seizures, although Maine had only one seizure on federal records for the two-year period. Territories of Hawaii, Puerto Rico, and Alaska also had seizures.

Also in 1924, as many as 336 rum ships were known to be bringing in contraband beverages. Specially equipped—syndicate-owned or free-lance—fishing boats operated from port to the anchored ships lying at the fringes of territorial waters. Some were equipped with special high-powered motors for speed and carried firearms to enhance their evasion tactics. The guns were needed not only against prohibition agents and Coast Guard patrols; the traffic was so hazardous that rum-runners were robbing rum-runners. By international agreement, territorial limits were extended from three miles to twelve miles, and the previously unprepared Coast Guard was making progress in the control of international rum-running.

Southern moonshiners and syndicate kings were not the only offenders in the annals of illicit whiskey making. Kitchen stills and bathtub-gin making was tried from the Atlantic to the Pacific, and the trial-and-error methods soon produced a palatable product. Buying of grapes, both fresh and dry, by home brewers sent grape prices skyrocketing. Little operators in service stations and stores along the major and minor highways contributed their share by either making it or selling the product of somebody else. Those, North and South, who could not make a passable distillate resorted to the use of beading oils (falsifying alcoholic strength by showing a bead—proof of alcoholic strength) or other chemical additives to convince a gullible customer that it was indeed first-class whiskey he was buying. Coloring, to imitate some brands of legal whiskey, was used by both the big and little operator. Prune juice was a favorite coloring—and even tobacco juice, food extracts, kerosene, ether, resin, junk battery acid, headache powder, stove polish, turpentine, coal tar, and a host of other ingredients were not unheard-of additives, especially if the illicit drink was sold in the ghetto areas.

Big names were becoming known and feared in the field of syndicate operation of illicit distilleries. Al Capone, Waxie Gordon, Dutch Schultz, and Eddie Fleischer were just a few of the more familiar. Gang slayings that made the hill-country moonshiner look like a kindergarten bully were taking place with increasing rapidity in the metropolitan areas; block by block fighting went on to establish exclusive sales rights in heavily populated areas. So powerful was the authority of the syndicate operators that wholesale groups of enforcement officers, prosecutors, judges, and politicians were influenced or controlled by them. Election results were often entirely dependent upon the support, or lack of it, from a gangland boss. Moonshining/bootlegging syndicates held similar sway over large financial institutions, with the business they controlled running into the millions of dollars, and huge financial and supply institutions sought their business eagerly.

By 1925 federal still seizures for one year had reached an all-time high of 29,087 and arrests topped the 76,000 mark. Prohibition-enforcement personnel now numbered 3,700 employees engaged in narcotics and prohibition work.

The automobile in this era became an important tool of both the prohibition agent and the moonshiner/bootlegger. Fast and effective transportation was a must, and the early automobiles and trucks were admirable machines. The average citizen old enough to remember the period has a clearer picture of the black sedans, with guns blazing out the windows, than of the reasons for the occasion. The number of deaths from car-to-car shootouts increased yearly during prohibition. Some of the gangster-owned cars of prohibition days have been on public display for years and still attract museum goers, with their powerful motors, excellent workmanship, and custom bullet-proof design.

The syndicate moonshiner kept trying to improve his distilling operation and distributional network as prohibition stretched onward. He was cornering more of the market every day, and he wanted still more of it. The small operator in the cities did not have the protection money, political influence, distributional set-up, or modern plant of his big-time counterpart. Home making of wine dropped off considerably, except among the foreign-born population who seemed patient enough to give such wines time to age. The wine industry had despaired of trying to dealcoholize its wine to make it legal for sale. The home brewers also abandoned the attempt to make high-alcohol beer. For the average city dweller, the job of carrying large quantities of barley or rye meal into his house and then living with the smell of fermenting grain were things he would forfeit to the professional moonshiner.

The syndicate moonshiner upgraded his operation in a number of ways as he sought more diligently than ever to satisfy the un-quenchable public thirst. He purchased or leased, in some camou-flaged fashion, yeast supply houses, grain companies, sugar whole-sale firms, plumbing establishments, iron and metal companies, and other businesses that would keep him in the supplies he needed for operation. If any of these arrangements failed for any reason, hijacking was as good a source as any—not necessarily as a secondary measure.

Syndicate bosses pushed their distillers even harder for improve-ments in volume and methods. The best distillers turned in a good performance by another breakthrough of importance: Fer-menting time of the sugar/mash had been cut to forty-eight hours and below, by the use of chemical additives called a "kicker" or "tickler." The additive used effectively to reduce fermentation time was a commercial chemical called urea. Some moonshiner/bootleggers used it undiluted; others preferred a mix, using in addition quantities of disodium phosphate, dead yeast, and calcium sulphate.

The bigger illicit distilleries took on the look of a legitimate commercial enterprise. Big column stills reached three stories into the air, and businesslike production records were kept. Elaborate exhaust systems were required to rid the area of distilling and fermenting fumes, for this was always a problem and one of the surest ways of getting caught. Syndicate vats looked almost like farm silos and ranged in size from a thousand to ten thousand gallons each. Disposal of spent mash posed monumental head-aches. There were no pigs around for the usual rural method of disposal, and syndicate employees found themselves as garbage-men trying to dispose of a smelly slop that must have seemed at times as voluminous as the foam on the Atlantic Ocean. They didn't dare flush it through city sewer systems for fear of instant detection, and if they had no waterfront location whereby the refuse could be piped out into moving water, there was no other way to move it except truck load by truck load.

The force of distillery employees comprised only a part of the syndicate operation. Payoff men, contact men, dispatchers, runners, procurers, and hatchet men all had their job to do. Everybody worked to produce the "alky" (alcohol), and a new name was added to the old list of illicit beverages.

To a casual observer the business of running an alky plant might have looked the same as running a soft-drink factory or a canning house. There were warehouses (usually referred to as "drops") and cutting houses where the high-proof alky was mixed with water to increase the volume and lower the proof—or sometimes blended and colored, or bottled in previously used bottles with counterfeit labels to appear as a first-grade domestic or foreign blend.

The production-control methods in the syndicate distilleries became efficiently managed to the extent that a reasonably good grade of alky could be made for approximately two dollars per gallon. Retail price of the same product in bulk quantity was approximately eight to twelve dollars per gallon. Selling price fluctuated greatly, depending on a number of factors: the working arrangement with the syndicate, volume purchased regularly, one time or repeating customer, pickup or delivery, and, not the least important factor, the risk involved in a particular sale.

Any purchaser having a wholesale buying privilege usually worked through the top echelon of the syndicate. In contrast to the retail price in bulk, ten gallons of high-proof alky (usually from 160 to 190 proof) cut for sale by the shot, would bring a speakeasy operator $500.00 or more, depending on how much the original alky was cut. This profit was fantastic for even the independent speakeasy operator, but consider for a moment the profit for the syndicate-operated speakeasy which was getting its drinks at distillery cost from its own operation. Some moonshining syndicates operated ten to twenty stills in one pool, capable of turning out 1,000 to 1,500 gallons *per day per still*.

It wasn't all roses even for the syndicate czar. Sometimes the runner (transporter/blockader) would get picked off by another syndicate team. Hijackers of spirits or supplies would sometimes be forced to yield to a second set of hijackers before they got home with the merchandise. Alky transported into small towns or villages outside the bigger cities had to pay off local authorities ("granny fees") to gain free movement. Such situations, called "grease spots" or "toll bridges," were taken care of in payoffs of cash or illicit liquor or both. Similar payoffs sometimes found their way into the pockets of prohibition agents and persons of the highest rank.

Another evolution in moonshine distilling was taking place that promised to be a permanent fixture of the future. The automobiles being shot up by the moonshiners/bootleggers and by the prohibition agents were hardly piled up in the junkyard before they were pounced upon. The eager scavenger was looking for radiators to serve as his condensing device. The old standby copper coil or worm now had a quick and easy substitute, and it mattered little if rust or lead cluttered the intricate tubing. The radiator condenser was a quick shot in the arm for the smaller operator, and he needed it. This simple device increased the activity of small operators in the moonshine business more than any other single factor. It gave the ghetto enterpriser and the poor man in general a tool he might otherwise have been unable to afford. An empty oil barrel, a homemade cap, and the junk radiator found him ready for business. On his back, he could carry a few ten-pound bags of sugar, a little corn meal, and a few cakes of yeast. Out of one hundred pounds of sugar and a few pounds of meal, our new businessman could make six to eight gallons of sugarhead. By working hard and adding a few extra mash barrels in his basement, it was entirely possible, with ten dollars worth of equipment, to make a profit of $250.00 per week, spare time. However, his clientele might have to adjust to his distillate, which earned its nickname "popskull" by producing the sensation of buzzing in the head and a thousand hammers pounding on the skull.

It is almost sacrilegious to imagine that sacramental wine requirements, which had already come under drastic regulation, might have been supplemented by a portion of sugarhead. And since the prescription privileges of physicians had also been more severely regulated by that same Supplemental Enforcement Act, doubtless many a menopausal housewife with a migraine headache found relief in a stiff dose of popskull.

The times were not devoid of humor. The flapper generation

seemed to project the atmosphere that all was right with the world and the time had come for all to "eat, drink, and be merry for tomorrow the speakeasy may run out of supplies or I might forget the password."

That was unlikely. What the syndicate and local moonshiner couldn't supply was coming north from the Southern moonshiner. His product was still good, and there were many who liked it better than anything coming off the big alky plants. But the same push was on the Southern moonshiner to some degree as on the city operator. The demand for white lightnin' exceeded his wildest dreams, and he still had his own local customers and general area to supply. He also had far too little aged whiskey on hand for the demands of the times. Before prohibition, the slow-moving mountain moonshiners had had the time to lay by a good supply in charred oak or maple barrels, but no longer. Under the circumstances, the best the moonshiner could do was sell his product "fresh" or direct the Northern buyer to another source—usually a wholesaler for the output of some of the big illicit rectifying plants along the south Atlantic coast, who were successfully faking foreign, quality liquors. Contacts were being made by the advance scout syndicate men, to ascertain the possibility of "manufacturing cooperation." They would add more than guaranteed orders and money, they said. New technical knowledge and ideas on more voluminous output would be other contributions toward a new arrangement. Sugar whiskey was among the first suggestions the Southern moonshiner was to hear. Some were already making sugarhead—especially the moonshiners newer to the business. The practice had spread quickest among those areas who had sent runners north and who in turn had passed on the city methods upon their return. The older moonshiner didn't take to the idea. He had his own formula and his own clientele who liked his distillate the way it was. The idea of sugar whiskey, the use of a rusty automobile radiator, all sounded like a child making mud pies. He would turn out his own product as quickly as he could, sell it "reasonable," and that was that. The mountain man would "think on it," but that greasy looking Yankee didn't make much of an impression and was, in fact, downright "unneighborly."

Such a man was soon in the minority. Stills in the South had quadrupled in number or more since 1900, and though many of the men representing those increases had gotten their stillin' experience from the old timers, they represented a new breed, open to new ideas and especially open to anything that looked green.

Another important juncture in the annals of moonshining history was occurring in this period, and the liaison with metropolitan moonshiners helped to propagate these ideas. Like the big push for sugar whiskey (which was becoming a misnomer in the absence of grain and more nearly a rum), the push was ever greater for improved distilling equipment and a more voluminous output. The majority of moonshiners in the various states did not have the big money of the syndicates or the connections to enlist the technical aid of imported experts in distillery design. They did, however, recognize the need from the earliest days of prohibition to improve upon old methods to meet a demand for moon, that proved astronomical in comparison with the best of "olden days." After the recognition of such a need, the small, low-volume pot stills of various shapes and sizes were found woefully lacking. Experimentation and improvisation, requiring the most exacting skill of the moonshiner, began to take place on a crash basis. Some of the moonshiners had always possessed mechanical ability, and this, added to the ideas coming from the metropolitan areas by way of Southern runners or blockaders and contacts with syndicate scouts, began to effect still design drastically. The new designs occurred only in pocket locations at first but soon began to spread rapidly. Bigger pot stills, which were simply huge tubs with wooden sides and wrapped in copper or galvanized metal, began to make their appearance. Such big tubs for stills would become known as "submarines" (see Chapter 12, Types of Stills and Their Application) because of the new, odd shape. In reality they looked more like an army tank, minus the tracks. Improved heating devices under the stills or cookers gained fast acceptance. Replacing the old wood fire were gas burners, which eliminated most of the smoke of wood and thus offered better immunity from detection.

Crude models of the metropolitan column still were made by welding barrels together in an imitation of the real thing. Pot still-column still combinations were tried by some, and the use of heat from coal, coke, charcoal, and oil became more widespread. Cooking the fermented mash by steam was another efficient method of production; a steam boiler generated steam, which was piped into an enclosed cooker filled with mash.

But by far the most important innovation for the pot and submarine distiller was the use of the "doubler" and "thump keg." The "doubler" provided an escape from the old method of running the distillate back through the still a second time to obtain high wines. The reader will recall from Chapter 6 the process of running low wines (first run) and then doubling (second run) to obtain a distillate of high alcoholic content. Understanding and use of the doubling device was almost unknown to the widely separated moonshining communities until prohibition days.

Some moonshiners consider the doubler and the thump keg two slightly different apparatus, but they are essentially the same thing, depending somewhat on the design and precisely how they are used. Figure 11 illustrates this evolutionary device. As shown, the doubler is placed between the still and the worm (condenser) box, and the vapor from the boiling mash enters the doubler on its way to the worm (or automobile radiator, whichever is used). As the steam empties into the doubler at the bottom of the pipe extension (called the needle), tremendous heat builds in the doubler, and before the steam vapor passes out the top of the doubler barrel, the vapor has undergone the effect of being double distilled or doubled. This operation, then, removed the need to run the distillate through the still a second time. This doubler barrel or thump keg is generally smaller than the still and can be made of wood or metal. The doubler is sometimes "charged" with distillate from a previous run or with fermented mash previously undistilled. Charging the doubler or thump keg allows the steam passing through the barrel to pick up vapor and add further strength to the distillate. The thump keg derives its name from the fact that a thumping noise is heard as the steam from the still "pukes" (moonshining vernacular) into it, carrying solid matter. This noise has been the downfall of many a moonshiner. It can be heard a good distance in the woods if all is quiet. The doubler-thump keg also serves the function of a filter. Solid matter that is carried out of the still is trapped during the passage of the steam vapor and, after too much buildup takes place, can be emptied. Not all moonshiners charge the doubler or thump keg with mash or distillate. For some it is used as a second boiling point for the steam vapor and as a filter, only. Another method of doubling (called the "piggy back ride" or "trick and a half"— a single doubler is a "trick") is accomplished by the method

Figure 11   Small pot still with the evolutionary "thump key"
or "doubler."

Lyndall Mason

illustrated in Figure 12. Steam vapor coming from the still is piped into a second (or even a third) barrel of mash where it passes through, picking up alcoholic vapor on its way to the last stage doubler and on to the condenser. This operation becomes more efficient as the unheated mash becomes hot from the steam passing out of the still. All sorts of cross combinations of this type were used frequently, but old-time quality suffered greatly.

The thump keg or doubler became the moonshiner's pride and joy, although the remark is still heard to this day from some of the old moonshiners: "I don't want nary a thing to do with that newfangled thumper keg, I'd druther do hit the ole' way." In a sense the old moonshiner had a point; the newer breed was making compromises from which it would never recover, but the two decades after prohibition began would show more evolution in still design than had been experienced in five hundred years by the small, noncommercial distiller.

Still seizures for 1926 and 1927 reached almost 51,000, and the

Figure 12 The "piggy back" doubling method.

Lyndall Mason

number of persons arrested for prohibition violations climbed to a figure of 152,457. More new states with near-negligible records of still seizures in the past began to show dynamically increased activity. Arizona, Illinois, Michigan, Wisconsin, Washington, Utah, Wyoming, Colorado, Idaho, and Nevada were but a few. The 1926–1927 still seizures did reflect a decrease over 1925 but hardly what the dry advocates might have expected. The wet forces were more sure than ever that prohibition was a disaster and were vehement in reminding a weary public of fluctuating opinion that the dry era had not been the idea of the metropolitan population and had been forced upon them by the states and rural populations. The drys were just as certain that industrial productivity, improved family life, higher moral standards among the majority of the people, and a multitude of other virtues was being accomplished in spite of the evils all about them. And there were the people of the in-between philosophy—those who wanted a drink but wanted moral and social order into the bargain. The public mood fluctuated from wanting the moonshiner/bootlegger locked up to not wanting him locked up because a source of supply would thereby be lost. Only the moonshiner/bootlegger seemed to be happy with the situation. This mood was not without reservation, but he had gotten more than his share of the breaks. Little had temperance forces ever guessed that the massive arrests would crowd the courts with impossible work loads of prosecution duties. Small percentages of convictions, mass confusion, and a worsening situation continued. Some of the public charged that speakeasies and blind tigers all over the cities had the sanction of law with cooperating policemen at every saloon door. The Prohibition Bureau, trying to do a good job under impossible circumstances, was having on occasion many of its own personnel going sour. Some agents were guilty of collusion with moonshiners and bootleggers, or a party to alcoholic-sales-permit abuses. Adding to the public unrest were cases of poisoning from contaminated moonshine both from the use of automobile radiators in distilling and converted alky from commercial alcohol, deliberately diluted and contaminated by the government in an attempt to discourage use.

It wasn't all bad news. General Smedley Butler, a marine career officer who took over the Philadelphia police department, did a commendable job in helping to rid Philadelphia of a large proportion of its moonshining population. Many prohibition agents were doing a brilliant job of enforcement, but they were suffering casualties like flies. High-speed automobile chases, gunfire from ambush, gunfire from still raids, and occasional accidents in line with the hazardous duty were all taking their toll. It was the age of Izzy Einstein, Moe Smith, and Elliot Ness's "Untouchables," when being a prohibition agent required skullduggery, disguise, impersonation, and every gimmick imaginable. Sometimes there was no satisfaction in the arrests, when as often as not the offender would go free under political influence, bribery, coercion, or any other of the escape methods.

Federal pleading with state and local authorities for the most dedicated cooperation in enforcement continued to receive mixed results. Some areas turned in good performances and others would handle both serious and light offenders with kid gloves. Judges in areas who depended upon their judicial positions by election support kept in mind the political overtones of too rigid a procedure.

Still seizures for 1928 took an upturn to 28,162, and arrests for violators hit an unprecedented high of 89,115. The following year, 1929, still seizures dropped to 26,465, and arrests were down to 80,364; but new factors entered the picture. The stock-market crash on Wall Street now became an issue, and writers, economists, historians, and the lot would speculate for decades over the influence of the depression on prohibition. In this writer's opinion, the first shock wave of the economic downturn slowed down every activity, including moonshining and bootlegging. There are, however, those who then, and now, argue that the new masses of the unemployed contributed greatly to the number of moonshiners and bootleggers. A contrary point of view would insist that, even if this were true, an unemployed population without weekly paychecks would be limited in its ability to buy the moonshiner's product. There is no doubt that the unemployed did add to the ranks of the moonshiners' total number, but that combined total had a greatly depressed potential market and a much poorer population to draw from in areas of sales potential.

The syndicate bigwigs would be the last to have any significant decrease in business, and the smaller moonshiners of the cities would feel the brunt of such a downturn first and hardest. The big boys were fighting hard to stay on top, though enforcement pressure on occasion kept their backs to the wall with increasing efficiency. Syndicate emissaries were still getting contraband liquor from cooperative sources abroad and transacting their business in code. Code breaking in this era was not the accomplished science it is today. When federal authorities began intercepting strange messages in code, it was obvious international bootlegging was becoming more sophisticated, and work on double-coding systems of intricate gibberish became a new task in prohibition enforcement.

The help of a woman who had gained the reputation of an expert cryptanalyst was sought to help solve one such case. A ship built in Canada for the purpose of transporting liquor was sighted by the Coast Guard off the coast of Louisiana and refused to respond to the "heave to and be searched" order. The vessel was pursued beyond the limits of maritime-law jurisdiction and sunk while flying the Canadian flag. A diplomatic embarrassment resulted, and the U.S. government was presented with a claim for $365,000, based on the assumption that the ship and cargo were Canadian owned. United States officials claimed that the ship in question (named the *I'm Alone*) belonged to residents of New York. After painstaking analysis of twenty-three previously coded messages subpoenaed from telegraph companies, Mrs. Elizabeth Smith Friedman, the woman cryptanalyst, was able to confirm Treasury Department information about the ship and her past operating violations. Not only did the decoded messages reveal shipping data on the contraband liquor, but further checking into the code names of the conspirators ultimately led to their arrest and established American ownership of the vessel. The Canadian claim was settled for $50,000 in lieu of the insult to the Dominion flag and for destruction to the property of Canadian seamen. The price seemed high, but another source of contraband liquor came to an end.

On July 1, 1930, the primary enforcement responsibility of the prohibition laws was shifted from the Bureau of Internal Revenue to the Federal Prohibition Bureau of the Department of Justice. This recommendation had been made by the Law Enforcement Commission, set up to make recommendations for improved enforcement of the prohibition laws. Previous commissions had made the same recommendations, and members of the judicial community had generally encouraged the change. Some temperance forces argued against the measure on the grounds that such a move amounted to "passing the buck" and putting enforcement procedure in the hands of nonveterans in prohibition problem solving. Such a suspicion had little foundation in view of the move of many of the same officers who had worked under the Prohibition Unit to the command of the Department of Justice. A weary public hoped against hope that the move would be more effective in the suppression of a criminal element that thrived in the midst of every effort by government to eradicate them. The Wickersham report of the Law Enforcement Commission submitted other recommendations that even for the times seemed rather drastic. Recommended was a change in law to permit the casual or slight violator to be tried before United States commissioners without trial by jury. The violator would have the right of appeal if he felt unfairly treated, but in the minds of some the whole idea looked too much like a kangaroo court to become a permanent fixture. The idea would relieve congestion in the courts, however, and a look at past history would reveal that the highest number of convictions among the less serious cases was obtained in this manner. In the past, simple pleas of guilty in mass trials became known among violators as bargain days.

Still seizures were down from 1929, though personal arrests were up. The records for 1930 showed 24,174 still seizures and 85,174 arrests; for 1931 both still seizures and arrests were down to 21,535 and 76,340, respectively.

In the fall of 1931, the kingpin of Chicago bootlegging and moonshining circles was running out of luck. Reputed to have under his control, aside from bookie joints, gambling houses, speakeasies, and brothels, was an ironclad arrangement to guarantee a commission on every case of illegal whiskey brought into Cook County. Illegal whiskey was not his ultimate downfall; the discovery of a diary-cashbook revealing a part of his big operation was the key that locked his cell. After painstaking inquiry into the affairs of the criminal giant, along with the cooperation of some Capone confederates, Capone was brought to trial. His summons to court was a close call that might have cost Frank J. Wilson, former chief of the U.S. Secret Service, his life. As the showdown date for trial approached, Al Capone imported a cleanup force to eliminate his adversary. After a tip-off, Wilson was able to evade the suspected attempt on his life and participate in the trial of Scarface Al.

It was still touch and go, for Capone was suspected of having influenced the jury. In a move that is still smiled about in judicial circles, Federal Judge James H. Wilkerson switched the whole panel of jurors with a fellow judge, trying a different case. In mid-October, Al Capone heard the verdict of guilty for his tax evasion, and one more ganglord was biting the dust.

In the presidential year of 1932, public outcry against the Eighteenth Amendment became a fighting national issue. The outcry was based on moral and constitutional grounds, with the recognition of unenforceability of the act no less a consideration. Some of the populace would compromise and accept alcohol in the form of light wines and beer of a strengthened variety. This was impossible under the present provisions of the Volstead Act, which still limited the alcoholic content of the beverages to .05 percent alcohol. Politicians played the issue with care, but the mood of the people was firm enough in this year to affect national party leaders in favor of repeal. The opposition was still great among temperance leaders and other influential people who felt sufficient time had not been allowed to judge the issue properly.

The presidential campaign of 1932 brought the issue to a head. The Democratic platform plank came out unreservedly for repeal; the Republican plank appeared to favor a compromise in the area of revising the Eighteenth Amendment with certain safeguards surrounding it.

In November of 1932 the Seventy-second Congress prepared a joint resolution for repeal of the Eighteenth Amendment. After submission through channels of government to the states, ratification was accomplished for the first time by conventions and not legislatures. On December 5, 1933, the Secretary of State certified the ratification, followed by the President on the same day, with a proclamation declaring the Eighteenth Amendment repealed. Federal prohibition was over, but states still had the right to remain wet or dry as the dictates of their people demanded.

The great experiment was over after almost one hundred years of preparatory groundwork. For almost fourteen years the issue raged and brought in its wake untold losses and maybe even some gains. It seems appropriate to add, in the closing of this phase of moonshining/bootlegging history, that the violations on record have given us only a glimpse at the illicit activities of an era. What would the real records look like?

But what does it matter. Prohibition was over, and illicit liquor making was a thing of the past. The moonshiner would toss his still on the scrap heap and go back to work. Or would he?

CHAPTER NINE

Post-Prohibition, World War II, and Moonshining of the 1950's

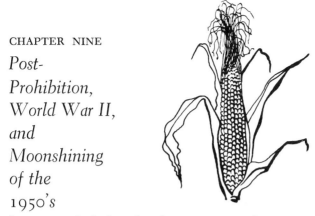

It appeared obvious by the year 1933 that a considerable number of stills were contributing to the scrap heaps of the nation, or being relegated to store rooms or attics. Still seizures were down to 16,465 as compared to 22,749 in 1932. Arrests were down slightly from the all-time high (throughout the entire prohibition era) of 101,317 for 1932.

The apparent downturn, however, would not be reflected until the 1934 report because all reports covered a fiscal year rather than a calendar year, and actual repeal had taken place on December 5, 1933, a period to be shown in the 1934 report.

One of the interesting statistics of 1932 and 1933 showed what must have been a vast, last-minute roundup of violators for both years, showing a total figure of arrests at 198,800, for those two years.

The 1934 report did show an immense drop in still seizures—9,869, the lowest figure since 1919. These late prohibition-year statistics are highly questionable, however. Did they simply reflect lack of enthusiasm for an unenforceable law?

The total figure of still seizures for the prohibition era was a staggering one. In the sixteen years, starting with wartime prohibition in 1919 and ending with the 1934 report, a total of 340,794 illicit stills had officially been recorded and seized by authorities!

A sigh of relief must have resounded across the land like a mighty hurricane. If it did, it was to be short-lived. Many members of government and most of the nation's citizens felt that the legal distillers could almost automatically take over their rightful place in supplying the nation's beverage needs. The states that still elected to enforce state prohibition could take care of their own problems with the help of federal enforcement agents, but national repeal would open up legal liquor to the vast metropolitan centers, and the problem would be over. The legal distilling industry knew better, and the war-weary Department of Justice and the Bureau of Internal Revenue of the Treasury Department, knew better. On May 10, 1934, the Federal Prohibition Bureau relinquished control of liquor-law enforcement to the newly created Alcohol Tax Unit of Internal Revenue. The hard-core moonshiners and bootleggers hadn't gone out of business to the same degree that the small timers had, and it was this problem that prompted the grave outlook of enforcement officials. The small, short-term, prohibition moonshiners had failed to see post-repeal possibilities, or their personal thirst had been their most important concern, but the more alert moonshiner/bootlegger had bigger plans.

There was hardly a breathing spell after repeal for the enforcement agency. Deaths, assaults, and injuries kept raising the toll. From January 1920 to May 1934, 126 agents lost their lives, ninety-six agents were seriously wounded, and 319 assaulted or otherwise injured by violators. The period had had its share of freak situations.

In addition to the more usual methods of casualty, agents had died from such oddities as scalding to death in boiling mash vats, heart attacks in the heat of a raid, overexertion, severe exposure to the elements, asphyxiation from fumes while raiding a still, ambush on the way to federal court, accidental discharge of firearms, and just plain disappearance.

The problem of liquor supply by the legal industry should not have been overlooked by anybody. The distilleries that had operated legally before prohibition were not ready to resume normal operations. Much of their equipment had been dismantled or required extensive repair. The work to be accomplished simply could not be done in so short a time.

Stocks of aged whiskey were very, very small and amounted to only 6 or 7 million gallons. An industry that for commercial purpose was practically dead in 1920 had on its hands the task of complete reorganization and re-establishment. Bootleggers and moonshiners on the other hand had vast supplies of aged contraband whiskey, alky from their own operations, and a variety of moonshine made by every possible formula. In short, whatever the public had a taste for, the moonshiner/bootlegger could still supply. Most of the syndicate moonshiners had long ago given up the attempt to fake-age alky or moonshine, for experiments in that direction had ended in the same frustration encountered by the legal wine industry in trying to dealcoholize its wine. When the aging was attempted, it usually took the form of filling charred, or sometimes uncharred, wooden barrels with the distillate and subjecting them to high temperatures. Storage in a closed room with temperatures in the 120- to 135-degree range was supposed to cause rapid absorption into the wood, to accomplish quickly what required much longer to accomplish in the legal distillery. This attempt (called "toasting" or "kiln aging" by the moonshiner) didn't fulfill his expectations, and caused rapid evaporation loss, too. Contraband liquor continued to be his best source for the aged product.

The syndicate moonshiner continued to maintain his contact with the southern moonshiner and occasionally with moonshiners in other geographical locations. This interest was particularly directed to the southern moonshiners, for they had always remained by far the biggest producers. Other states had become large in the illicit operations, but after supplying the needs of their own areas, seemed to have less surplus. States outside the South and Southwest still large in moonshine operations after repeal were Illinois, Indiana, Maryland, Michigan, Minnesota, New Jersey, New York, Ohio, Oklahoma, Pennsylvania, and Wisconsin.

The relationship between the syndicate operations and the independent moonshiners of the South fluctuated in success and in geographical locations. Considering the entire situation of the period, it can be concluded the syndicate was successful, but it came nowhere near to organizing the southern moonshiners as one vast supply group. One might say that the syndicate operations courted the southern moonshiner, made love to him, but never was able to marry him. The southern moonshiner could not be tightly organized for long then, nor could he at any future date. His temperament, heritage, individuality, and way of doing business simply would not lend themselves to such an arrangement on a mass basis. If it happened, it would be among a younger generation, and primarily, with rare exception, near the industrial centers and not the back country.

In some instances, however, syndicate penetration into the South met with resounding success.

In the author's home state of Virginia, one such operation was uncovered, making national headlines and exposing to view an impressive list of county, state, and federal authorities who had participated, or were suspected of participation, in the fraud against the government. Three other things developed in this trial which were not the rule in southern moonshining: First, the government sought in its prosecution of the case to prove widespread conspiracy to commit tax fraud in addition to illegal distilling; second, this vast moonshining/bootlegging operation sought to eliminate competition from the little, independent operator and force him into the conspiracy; third, the area of illicit operation in question had been blocked off in sections with kingpin moonshiner and a state officer for each section. The arrangement must by now have a familiar ring to the reader, recalling an earlier chapter dealing with the block-by-block takeover by syndicate gangsters of the metropolitan areas of the North.

The case resulted in the indictment of thirty-four men for conspiracy against the government. Among them was a former federal prohibition agent, former member of the state legislature, a commonwealth attorney, county sheriff, former state prohibition officer, and four deputy sheriffs.

Named as co-conspirators but not indicted were a former sheriff, two former deputy sheriffs, and fifty-three additional citizens.

The trial began on April 22, 1935, and was attended by the noted author Sherwood Anderson. The following is his account of the trial written for *Liberty* magazine in November 1935*:

> What is the wettest section in the U.S.A., the place where, during prohibition and since, the most illicit liquor has been made? The extreme wet spot, per number of people, isn't in New York or Chicago. By the undisputed evidence given at a recent trial in the United States Court at Roanoke, Virginia, the spot that fairly dripped illicit liquor, and kept right on dripping it after prohibition ended, is in the mountain country of southwestern Virginia—in Franklin County, Virginia.
>
> Franklin is a big county and practically all mountains. It lies just south of the county seat, Rocky Mount, and some twenty-five miles due south of the industrial city of Roanoke and a few miles from Lynchburg, home town of Senator Glass.
>
> These big towns and others, growing factory towns, Staunton, birthplace of President Wilson; Winchester, place of many

battles during the Civil War, home town now of Senator Harry Byrd; Lexington, home of Stonewall Jackson and the place where Robert E. Lee went to become a schoolteacher after Appomattox—a Lee was among others recently being tried in the United States Court—all of these towns lie in the famous rich valley of Virginia, the Shenandoah Valley. Lynchburg, as you go west from Tidewater Virginia, is really the beginning of the mountains—Virginia's portion of the famous Southern highlands, land of moonshiners and of the feuds.

Involved in the trial at Roanoke were some of the solid men of the big mountain county. There were merchants, automobile salesmen, liquor financiers, sheriffs and deputy sheriffs, a member of the state prohibition force, a federal revenue man—makers and more makers of moon—and the charge on which these men were tried was not alone that of liquor making, but of a conspiracy to beat the government out of the tax on liquor. Carter Lee, a grandnephew of Robert E. Lee, was up there, facing a possible prison term, and the South was shocked. He came clear. The jury declared he was not guilty. He is the prosecuting attorney of the mountain county and, of all the men indicted, he and two unimportant deputy sheriffs were the only ones who did come clear.

As to the amount of liquor made in the mountain county right on in the years after prohibition ended, some notion may be had by the figures given in the testimony.

Fred O. Maier, representative of Standard Brands, Washington, D.C., testified that 70,448 pounds of a single standard brand of yeast, such as is used in distilling, was sold in the county in four years. The yeast was sold in pound packages, each containing thirty-two pieces. That sounds something like 21,000,000 brews. A lot. Franklin County, Virginia, has a population of 24,000. The City of Richmond, with 189,000 people, used 2,000 pounds of yeast during the same period. There were said to be single families in the county that used 5,000 pounds of sugar a month.

There were other startling figures introduced by the government. These, totaled by government statisticians, revealed purchases of commodities useful to illicit liquor makers as follows: Sugar, 33,839,109 pounds; corn meal 13,307,477 pounds; rye meal, 2,408,308 pounds; malt, 1,018,420 pounds; and miscellaneous grain products, 15,276,071 pounds.

Some one had invented a five-gallon non-gurgling tin can. That was an idea. Most of the liquor made in this Virginia mountain county had to be run out to some distant city, and one of the pests to the rumrunner is the gurgling sound arising from containers on rough roads. The non-gurgling cans apparently worked.

And they sold. Into this one mountain county during a four-year period there were shipped 205 carloads of 516,176 pounds. One witness testified that a carload runs about 3,000 cans, which means that the county consumed more than 600,000 of the five-gallon cans.

That would account for some 3,501,115 gallons of moon liquor pouring down out of this mountain county, being rushed at night in fast cars into the coal-mining regions of West Virginia, to the big Virginia towns along the valley, to Roanoke, Lynchburg, Norfolk, and on into Eastern cities. The business, once organized, kept growing. They were at it up to the moment when some thirty-four of the more prominent citizens of the county, were brought into the United States Court.

In this mountain country in the very heart of America, the government in its recent wholesale raid didn't pay much attention to the little moonshiner. He exists everywhere but he doesn't count. On the witness stand at the big trial some of the big makers spoke of these little picayune makers, and always contemptuously. "These little cobwebs," they said, meaning the poor little hillside farmer, the poor mountain white, who creeps off up some mountain stream, under the deep twisted laurel, with a homemade still, to run himself off "a leetle run" for his own use, or perhaps to sell a gallon now and then.

In Franklin County the little fellows were out. The officers, it seemed, had to make a show now and then, a few stills captured and cut up. So they got the cobwebs. Any number of the little fellows testified at the trial. "I tried making a little run but I got caught."

Sometimes one of the big fellows, or a county or state officer, came to call on such a little cobweb.

"Howdy, Jim."

"Howdy, Jake."

"You been making a little now and then, eh, Jim?"

"You know I have, Jake. But I ain't had no luck."

"You got your still cut up, eh?"

"I sure did, Jake."

A smile from Jake. "Suppose, Jim, you go see Jeff. You know who I mean. You talk to Jeff." (Jeff would be one of the big shots.) "I think, Jim, you might have you a little better luck than you been having."

It was the contention of the government in the conspiracy trial that the little fellows, the old-fashioned rifle-toting mountain moonshiners of romance, had been quite put out of business in this section.

The county had been divided off into sections, a big blockader and a state officer for each section. Some of the really big operators didn't make any liquor at all. They let out the job to other mountain men. "Jim, I'll be up your way next Wednesday night at about ten. Where'll be a good place to leave the stuff?"

Witnesses at the big trial, testifying:

"So I was working for Jeff [or 'Henry' or 'Peg']. I was hauling. So I hauled the yeast out, the sugar out, the meal out."

"Where'd you leave it, Ed?"

"I left it just where I was told, sometimes by a bunch of trees or laurels just off the road—maybe ten, fifteen, twenty hundred-pound bags of sugar, so much meal, so many cans, so much yeast."

"You just dumped it down there in the dark? And there was no one there to receive it?"

"There may have been some one there. I dunno. It was black night. I didn't see no one."

"And what did you get for this, Ed? Bear in mind, Ed, you were running the risk of going to prison every trip you took."

"Yes, I know. I got maybe a dollar, maybe a dollar and a half."

There was plenty of testimony of that sort. Men running stills, back in the mountain laurel, for the big fellows, working for the big fellows—some of them testified, turning out moon at ten cents a gallon.

There should have been money in that for the big fellows! There was.

There were plenty of romantic figures at the trial. The government had two attorneys and the county men had some ten or twelve. In a United States Court the judge can question witnesses. He can make comments.

One of the lawyers pleading to the jury for a mountain man: "Men, send him back where he came from. Send him back to his mountain home."

The Judge: "You mean, send him back to keep making the same kind of mean whisky he was making."

There was Willy Carter Sharpe on the witness stand. She is a rather handsome slender black-haired woman of thirty. It came out, when she was questioned, that she had been a mountain child from a neighboring county, and as a child had gone down into a Southern industrial town to work in a cotton mill. Then a spell in an overall factory and a job in a five-and-ten-cent store. She met and married the son of a big shot.

"I began selling liquor around town, drumming up trade."

She had, however, a passion for automobiles and developed into a fast and efficient driver. A Virginia businessman at the trial, full of admiration, whispered of her accomplishments: "I saw her go right through the main street of our town and there was a federal car after her. They were banging away, trying to shoot down her tires, and she was driving at seventy-five miles an hour.

"She got away," said the businessman. He liked her, as did every one in the courtroom. She told her story frankly, as did many other witnesses. It was evident that something new had sprung up in the mountains—big business, mass production, introduced by a few shrewd determined men, the plan being to make the little fellows work at a dangerous occupation—prisons staring at them—for little more than a day's wage.

There were mountain boys and men working nights at the stills—big stills some of them, 1,000- or 2,000-gallon capacity. Men hauling the meal, sugar, yeast, and containers back up into the hills at night.

"What did you get?"

"Oh, I got a dollar a trip."

The lawyers for the defense didn't even cross-examine Willy Carter Sharpe. She told a story of how mountain men become big-time promoters, convoys of cars on the roads at night, herself in a fast car acting as pilot, government men, not fixed, coming in from Washington, the chase at night, cars scattering, dashing through the night streets of towns, the big business carried right on after prohibition ended.

Men in the crowd in the courtroom whispering: "This is the biggest it's ever been in the mountains. This'll clean things up."

One of the men accused—he had pleaded guilty and faced prison: "I'm glad it's over. It had got too big. We don't want our county to be like that."

After she had been on the witness stand and had told her story, Willy Carter Sharpe talked freely. "It was the excitement got me," she said, and spoke of other rumrunners employed by the big shots. "They were mostly kids who liked the excitement." There were women, some of them of respectable families, who came to her—this after she had been in jail, had been in the newspapers. "They wanted to go along with me on a run at night. They wanted the kick of it," she said. She refused to tell who they were. "Some of them had in their veins what you call the best blood of Virginia," she said.

The trial was extraordinary. Even some of the big shots— mountain men who had gone into the outlaw liquor business in the new big way—came down out of the hills to testify for the government. The jury was made up pretty much of mountain men from neighboring counties. The mountain men came down, some of them, to convict themselves. They semed to want to go back to the old ways.

The big way was too cruel. It brought out too many ugly things in men.

Sentences for those found guilty at the conclusion of the trial ran from fines of $5,000 and two-year imprisonment down to suspended sentences. An interesting aftermath of the trial was the indictment of twenty-four persons, nearly one year after the trial, for conspiracy to influence the jury. Two of the conspirators had been federal prohibition officers. A Virginia daily was subsequently to make the comment in satiric humor that, even during the appeal of some of the defendants, their moonshining activities were not suffering.

To the rapid reader who might have passed over the figures brought out in court testimony and revealed in Sherwood Anderson's story, a quick review is suggested. If forty-seven *entire* states on an average produced *just* ten times as much moonshine as that produced by just *one* Virginia county (for the four year period brought out), the total national output would be 1,645,524,050 gallons! What the national output of illicit whiskey really was is only a guess. The rest of the counties of Virginia and the other states had had over sixty thousand still seizures for that same four-year period. What would the output from those operating before seizure have been—and the countless others which were undetected?

The whiskey tax had been lowered in 1934 to two dollars per gallon, and based on this tax (which would not have been applicable in three of the violation years), tax loss to the federal government on the speculative four-year figure above would be $3,291,048,100.

The lowering of the federal excise tax served to keep down the price of legal liquor. Thus it helped to counter moonshining operations, by closing the gap between retail liquor prices and prices on the moonshine market, and at the same time gave a boost to the legal industry. Up to this point and by a rough rule of thumb, moonshiners, from the very beginning of the tax in 1862, had been able to supply moon at prices approximately the same as the federal tax figure alone on legal liquor. There were exceptions, both up and down, and these exceptions were particularly true in time of war or when the government was making a special effort to eradicate moonshiners by bargain tax rates. During the author's field research, a moonshiner was interviewed who made white lightnin' for a syndicate operator on a contractual basis for ninety cents per gallon at the still or $1.70 per gallon delivered to Washington, D.C. (the year was 1939). What the bootlegger sold it for is unknown. Of course, this was bulk quantities, and the moonshiner's output was eight hundred gallons per week—still not a bad income for a mountain man who otherwise might have earned $25.00 weekly at a more normal job.

Federal still seizures held steady throughout 1935 and 1936 at a figure fluctuating between fifteen and sixteen thousand annually. The following year saw a small increase, and still seizures for 1937 were 16,142.

Seeing another upward trend in illicit activity, enforcement authorities pressed harder along every avenue of enforcement to put the moonshiner out of business. Strenuous new effort was made to trace the sale of large volumes of sugar and, as a result, establish a trail leading to the user and supplier. The same system of product surveillance applied to corn and rye meal, malt, molasses, and even whole corn. The system worked fairly well in the metropolitan areas where all of these items had to be bought—and even in the South where big moonshining operations demanded such a large quantity of these products that sales and sources of supply from big commercial houses could not be adequately covered up. In the medium and smaller operations of the South, however, many of the moonshiners were still raising their own corn and rye and making their own malt. Even those who were not could find a perfectly safe source of supply from the hundreds of small grain mills that dotted the entire South. The barter of whiskey for products or services existed plentifully well past World War II. It is still used today, though on a much smaller scale.

The matter of sugar was another problem. During the latter two thirds of prohibition, and after, such a vast majority of moonshiners were distilling from sugar that those who were not using it probably numbered fewer than fifty in each high-producing Southern state.

Molasses distilling up to this period had never been widely practiced over the entire South, although there were spotty instances where it was tried briefly, usually in the coastal areas of Florida or Louisiana. The heavy population areas of the Northeast had been the bigger practitioners of moonshine rum making. It goes without saying that, in this era of moonshining, the difference between rum and whiskey was not always distinguishable. The true definitions of the various beverages had become so intermixed or mismixed from the clear definitions of the legal industry, it is doubtful that in most instances the drinking customer knew what he was getting. The moonshiner might have been equally confused about the true definition of what he was making—but it mattered little to him if it would sell.

Many of the syndicate distilling mills preferred black-strap molasses for distilling, claiming that it produced a quality distillate. Fermenting time of the molasses, too, was said to be about one half that of cornmeal and sugar.

The concentrated effort of enforcement authorities seemed to be making headway. Still seizures for the whole country dropped to 11,407 in 1938, but the government excise tax inched up to $2.25 per gallon. All things considered, the revenooers had some success to be mildly optimistic about. Still seizures now stood encouragingly close to one third of what they had been during the worst year of prohibition. Then, too, the employment situation was getting better, and possibly this would take some of the practitioners out of moonshining (they hoped it wouldn't also send purchases up with the new money in circulation).

Still seizures took another healthy drop in 1940, down to 10,633 for the year. Again the excise tax was increased—this time to three dollars per gallon. War clouds loomed in Europe, and soon the whiskey tax would help to support war costs as had so often been the case in the past, but this time stocks would come partially from inventory storage. Distilleries would be concentrating on war production.

With the coming of 1941, still seizures jumped to almost twelve thousand. Increased excises were only part of the answer. War anxiety and the higher liquor consumption that always accompanied it was another part of the explanation. Partial conversion of the legal distilling industry to wartime needs of medicine, industrial alcohol, and so forth, again gave the moonshiner the impetus for increased activity. Declaration of war in the last month of 1941 and excise tax increases to four dollars per gallon would have a bearing on illicit activity, as would the continuing success of local-option sentiment.

The excise tax increased again in 1942 to six dollars per gallon on whiskey for beverage use, and local-option elections were scoring vast gains for the dry forces. During this year, local-option elections in approximately 1,500 geographical locations showed more dry gains than the previous eight years. Of the previous period, when over twelve thousand local-option elections were held, dry sentiment prevailed in almost two thirds of them. Dry sentiment was still strong enough that an established 36 percent of the national population favored wartime prohibition. Many forces combined to offset a national move to prohibition, however. But even without it the moonshiner had a bright future if he could overcome some obstacles.

One of these obstacles was an effort on the part of federal, state, and local governments to restrain drinking in favor of the war effort. Legal compulsion seemed soft-pedaled in favor of an appeal to patriotism and dedication to the task at hand. Many influential leaders lectured the public on the unwisdom and unpatriotism of excessive drinking in wartime. Regulation of selling hours of intoxicants and restrictions on advertisements pertaining to the sale or drinking of hard liquor also were effective. And, needless to say, there were thousands fewer young men to drink the legal or illegal brew.

Still seizures for 1942 dropped by an encouraging 454 from the previous year. Lt. Col. James Doolittle was bombing Japan; the battle of Midway and the horrors of the Bataan death march had the attention of the American public as the country fought on in the most devastating war the world had ever known. With millions of American young men away at war and severe rationing previously unknown, it was to be an entirely new world for the moonshiner.

By 1943 still seizures had dropped to 5,654, the lowest figure since 1918. The syndicates and other independent city buyers kept calling for the merchandise, but the ability to supply was running into trouble. Sugar was the big item, and it was as scarce as the proverbial hen's teeth. Grain shortages could be overcome by the little man, but the bigger operations failed to deliver. Second only to the shortage of base products for mash making were the lack of metal supplies for still construction. The still, like a wood-buring stove, burned out frequently after continuous use and needed replacement. Copper was not to be had and certain to be traced if it was; the substitute, galvanized sheet metal for the big pots and submarines, was equally hard to come by and when the moonshiner resorted to using tin originally made for barn roofing, that worked only for a fleeting period of time. Copper tubing for the worm was even scarcer. If all the copper hadn't gone to war, there were few moonshiners who knew where to find it. Junk automobile radiators, which had been adequate in supply since prohibition days, were becoming just as scarce. A horde of non-moonshiners had found a use for them, keeping the diminishing number of American automobiles in service. And behind the garages and mechanics came the junk dealers who would collect and sell anything that felt hard at premium prices.

It wasn't unusual in moonshining country to see a number of vehicles coming down the highway with the grilles removed. During the week, the family car would be minus a radiator and have it put back for the Sunday trip to church. What was the use of putting the grille back in place—it would just have to come out on Monday.

The moonshiner improvised in a thousand ways during the hard years, grumbling all the while that the son, nephew, or neighbor who had stood by his side and helped with the stillin' was now "across the water fittin' the 'slant eyes' and 'notsies.'" The younger ones could be replaced at the still but not so well at the wheel. The expert drivers were probably handling tanks or convoy trucks by now. The older men had lost their nerve—the U turn at high speed was for the youngsters, and no amount of money would make them attempt the beautifully executed "deluxe turnaround" if confronted by the ATU boys (Alcohol Tax Unit agents.)

The deluxe turnaround was the pride and joy of young moonshining runners. It took raw courage and timing executed to the split second. The maneuver consisted of throwing the car into a skid and applying the emergency brake (emergency brake held only the two rear wheels) lightly; then giving the steering wheel full circle turns while at the same time jamming the accelerator to the floorboard. Done properly at high speed, the action would give the feeling of leaving the eyeballs looking south while the knees were headed north; done improperly the driver was already dead.

Vehicles used for running were mechanical masterpieces and kept in the finest condition. Often they had under the hood Cadillac or special racing motors to outgun the ATU agent in races across mountain roads, sometimes exceeding a hundred miles an hour. Heavy springs and extra gas tanks (for moon storage—not gas) were frequently used to enable the runner to haul a heavy payload. Often a pistol or shotgun lay in the front seat for use against the "federal boys" or a competitive moonshiner/runner. During this period, the 1940 Ford coupe was the favorite car of the professional runner. Characteristics of balance, construction, maneuverability, and speed made it ideal for the job to be done. It was a thousand dollar-a-week job if the driver worked every night and lived through it.

Cars, too, were another problem of the war years—'40 Fords or any other make suitable for the job. It became the age of the taxicab runner. Cab companies with a more generous gas allowance than that of private citizens became very active in running moon during the war years, and some cab and cab company owners were successful bootleggers. Their runs were generally short, to nearby cities, but they helped conserve gas for the long-distance runs.

With all the obstacles involved, the moonshiner managed to keep going. Losses of stills were heavy, and they hurt badly with replacements so difficult to obtain. Losses by seizure in 1943 totaled 5,654 stills.

It must have been a time when the Southern moonshiner sometimes wished he was owned by the Northern syndicate operation—especially if the syndicate's supply sources were better than his own. Some few of the syndicates were better off in that regard but only if they had captive businesses which could help provide such needs, or connections which bypassed normal procurement. But the North and Midwest were not the illicit centers of former days. New Jersey, Pennsylvania, Maryland, Ohio, Indiana, and Michigan were passing out of the picture. Only New York seemed to have the spunk of the old days. If the illicit banner was to be carried to the end of the war, the Southern moonshiner would have to do it. Every moonshiner seemed to be more and more on his own, and government people were everywhere—price checkers, ration-book checkers, meat checkers, gas and vehicle-tire checkers, and hordes of others.

The need for further improvising taxed the ingenuity of the Southern moonshiner as national shortages became even more severe. For a man cleaned out and unable to buy a good still, he was now faced with using discarded oil barrels, zinc laundry tubs, discarded hot-water heaters, junked soft-drink coolers, and anything else that could be formed into a still. Occasionally he would find an old-style refrigerator condenser which could be used. The worm or condenser had a reasonably long life but seized stills, working at the time of capture, were usually destroyed on the spot by dynamite or the swinging axes of the ATU agents. Worms and caps were generally chopped up for good measure or brought back to headquarters scrap heap. After a run is completed, the moonshiner will always carry away the cap and condenser. These are portable and represent an important part of his still setup, and in case of loss cannot always be replaced quickly. When a still is found by agents not operating, it is rare to find the cap and condenser in place.

Other methods of improvisation took the form of experimenting with new distillable base products. Men tried distilling cabbage, potatoes, and even tomatoes. Honey was used often as a sugar substitute and so was home-grown cane molasses and homemade maple syrup. Many moonshiners had their own beehives, but cane for molasses making or producing trees for maple syrup supply were more regional in nature and more limited in usage.

Occasional occurrences of sickness, lead poisoning, and blindness made headlines amidst the news of war. Driven by greed, the moonshiner went to greater and greater extremes in whiskey making, and contamination was the obvious result. He was probably guilty of making more rotgut whiskey during the closing years of the war than at any other time in history. "Rotgut" is a term used in a very broad sense to define any kind of illicit distillate which was too worthless for human consumption. It was possible and often probable that the very first run a moonshiner made was nothing but rotgut in the technical sense. If spoiled or contaminated fruit—rejected or moldy grain—were used, which was not a rarity at all, nothing he turned out would be anything but rotgut. Normally, the rotgut portion of a run was the last run made and came about in the following manner: If sugar was used by the moonshiner, and almost all by this time did so, his first mash would be made with fresh yeast, newly ground cornmeal, and malt, with the sugar thrown in according to his formula. After fermentation, the still beer would be run through the still and the distillate from that run would be called "first sugar." The mash just distilled would be cleaned out of the still and put back into the original mash boxes to scald down a small quantity of fresh meal, and later on a little yeast would be added. On top of all this would be added a heavier concentration of sugar. This is called sloppin' back. All the mash boxes would be done this way as they were emptied of the *original* mash. This second mix would sit for three or four days, until fermentation was complete and the moonshiner was ready to go again. The distillate he would get this time would be called "second sugar." The same thing would be done over again and again for "third sugar" and "fourth sugar." It was a method formulated to use the same mash over and over again by just adding fresh sugar and yeast and perhaps a smattering of fresh meal. It is not hard to imagine what the mash looked like after three or four runnings. Any run after the second-sugar run or certainly the third-sugar run was rotgut, aptly named. Millions of gallons of rotgut were sold during the prohibition, depression, and World War II days. While it could not, in most cases, be successfully pawned off on an experienced buyer, it was sold successfully in ghetto areas, logging and mining camps, and anywhere else a cheap drink would sell well. Often the entire output of any given still would be divided and sold to three ranges of customers. Syndicate or independent bar owners, professional bootleggers, or other such people would get the first-sugar and second-sugar runs; the third-sugar run would go to the small-time bootlegger and the fourth-sugar and rotgut to slum areas and centers of lower-class working men. Many moonshiners sold their whole output and made no distinction whatever in the various runs, allowing a buyer to believe, or even telling him, it was all first and second sugar. If a man got away with it, fine—if not, there was always another buyer waiting.

The second-sugar run was almost as good as the first-sugar run, and some buyers and users liked it better. If the spent mash from the original run was used, the whiskey resulting was sugared, "moonshine sour mash." It was not sour mash in the proper sense of the early moonshiner, for he used no sugar whatever.

Moonshine brandy sold well during the war years and would have sold better had the moonshiner made more of it. Most moonshiners didn't like to distill it regularly, because it took longer to make and tied up his equipment. Crushed apples, crushed peaches (seeds, worms, and all), plums, apricots, pears, or cherries could be used, but fermenting time was lengthy. Whereas a corn-meal, malt, sugar, and yeast mixture would be ready for running in three to five days in hot weather, fermenting time for "pum-mie" (the name moonshiners use for fermenting mash for brandies) would take from three to six weeks. Even with sugar added in quantity, three weeks was about the minimum. The moonshiner preferred to use sugar to hurry fermentation and in-crease the output of his still, but if he didn't have it, he could still make moon brandy from nothing but the crushed fruit or fruit juice.

The brandy sold well and brought a higher price than the corn/sugar whiskey, mainly because it took so much longer to make. One thing that forced the moonshiner to make it was the wartime shortage of sugar. A combination liquor was also fre-quently made and sold which contained half brandy and half corn/sugar liquor. Aside from mixing two distillates to obtain the combination, the same thing could be accomplished by the dis-tilling process. The still would be filled half with pummie and half with still beer made of cornmeal, malt, sugar, yeast, etc. (this was called "crazy apple," "scalding the apple," and a dozen dif-ferent names). Every combination possible to make an alcoholic drink has, without a doubt, been tried by the moonshiners. One moonshiner I encountered during field research made a distillate from green peppers, tomatoes, and garden beets (tops and all). He told me that "it had the purtiest hue you ever seen, and I couldn't hardly wait to drink it. Reckon I should'na done it, though. Me and Clyde [his still hand] both had whelps allin' over us as big as peach seeds for nigh to two weeks." It is impossible to say what caused the "whelps." The moonshiner admitted, somewhat reluctantly, that he had sold the rest of the green-pepper distillate to a power-line construction crew.

Still seizures were 6,801 in 1944, up uncomfortably by nearly one thousand from the 1943 figure. The whiskey tax also went up to nine dollars per gallon, the sixth increase since 1934. Another up in late 1944 was American hope for the foreseeable end of the war. General MacArthur had made a triumphant return to the Philippines, and in the European theater, beverage spirits were also a topic of conversation. Some months previously, Gen. Lawton Collins had asked Col. Mason J. Young what prize he desired for building a Treadway floating bridge across the Rhine in twelve hours. Colonel Young answered that he asked nothing but a few cases of champagne for his engineers. The floating bridge was completed in ten hours and eleven minutes. General Collins paid up, and none of the temperance forces in America was reported as having made an issue over the matter.

By May of 1945, General Eisenhower announced the surrender of the remnants of two German armies. In the same year the moonshiners were still making their contribution with the surrender of 8,344 stills, and the legal industry could envision normal production of alcoholic beverage making. The big effort at moonshine making and the even larger volume of consumption for that year was almost forgivable. There was indeed much cause for celebration.

The young moonshiner returning home to the southland after the war was not the same young man who left. He had seen the world now. The pleas to return to stillin' seemed to fall on deaf ears. There were new ideas in his head—the chance to practice the mechanics trade he had learned, maybe even the chance to go to school and learn a little more than his father knew. The GI Bill and the on-the-job training programs offered enticing alternatives to the old task of stillin'. Though the world seemed flooded with returning servicemen, some of whom might not find their niche in society, on the whole the hope of a brighter future was present.

Moonshining activity was not to change much in the three years after the war. There were still shortages of metal, and an automobile could be had only at a premium. Purchases with mustering-out pay, in addition to the heavy demand of the civilian population which had waited four years for its chance, was forcing the automobile market to unheard-of price ranges. If a new car was to be had, it generally carried with it a thousand-dollar "greasy palm" payment in some form. The moonshine runner either had to make out with his old transporter or pay black-market prices for a new one.

For the three years of 1946, 1947, and 1948, still seizures held steady at an average of 6,500 annually. The South was by now almost all alone in moonshine making. Even New York had dropped to only seventy-six in 1946 and forty-seven in 1948. Arkansas, Illinois, Maryland, Pennsylvania, and Texas had all dropped under eighty still seizures per year. The only state outside the South still showing moderate activity was Oklahoma. Of the 6,757 still seizures for 1948, 6,020 of them were accountable to nine Southern states. Georgia led in greatest number of violations, then North Carolina, Alabama, South Carolina, Virginia, Tennessee, and Mississippi, with Kentucky and Florida tying for eighth place.

The controlled level of moonshining activity after the war was not attributable simply to the problems and shortages the moonshiner encountered. Outstanding work by enforcement authorities was a prime moderating influence. The extent of this force was in one way evidenced by the deaths of twenty-six additional agents in the line of duty, since the repeal of the Eighteenth Amendment. Another important factor, which was to have increasing influence in liquor-law enforcement, was better and better participation by state enforcement agencies. A burden that had for years been primarily on the shoulders of federal authorities was now more equally shared by state and local enforcement agencies. With the cessation of war and the alleviation of the manpower shortages, the states having alcoholic-beverage-control boards or similar agencies continued to upgrade their methods and personnel. Most still raids continued to be made with enforcement personnel of both agencies, but state strength progressed to the extent of making raids unaccompanied by federal men if the occasion called for such action.

Sometimes the good work was all in vain, for many areas continued to have a policy of leniency for the moonshiner. Numerous judges of the South were accused of outright benevolence toward the illicit operators. A radio newsman would occasionally bring to the public attention news of a judge who would give stiff sentences to the moonshiners during morning hours of court—for benefit of the newspaper reporters—then in the afternoon, when no newsmen were present, suspend the sentences.

The level of moonshining activities took a sharp upswing in 1949; the federal seizure figure exceeded eight thousand. Several factors explained this increase. In 1948 and early 1949, the Southern economic picture was akin to a recession, and unemployment figures started to rise. Younger men, and especially the former servicemen of less educational background, were not being taken into the ranks of industry as fast as hoped. Many of them, married with children to feed, now had second thoughts about the possibilities of stillin'. The temptation was especially severe if they had had ties to the illicit business in former years or if members of their family circle were yet active. Some of them had resisted the occasional reminders from elders, in postwar years, that "sugar's plentiful now, Ed," or "Wouldn't you like to load that Plymouth down and take a little trip to Baltimore?" It was quick money, but the federal ATU and the state ABC boys were getting better in their surveillance. There were rumors around the still that those little planes overhead could see what was going on below, and it unnerved the moonshiner. The more knowledgeable ex-serviceman, who might be carrying in the grain and sugar or carrying out the white mule to market, indeed confirmed that long-range camera lenses could record activities over long distances. Another factor was the brooding ex-serviceman who seemed overcome with the obstacles of his future and needed a little "snort" to pacify the days. His meager finances had no surplus to pay for legal drinking likker, much less a federal tax of nine dollars a gallon and a state tax to boot. There was plenty of reason to believe many others were having the same problems and that maybe a little more makin' could do two people a favor and help their economic lot as well.

Federal still seizures rose again in 1950 to 10,030—and yet again in 1951 to 10,177. Part of the picture was greater effectiveness by the revenue men (they were fewer in number since 1939, but the capture rates were higher), but in the majority of cases for every still seized another took its place to fill the void in the market and replace the "shiner" who might be on probation or doing a little time. The biggest single factor at this time, however, was one of simple economics: The federal whiskey tax was raised to the staggering figure of $10.50 per gallon—the by now familiar war tax, this time for the Korean conflict. State taxes were raising it even further. The time had come when the moonshiner could make and sell his best white mule for half the amount of the taxes alone. The smallest still in the mountains could now turn out $500 worth of illicit whiskey per week and rest on Sunday. Federal figures for the average daily producing capacity of all seized stills was twenty-eight gallons per day per still.

Whiskey tax rates wouldn't be the only thing going for the moonshiner. The economy was in high gear again, and war anxiety whetted the drinking appetites encouragingly. The legal distilling industry wasn't expected to close up shop with the advent of the Korean War, but the evidence indicated there was no need of it— the tax gap was in itself enough to provide plenty of work room. The moonshiners would lose some of their sons again or perhaps brothers, but the ex-soldier would return home to find the illicit industry more successful than his wildest dreams.

Strange things had been happening as far back as the late 1940's, which had government officials scratching their collective heads. There was something wrong with national consumption figures relating to beverage alcohol. Sharp drops in legal whiskey sales and a consequent drop in revenue didn't seem to tally altogether with the number of annual seizures and estimates of output based on those seizures. The dragging economy of the pre-Korean War period could account for part of the question but not all of it, and wartime buying had not brought legal sales figures up to expectations.

At this point some conclusions were drawn. State and local seizures, added to federal seizures, were showing illicit activity far and above what authorities had thought to be the true state of affairs. In prior years, state records were either not kept, sparsely kept, or discounted altogether for fear of duplication with federal records. It was true in the past that a majority of raids took place with both agencies (and sometimes local agencies) involved. Now, however, increasingly better-kept state records were an important step in better enforcement. The conclusion was drawn by more federal authorities than had ever been convinced before, that seizure records were only partial guides to the determination of illicit activity.

In short, seizure records could be only a guess at how many stills were in operation. In prohibition days, most of the top-echelon people in federal enforcement knew this, but after prohibition was over, the necessity of pursuing statistics seemed not so necessarily pressing an issue.

Now it was time to take another look.

Officials inspecting still-seizure records and scrutinizing scientific analyses of all factors of data realized that something profound was happening to the profession of moonshining. A massive move was under way to capitalize on the whiskey-tax advantage held by the moonshiner. With no state or federal taxes to pay, small overhead, no aging worries, and a multitude of other advantages, the future looked almost as bright for the moonshiner as prohibition days.

Illegal whiskey was gushing out of the South at prices of three to four dollars per gallon wholesale, and being bought by an army of purchasers at two dollars per fifth, and below. Other areas, where illicit distilling had been intermittent, began to get into the act. Moonshining had younger blood, better brains, and more money than at any time since prohibition, and its exploitation was plotted fully.

Two things in the early '50's had federal authorities worried: Moonshiners were building bigger stills of greater output capacity, and at least some of them were emerging from the more remote locations and setting up operations nearer the cities. Part of the movement could be traced to locations in the "soft" judicial districts—areas that had a reputation for dealing lightly with the moonshiners. Moonshiners were quick to learn of and grasp this opportunity. Both the movement of moonshining activity and larger, more expensive operations were having a dangerous side effect—they were throwing operators and bootleggers into closer contact and requiring higher financing, which would lead to the formation of semi-syndicates.

Many of the highest producing states had independent enforcement programs, and some had a policy of joint federal-state seizure. This was further complicated by the fact that some states had no state alcoholic-beverage-control boards or similar agencies but vested all enforcement in local officials. Still other states had no active enforcement at all except that by federal ATU personnel. By 1952 every fear of the magnitude of moonshining organization and output was being confirmed. The data on state and local seizures, when added to federal statistics, was enlightening to the point of shock. These combined totals nearly doubled federal figures alone.

In the North illicit activities were not growing high numerically, but seized stills were often of a very large size with heavy-producing capacity. Such stills could distill from five hundred to two thousand gallons of high-proof alky per day. Federal officials admitted that the production capacity of all stills seized in the decade of the '50's, going by their size and the volume of mash destroyed, had a total production capacity greater than that of the legal industry.

Enforcement officials fought back energetically against the growing tide of illicit distilling. Supply surveillance was stepped up, and a policy of "sell and tell" was encouraged among suppliers. By this method a legitimate supplier of grains, sugar, yeast, malt, etc., was encouraged to be more forthright in reporting a suspected purchaser. Occasionally moonshining activity would come to an abrupt halt in a certain locality, but at a tragic cost. In 1951, one district in Atlanta, Georgia, had an outbreak of death from poison moonshine that took the lives of forty-two people. Retail sales of legal liquor skyrocketed as a result, and moonshiners hurt for business. But only for a while. The bargain-price rates were too great a temptation, and before long, most customers were coming back, in a gamble against their lives.

Poisoning from moonshine can occur in a number of different ways: toxic lead salts deposited by the reaction of moonshine with metal in the still equipment (and particularly in contaminated auto radiators); poisoning from cutting illicit alcohol with methyl alcohol or paint thinner (and if death does not occur from such exposure, blindness is often the result); and an overdose of unfiltered congeners from a run of moonshine is also poisonous.

In the early '50's Licensed Beverage Industries, an organization of the distilling industry, began national data collecting from federal, state, and local enforcement authorities regarding still seizures, sales, interstate movement, and so on, to assist in formulating a more complete picture of illicit activity. By 1952 their findings indicated combined still seizures running at twenty thousand plus. No doubt now remained—moonshining was approaching prohibition levels. Of course there were chances of error from duplication in the combined reports, but on the other hand, information from many state and local authorities was missing entirely.

As to how many stills were in existence, the most conservative estimates among enforcement authorities was one for every one captured. Such alarming data, coupled with statistics on mash discovery and destruction, made it pretty clear that 20 percent of the distilled spirits sold in America was moonshine whiskey. By 1954, with still seizures from all sources totaling 22,913, suspected production of illicit whiskey ran to 35 million gallons. If, as believed, one still was operating for every one seized, national output of moonshine whiskey could be approaching 70 million gallons annually.

Federal agents in the field in 1954 totaled 812, as compared with 1,022 in 1946. Though fewer agents were closing down more illicit stills, the situation was clearly getting out of hand, even with excellent support from many state and local authorities. Moonshiners were shipping vast quantities of moon into the North, Northeast, and Midwest metropolitan areas by car, small truck, and trailer truck.

Arrests were averaging one person for every two stills. With even a small still needing at least two operators, the escape ratio was not encouraging. Of the number captured, a survey by Licensed Beverage Industries indicated approximately one third went free with no jail sentence or fine. The escape ratio involved some overly sympathetic judges, legal technicalities, belief that hirelings and not main culprits had been caught, and a variety of other reasons.

By 1955, combined totals of still seizures were believed to be passing the 23,000 mark. With the bare minimum of two operators per still and two more handling transportation and distribution, the absolute minimum figure of persons employed in illicit distilling would be near a hundred thousand people.

Combined still seizures from federal, state, and local sources showed 1956 as the biggest year in the illicit business since the height of prohibition; moreover, the 25,608 still seizures of that year came dangerously close to the prohibition high of seizures in 1925 (29,087), second high of 1923 (26,050), and exceeded the 1924 seizures of 25,318.

The comparison of 1956 illicit activity to the high marks of the prohibition era was not, however, altogether a fair one. Prohibition statistics were based on federal data only, and now improved state and local figures were showing a more accurate picture. In addition, prohibition activity was so rampant over a larger area and, in some instances, so much better hidden, that the best educated guess could only begin to imagine the real depth of law violation. However, one thing was certain: Illegal whiskey making was at its highest peak since repeal.

How to stop it took precedence over statistical juggling. The moonshiner was like a ten-headed dragon. Capture a still and maybe a man, and two more of each popped up to replace him. New moves obviously had to zero in on the man himself.

By 1957, Alcohol and Tobacco Tax agents (the old Alcohol Tax Unit of 1934 had been expanded), by administrative directive, plotted a more pressing attack on the adversary. The attack was two-pronged: (1) Efforts were stepped up to stamp out the moonshiners' sources of sugar and other supplies; and (2) Still seizures were delayed until agents could catch the operators at work.

In past years a still was often destroyed when found, whether the operator was in attendance or not. The new policy meant close surveillance of the still site, but if the moonshiners could be caught operating the still, not only would they be the prize, but their output for at least one run might be captured, along with fresh mash, sugar, and all the components of their still.

The plan seemed to be working. Still seizures from all agencies dropped to under twenty thousand for 1957 and held to just over twenty thousand for 1958. But it was still tough going. Moonshiners, in spite of advancing living costs of the decade, were still selling bulk quantities of moonshine from $4.50 per gallon to $10.00 per gallon, depending on the state in which it was made and sold—$4.50 in South Carolina and about $10.00 in Kansas. The illegal retailer sold pints for $1.00 to $2.00. Small sales at the still were any and every price, depending on the whims of the moonshiner.

With output so vast, state-to-state shipments were adding to the complexities of stopping the moonshiners. It was suspected that 15 to 30 percent of illicit whiskey was being shipped across state lines. Only 25 to 55 percent appeared to stay within the county of manufacture. Distribution outside the county accounted for ranges of 10 to 50 percent, all depending upon the geographical area in question and the moonshiner's particular method of doing business.

There is one type of bootlegger/runner who is especially hard to catch and/or control. Individually, he is a small operator, but collectively he comprises a very large segment of the intrastate and interstate movement of illicit alcohol. The man referred to is tagged by his suppliers as a "tote and tell" man. He is a former resident (and sometimes former practitioner) of moonshining country who has moved away and is most probably working at a skilled or semiskilled job in a Northern industrial city. When he makes return trips to his home county, he totes all the moonshine liquor he can haul, in addition to his family and baggage, back to his city of employment and tells his trusted associates that he has such a tax-free product for sale. This sideline enterprise serves a number of functions. It provides the transporter his own drinking liquor; the profit of his sales helps to defray the cost of a vacation trip; and it helps the folks back home to sell to a safe buyer who will pay a premium. Twenty-five to fifty gallons of illicit liquor can usually be hauled without very much danger of detection. Although this high gallonage causes the vehicle in which it is being hauled to "set low," state police are not particularly suspicious of a low-slung vehicle if it is full of small children, an obvious wife, and baggage tied to the top of the car.

The tote and tell man has existed from prohibition days down to the 1970's. Closely akin to him is another type of bootlegger/ runner whose activities were widespread in the period 1920–1960. This man was the campus peddler—the young man who helped work his way through college by buying wholesale at the still from a relative or friend and reselling to his friends on campus. His fellow students liked the price, the product, and the feeling of being a part of an illicit act. The modern-day interest in drugs on most college campuses has all but replaced interest in illicit liquor, however.

Distribution patterns were but one of the complexities of twentieth-century moonshining. There were so many types of moonshining activity, they almost defied description. Very broadly, they fell into the following patterns: the kitchen or basement moonshiner, with a small still of twenty-five- to fifty-gallon capacity; the swampland or mountain moonshiner with a small pot still of two hundred-gallon capacity or below; medium-sized moonshiners with pot, submarine, "groundhog" (buried), or small box stills of three- to eight-hundred gallon capacity; big independent operator with large pot, multiple submarines, groundhogs, or boxes, with capacities of seven hundred to two thousand gallons; semi-syndicate operations with one or more locations, having stills of eight hundred-gallon capacity and up; syndicate operations with both intrastate and out-of-state financial backing and large stills of pot, pot-column, or box type, all usually over one thousand-gallon capacity (see Chapter 12, Types of Stills and Their Application).

Moonshining activity of some kind was reported in twenty-nine states during the '50's, but even without 100 percent participation in the illicit business, moonshiners, particularly those of ten southern states, managed to turn out an estimated yearly 40 million and possibly 60 million gallons of nontax-paid whiskey. Revenue loss to state and federal governments would be a minimum of $575 million.

Combined still seizures from all agencies did decline to 20,416 in 1959 and still further to 18,801 in 1960. Perhaps the '60's would find the moonshiners with their backs to the wall and preparing to close up shop.

CHAPTER TEN

Moonshining in the 1960's and the Still Raid

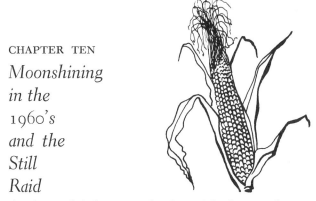

As the 1960's began, a backward look into the 1950's indicated almost one out of five gallons of liquor consumed by the drinking public was moonshine whiskey. Such knowledge was not encouraging news with which to begin a new decade of work, but it stiffened the backbone of every enforcement officer and administrator from Constitution Avenue to the high mountains of the back country. But all was not gloom, and two factors in particular were working in favor of federal, state, and local authorities. National still seizures were dropping, and 90 percent of the problem was confined to ten Southern states (although some illicit activity was found in a total of twenty-nine states). One thing was certain in the beginning of this new decade: The moonshiner of the mountains was losing his historical image as a small backwoods operator. Total still seizures were down, but those captured were bigger, higher-producing units and much more sophisticated. Fears of the 1940's and increasing evidence of the 1950's left little doubt on this point.

In addition to their efforts at stopping the manufacture of illicit whiskey, authorities mounted a strong campaign to induce the drinking public not to buy the illegal product. That, too, was not to be an easy job. Sales of moonshine in some Southern states accounted for as much as 50 percent of total liquor consumption. Only occasionally did the tide abate and usually only for a short duration. Such sales fluctuations usually resulted from outbreaks of moonshine poisoning in high-consumption areas. Atlanta, Georgia, and Winston-Salem, North Carolina, both were hit by massive epidemics of deadly lead-salts poisoning or sickness and blindness resulting from liquor contamination with paint thinner, ether, rubbing alcohol, or antifreeze. Laboratory tests confirmed the already grim picture by estimating a good 30 to 40 percent of all moonshine whiskey contained some concentration of lead salts.

Public-education programs were another tool used by a combination of agencies toward wiping out the moonshiner. It was hoped that a public aware of the potential danger of moonshine drinking would not be such a willing purchaser. A concentration of lead salts two thirds the size of a pinhead makes a quart of white lightnin' a dangerous drink—a fact few moonshine lovers had ever heard. And to be told that .0004 of one ounce will kill was a downright shock to even the most loyal connoisseur. Sometimes hearing was not believing but there would be little room for doubt when the moonshine drinker experienced the abdominal pain, nausea, and a stuporous condition resulting in coma if not death. If he went a step further, he could find out that an immediate illness was not always the result of drinking moonshine; serious illness could occur a year after drinking, and continual drinking of even very low amounts of lead-salts liquors could build up a deadly concentration in his body. Public education helped but not enough. There were 18,800 still seizures made by all agencies in 1960, evidence aplenty that the moonshiner was still a worthy adversary. He still had a record of producing and, through a national network of distribution, selling one out of every seven gallons of liquor consumed in the United States. His tax fraud against the federal and state governments was rapidly approaching three quarters of a billion dollars annually, and he smiled in contentment. When federal and state authorities curtailed his activities in one area, he would move to an adjoining area and operate from there. Local and regional sales were only a part of the picture. Some boasted that 90 percent of their output was going to Chicago, St. Louis, Detroit, Cincinnati, Columbus, Baltimore, Washington, New York, Philadelphia and a score of other industrial cities. It is a popular product, and increasing evidence supports the idea that not only importing but manufacturing is increasing in those areas. Cleveland, Youngstown, Philadelphia, and Detroit, in particular, seemed destined for greater hometown makin'.

Public education on the subject of moonshine drinking came into sharp focus in 1962 in South Carolina. It was the latest effort of enforcement authorities and aptly termed Operation Dry-Up. Coupled with a heavy bombardment of public information and a sweeping dragnet of the countryside, it seemed highly effective. Moonshine sales and production suffered in years to come, and legal whiskey sales rose. Though moderately successful in the state, later facts indicated that some of the moonshiners had merely been pushed into neighboring states, where they continued to operate and possibly later moved back. As enforcement authorities became more mobile, so did the elusive moonshiner. He also pulled new tricks out of his bag or at least tried old ones more often. Mobile moonshining units became subject to capture more often. Trucks, both large and small, boats, house trailers, and campers became moving units of moonshine manufacture. Dummy lumber and transport trucks would mash in in one county or state and run off in another. Complex networks of distilling equipment were set up in houses, warehouses, dairy barns, barges, coal mines, legitimate business buildings, and occasionally under a backyard swimming pool. Electric pumps and pushbutton control panels did the work of the olden-day still hand. Enforcement agents were not in the least in doubt that the moonshiner of legend was going modern. Catching the distiller at his still was yet effective, but less and less was the captured man the real owner and money man of the operation. The little pint-and-jar man of an earlier era was less and less the problem.

Second only to the problem of stopping the still was stopping syndicate distribution, which appeared to have well-organized supply lines stretching all over the country. In another area the moonshiner had proved evasive: Tracing large sugar and other supply sources was becoming more complex. It was no longer rare to find evidence of a gigantic sugar purchase in Louisiana for use in a North Carolina still, with the illegal distillate going to New York. Neither was it unusual for a moonshining ring of the early '60's to use a rented helicopter to fly over his own still site, inspect it, and make sure it was well hidden from view. If the site looked the least bit suspicious, it would be moved, painted green, or covered with camouflage netting.

The big moonshiner of the early '60's had his own walkie-talkies and employed a series of subterfuges. For one thing he had started to add deodorant to his spent mash and would sometimes color it to prevent detection. He would go a step further and booby-trap his own still, never approaching it without first taking a long look around from a safe distance with the aid of field glasses. If his eyes were sharp, he could tell if anything had been tampered with. Better than 18,500 still seizures in 1962 proved he was often outsmarted. Some evidence of chain operation of widely scattered stills gave authorities cause for concern in the early years of the decade.

The era of prohibition seems a terribly long time ago, and yet there is today a similarity of daily occurrences which approach those days more realistically than the average citizen is aware. The city of Atlanta seems unable to eradicate the "nip joints" which plague its alleys and back streets. Some of the estimated 35,000 gallons of moonshine per week, said to be consumed or sold there, is provided by stills operating within the city itself. Like it or not, Atlanta is the moonshine capital of the nation. Tennessee has a problem almost equally severe. Moonshine liquor reportedly flows into Chattanooga at the rate of a thousand gallons per day and into Memphis at the rate of 1,500 to 2,500 gallons per day. Perhaps, as many enforcement authorities believe, illicit distilling is impossible to control, much less wipe out.

The bargain-basement product finds an equally good reception as far north as Buffalo, New York, and Detroit. It is easy to understand why such a cheap whiskey would be hard to give up—from the view of the moonshiner, bootlegger, and consumer. With costs of the early 1960's considered, the moonshiners make their product for about $1.00 to $1.50 per gallon, and by the time it reaches the consumer the price is $2.50 to $3.50 per quart. With the moonshiner selling at $8.00 to $12.00 per gallon wholesale in case lots to the bootlegger, there is still the kind of profit men would die for. The retailer has the option after purchase to cut the liquor, and drinks by the shot at twenty-five to fifty cents each are the real bonus of the business. The competitive edge against legal liquor at an average retail of $5.95 per quart can be readily seen. Moonshine whiskey—costing twenty-five to thirty-five cents per quart to make, and having no tax, advertising, little overhead, no factory maintenance, no license or fringe benefits— has a built-in profit of better than $3.50 per quart. Legal liquor on the other hand, after overhead costs and applicable taxes, might produce a profit of forty cents to one dollar, depending on the brand and local situation.

When and if the moonshining business in America is ever brought to a halt, more than illicit distillers and nip-joint operators will be unhappy. Related work in this illicit field is estimated by authorities to employ more than 200,000 people. Not all are distillers of course, and their activities range from being professional sugar gatherers to craftsmen engaged in making the stills.

There are many interesting facts about moonshining that escape public attention. One is the fact that moonshining has always been a spare-time occupation. This has been so for a variety of reasons. In the earliest days, illicit distilling was worked in conjunction with operating a farm and was an integral part of the food raising–food conversion process. In still later years, moonshining was carried on for the most part in conjunction with another type of work, whether self-employment or a public job. Waiting between periods of mash fermentation allowed plenty of free time to pursue other jobs. Some occupations just naturally went well with moonshining. For a farmer, logger, cattleman, sawmill operator, coal miner, fruit-orchard proprietor, fisherman, barge operator, grain-mill operator, poultry farmer, trapper, railroad-maintenance worker, fruit picker, and countless other workmen, it was the ideal sideline. The occupation of runner or transporter-blockader also helped to train some of the best race-car drivers in the nation. Some of these men have publicly conceded their rum-running days as being the earliest training ground for race-driving experience. But as for the moonshiner, his having a legitimate job served a secondary purpose—it gave him some measure of respectability, allowed a greater freedom of movement whereby his need for sup-plies could be obtained with less suspicion, and made him less suspectable of illicit activities.

The moonshiner of today has more problems regarding concealment than did his predecessor and more trouble with procuring supplies. He is most likely finding that, if he keeps two jumps ahead of the enforcement officer, it is near to a full-time job.

Alabama continued to lead the nation in still seizures when 1963 statistics reached the computers. Total seizures made by federal, state, and local authorities for that year totaled 18,460. Of that number Alabama seizures accounted for 5,010. Not far behind Alabama was Georgia with 3,701, and North Carolina trailed in third place with 2,851. Fourth place in the ratings went to South Carolina, fifth to Tennessee, sixth to Mississippi, seventh to Virginia, and eighth to Florida. Ranked ninth was Kentucky; tied for tenth place in national ratings were Arkansas and Oklahoma; eleventh place went to the northern state of Michigan; ranked twelfth was West Virginia, and in thirteenth place was Pennsylvania. California, Indiana, Maryland, New Jersey, New York, Ohio, and Texas showed some troublesome activity but looked small compared to the big states.

In spite of the efforts of enforcement authorities, moonshining operations were either increasing rapidly or seizure efforts were more effective than expected. Still seizures jumped in 1964 to very near the twenty thousand mark. The real picture was hard to gauge. Authorities had years ago concluded that statistics on still seizures were only a partial guide to the moonshiners' activity. In areas where enforcement authorities were able to concentrate their forces, many illicit stills were closed down, and results were most encouraging. But in other areas, temporarily ignored for a massive concentration elsewhere, activity went on steadily or increased at a furious pace. One of the reasons came to light quickly with every close-up view of a captured site: Stills were getting bigger. Large bubbling continuous stills and huge steam cooker units were not a rarity, and mash seized at each still was growing in volume by as much as 60 percent. The year ended with the near-unanimous opinion of experts in the field that at least 50 million gallons of moonshine whiskey had been made and consumed for an illicit profit of nearly $700 million!

The question invariably arises: What is the reason for such enthusiastic acceptance of a product known to be at times poisonous, supposedly inferior in quality, and always illegal to make, sell, or consume? First of all, millions of people really like it—swear by it, in fact. Long, habitual drinking of the dynamitelike liquid makes all other drinks seem childishly mild in contrast. To some laboring-class men, if a drink doesn't take the top of your head off, you've been cheated.

An opinion of my own, developed during the field research for this volume, is that addiction to drinking moonshine is somewhat different from normal alcohol addiction. Rare is the heavy moonshine drinker who will touch the best bourbon or scotch; he likes the raw, fiery taste of the harshest of moonshine runs. But his inclination goes beyond preference to a unique need. Perhaps one or more of the congeners found in the illicit product enslave his system as heroin enslaves a drug addict.

Then there is the matter of economics. In various geographical areas the illicit drink can be had for one fourth to two thirds the cost of legal whiskey. If the buyer wants to stock up and buy by the quart, gallon, or case, his drinking liquor costs only a fraction of the taxed distillate. Such a man is not the least interested in paying the $10.50 per proof gallon federal tax. No more bearable are the state and local taxes that might add on two, three, or more dollars. At such discounts he will even buy liquor he knows is bad. Unskilled or semiskilled laboring men are prime customers for moonshine, and so is almost every ghetto section of the nation. The dollar of these people must go a long way, and the bargain-rate moonshine supplies their need and saves their dollar. No moonshiner anywhere would last a year without this market, and as long as the market exists, so will the moonshiner.

Yet another reason is the resentment of such people against what they feel is unreasonable taxation by their government. By purchasing and consuming the illegal drink, they fight back. Excessive drinking is closely related to poverty and ghetto life, of course, but prohibition taught us that cutting off legal sources of supply solves nothing. Human nature being what it is, there is no way to view the problem except within the scope of reality.

It would seem the moonshiner/bootlegger has little to worry about. He has always been with us and always will be. Maybe so, but his lot is getting tougher in some respects. His great-grandfather could always find a secluded patch of woodland in which to make his product, but twentieth-century America is closing up fast. His problems of operation will soon be compounded. Hills, hollows, swamps, and mountains will not be so remote in the future. Deserted warehouses, old mines and caves will not be free of scrutiny as the population swells. More scientific detection equipment and at least a part of society will keep the pressure on. A greater accent on the purity of foods and beverages will turn the tide for a few of his sympathizers. A higher standard of living for more people and possible beverage-tax adjustments will cut into his market. Judges are giving sentences more severe than ever, and the county sheriff, who in years past was justly accused of looking the other way, no longer is so anxious to do so. Laws more severe against shinin' are getting eager sponsorship, and fines are more than tokens of public appeasement.

Harold A. Serr, former director, Alcohol, Tobacco and Firearms Division of the Internal Revenue Service, gave his men and an interested public a more specific directive: "Moonshiners must no longer feel comfortable in the community."

Enforcement officers, on the local level in particular, have come a long way toward reversing the old state of collusion with or at least apathy toward, moonshiners. In some areas outstanding work in this direction has been done and at times with tragic consequences. One of my more memorable field trips involved a visit with Bufford Pusser, sheriff of McNairy County, Tennessee. Pusser has gained a reputation as a two-fisted lawman who declared his own personal war on moonshiners. Before many years in office, he had bankrupted too many moonshiner/bootleggers and helped to send a dangerously high quota to prison. Threats on his life thereafter began, but he refused to let up the pressure, which had moonshining and other organized crime at a standstill in his domain of southwestern Tennessee. One of the syndicates he had hurt the most decided, if there was to be moonshining and bootlegging, there had to be one less sheriff. Finally the ambush was plotted at 4 A.M. on a Saturday morning in 1967, when Pusser started to leave his home to answer a routine disturbance call near the state line, separating McNairy County, Tennessee, from Alcorn County, Mississippi. Pusser's wife decided to ride with him, since the call was routine and had come near their normal morning rising hour. Minutes later, as they drove over back roads to shortcut the distance, car lights flashed in their rear-view mirror, and in seconds the trailing car had pulled alongside the Pusser vehicle and started firing with high-powered rifles. The first bursts of gunfire killed Mrs. Pusser and seriously wounded Sheriff Pusser. He had recovered before my visit, but visible bullet scars were a grim reminder that a hostile brand of moonshiner/bootlegger is still around in the 1960's.

Other unheralded officers and agents of the county, city, state, and federal level have had similar experiences in their fight against a doggedly persistent adversary. Theirs is a hard and often thankless job, and moonshining history without them would paint a grim picture of rampant lawlessness. Fortunately, the death rate for modern-day enforcement officers does not compare with that of earlier years.

Finding an illicit distilling operation in the 1960's is sometimes more scientific than it was only a few years ago, but quite often it is not. The same method of watching for smoke, trudging the hills and hollows, tasting the water from a mountain stream for the presence of mash or still beer are still approved methods of detection. Raiding a still has changed little for a hundred years.

About the biggest difference is the mode of transportation to the still site. In the interest of history and perspective, let us first return to a still raid which happened ninety-seven years ago before a more modern experience of the same type of venture. The first still raid depicted is narrated by E. F. Madden, Louisville correspondent for *Harper's Weekly*, and took place in Hardin County, Kentucky, in 1877:

> Leaving Louisville early one evening, we set out for Hardin county, arriving at Elizabethtown a while before the interesting hour when church-yards are supposed to yawn. Lunching first, we then awakened the proprietor of a livery stable, and procured the three best horses he could offer. Half an hour after our party left E. town, as its inhabitants are pleased to designate their pretty village, for a point twenty miles distant, the moon shone brightly through the trees, the air was mild, and balmy, and sufficient wind moved to make traveling by horse as pleasant as possible. As we galloped on towards our destination, however, and in two hours after starting, the wind increased, the moon became partly obscured by fast floating clouds, and large drops of rain fell ever and anon. These continued to grow large in size until, at half-past three, quite a sharp shower was in progress. Riding now became decidedly disagreeable. A miserable rocky road added to the discomfort first brought on by the rain and darkness. The horses ceased galloping, and picked their way along in a quick walk. The moon disappeared entirely, and darkness most intense enshrouded the earth. We could hardly distinguish each other, and having entered a forest several miles in length, full of narrow, winding paths, tall thick trees, and overhanging vines, and bushes of all descriptions, were compelled to proceed with exceeding care and caution.
>
> Deputy Marshal Wyatt rode a white horse, the writer a bay, and Deputy Marshal Whitaker a gray. In order that all could keep together, Mr. Wyatt went in front, hoping that the other two could always perceive his white horse. For a time we were enabled to do this, but by-and-by, as the darkness grew deeper, not even this animal's snowy color could be seen. The path we were following led through creeks, up and down hills, through brush, through briers, and across fields, forests and meadows. Thus seventeen miles were passed before halting. When a stop was made, the gray signs of daylight were appearing in the eastern horizon. The rain poured down as incessantly

as ever, and the three of us were drenched through and through. Changing horses we went forward once more, anxious to reach the still-house for which we had started, before day had fairly come. By some mischance the wrong road was taken, and after traveling in all twenty-two miles, a second halt was ordered. Day had now appeared, and, lest we should be seen by moonshiners, the marshals thought it best to find shelter.

Observing an old farmer feeding hogs, we signaled to him, and on his coming up to within a few yards of us, Mr. Whitaker asked for shelter for man and beast. The old gentleman did not seem particularly desirous of complying, and the others dismounting, ordered him to move aside and allow them to pass. He obeyed, and shortly afterward we were before a warm fire, and our beasts under a warm cover. Breakfast eaten, the old man, a Mr. Gibson, was asked whether there were any still-houses in his section. He answered that there were, but declined to locate them, saying he might involve himself in trouble by so doing. Persuasion was of no avail, reward was likewise ineffective, and the only alternative before us was to try his son. The youth proved only a chip off the old block. Not caring to dally more, the marshals produced pistols and told young Gibson to mount and lead them to the nearest still-house. He obeyed, very reluctantly, going to a place four-and-a-half miles distant in the midst of a heavy wood. There he drew rein, and remarked, "I think it's right close," referring to the location of a still-house. All dismounted, and creeping forward soon observed a light smoke curling gracefully upward from a deep ravine. Another peep showed a still-house, beside which sat a man whittling a stick, and occasionally stirring a fire. The pattering of the rain drowned the noise of our approaching footsteps, and not until the three men stood before him, did the solitary one seem apprised of their coming. Mr. Whitaker's voice first startled him. The marshal said, before he himself was seen, and as the moonshiner sat whittling, "stranger, how are you?"

Leaping to his feet, the other cried, in tones of astonishment, "the devil!"

"Oh, no," said the officer, "Whitaker, Louisville—Marshal for Uncle Sam, you know. My friends, Mr. Moonshiner, Wyatt and Mr. Madden, all true blue, you bet."

The fellow was too astonished to utter a word. He gazed at those before him for five minutes, and then, turning his eyes on Mr. Wyatt, bellowed out, "Oh, say, you've watched the wrong fellow, I swear you have, by gosh! I'm innocent, indeed I am, Mister. I'll bet twenty dollars, and it's all I've got, that I can prove my innocence to any man around here. Yes I can, by gosh."

"No doubt, no doubt," said Mr. Wyatt, "but can you show me a man about here that hasn't got something to do with stilling?"

Before an answer could be given, Mr. Whitaker suddenly ejaculated, "Behind the barrels, boys, here's more coming."

We were hidden in an instant.

Mr. Whitaker said, "Here, you moonshiner, dare give those fellows a sign, and I'll bullet [shoot] you! If they're engaged here, motion with your left hand."

The prisoner did not comply.

Mr. Whitaker cried, "Quick, quick, now. Is either of them connected here or not?"

"Yes, the one on the left, the other is not."

The two individuals continued to approach. When within pistol range, the two marshals sprang up suddenly, and bade them "throw up your hands, and come forward." They answered, "we have no weapons, and will surrender." The three were then searched, and told to sit down and await the coming of more. An hour later young Gibson, the guide, and a stranger, came in view. At the sight of Gibson, the first prisoner, Frank Carter, and the one he had pointed out as concerned in the illicit work, conferred together a few moments. Shortly after, Carter burst forth in a violent torrent of abuse, cursing Gibson and his family, in the vilest language, and calling on God to give him an opportunity to thrash him. His companion, a beardless youth, Silas Pendleton by name, said:

"Clay Gibson is mad with both of us. He piloted you men here, and as I live, and as God lives above me, he had better kill me now! He'd better get evidence to hang me, too, for, as I hope to get my liberty, I'm coming back to make him die for this. I am, so help me God." "I've a notion to do it now," said Carter.

Gibson grasped the revolver of the writer from within his overcoat pocket. His face was as white as a sheet. He looked at his enemies and said, "You accuse me wrongfully. I did not give you away. Say what you please, Carter, about me, but speak of the old folks again as you did just now, and I'll lay you out, though I hang as high as the tree tops. Mind, now, mind, I say, for my blood is up, and you'd better take care."

"Quiet, quiet, both of you," put in Mr. Whitaker. "Carter, hush. Young fellow, leave at once."

Gibson then walked away, the others sending after him a torrent of abuse.

Noon had arrived by this time, and no other moonshiners having made their appearance, the officers demolished the still, numerous barrels of mash and beer, a lot of corn meal, a bed whereon a sentinel had been accustomed to sleep, and all the appliances generally used in the manufacture of moonshine. The man who had last come up, gave his name as Daniel Roberts Greggston. He was made prisoner, and told to follow the others. Greggston said he was under promise to appear before a civil court, next day, to answer the charge of arson. The others substantiated this, but the marshals compelled him to accompany them notwithstanding their assertions. The youth, who had come up with Pendleton, gave his name as George Carter. He seemed to be a born fool and was suffered to depart in peace. The remainder were placed together, and all then galloped away to another still-house, the location of which the officers had been informed of.

Before speaking of this adventure, a description of the previous still-house should be given. Its situation was in the most desolate, dreary, out-of-the-way spot imaginable. In the heart of a dense forest, at the base of two hills, almost mountains they were. Under a cliff, and surrounded by tall, thick limbed trees, and innumerable bushes and brambles, were the still and its accoutrements. The tell-tale smoke alone gave indication of its presence and by this were the officers guided to it. A small branch of water ran down the hill-side, and a stream of this necessary adjunct in making moonshine, was trailed into the still by means of a sapling hollowed for that purpose. The still and its parts were constructed very crudely, yet, all in all, answered their purpose as well as those more elegantly made up.

When the officers left this spot, they set out for another still-house eight miles distant. The rain was falling as hard as ever, and a cold wind pierced us through and through. We galloped through field and forest for three hours, without success, the most careful search failing to reveal the still we had hoped to find. Night coming on, the party rode four miles farther to a place called Big Clifty. Here we remained over night, the landlord entertaining us with an excellent supper, the sudden, indeed it may be said, the very sudden disappearance of which astonished the host exceedingly. In the morning, early, after breakfast was eaten, a start was made for another still-house. Four miles of galloping, and a halt was ordered.

"Any moonshining about here?" we asked of a man in the road.

"Not as I knows of," was the answer.

"Show us where that still is, or I'll end your career in a jiffy," cried Mr. Whitaker.

"All right sir, all right," said the countryman; "follow me and I'll take you thar."

We followed, and half a mile on heard the sound of wood-chopping. Our guide was released. Peering through the bushes, we saw an old man chopping wood. Beyond him we could see a small wooden house, probably eighteen by twenty feet in size, and not more than nine feet high. A drove of hogs grazed between the axeman and the house. Understanding their fondness for refuse matter, we felt sure that an illicit still was near. In order to reach the axeman we had to descend a hill-side five or six hundred feet deep, clinging to bushes as we went. When the axeman was reached, Mr. Wyatt said, "How d'ye, stranger?"

"Morning," answered the one addressed.

"Old boy, how's moonshine?" continued Mr. Wyatt.

"Thar's none 'bout here, sir."

"Aint that a still-house?"

"No siree; not as I knows of."

"Whose hogs are those?"

"Mine."

"What is your name?"

"Pearl, sir; Jeems Pearl."

"Aha!" continued Mr. Wyatt, "so that's not your house, but them's your hogs. A sort of pearl among swine, you'd have us think, eh? Guess that's the house Jack built. Burst that door, Walter."

The last remark was addressed to Mr. Whitaker, who thereupon forced open the door. A glance within disclosed a still, and fourteen mash tubs. Nearer inspection revealed many other things necessary for making whisky. Two gallons of pure moonshine were rooted out of concealment, and so were numerous sacks of corn meal, some malt, and a quantity of corn. Fourteen tubs contained mash and beer, and an eighty-five gallon still reposed on the dying embers of a recent fire. Mr. Whitaker remained to guard the prisoners, and Mr. Wyatt left for the purpose of securing a yoke of oxen to carry the meal, &c., to the nearest station, from there to be taken to Louisville on the railroad.

On the way he met William Wakefield, an old man of seventy-eight. He acknowledged himself to be the owner of the land on which the still was situated, and was therefore arrested. Obtaining the necessary oxen, Mr. Wyatt returned, and left the prisoner Carter, in charge of them for a few minutes. He had scarcely been absent a quarter of an hour, when two men springing out of the bushes, pointed pistols at Carter's head, and bade him free the oxen, also cursing him roundly for being with the officers. Carter explained that his coming had been compulsory, and watching his opportunity to escape, seized upon a moment when the newcomers were engaged in conversation, and dashed behind the oxen, at the same time calling lustily, "Ed, Ed! quick, quick, this way!"

The marshal heard the call, and fearing trouble, came rushing through the bushes, with pistols pointed and hammers raised. The two strangers hearing him approaching, ran for dear life, disappearing behind a cliff just as he came in view of their flying forms.

Without further trouble the prisoners and booty were removed to Big Clifty, the nearest railroad station, and thence taken to Louisville.

It is hard not to share the feeling of adventure related by Mr. Madden and to have seen the caged moonshiner caught in his own snare. More contemporary writers of national reputation have felt this same inclination to see this denizen of mystery and legend operating in the confines of his lair. The late Drew Pearson for years harbored a curiosity and awe regarding the publicity-shy practitioners of the nocturnal art. Pearson's curiosity was satisfied in January of 1956 by a trip to Virginia mountain country, where he was a participant in a real-life raid. Here is his personal account, originally carried in the *Washington Post and Times Herald**:

> My wife and Harry Truman claim that I never tell the truth. Mr. Truman hasn't been so vocal on this point of late, but my wife still seems to agree with his original point of view, and the other day it's possible that she caught me in an untruth by-reason-of-silence.
>
> She came into the office to hear Miss Canty, my efficient

---

* "Washington Merry-Go-Round," syndicated column by Drew Pearson, January 13, 14, 1956.

secretary, say, "Well, we finally got Mr. Pearson's reservations to Roanoke, Va., but I certainly had a hard time doing it."

"What!" exclaimed Mrs. P. "I've invited a lot of people to dinner tonight! Mr. P. knew this weeks in advance and assured me he would be here."

"Well, maybe I wasn't supposed to tell you," confessed the usually discreet Miss Canty. "But he's going to Virginia to raid a moonshine still."

Mrs. P. was then doubly irate. She figured I was going to be shot.

"I was going to break it to you gently," I tried to explain. "But Mr. Avis of the Alcohol Tax Unit promised me some time ago to let me go on the next big raid and televise it. This raid is all set and it won't wait. Besides, I'm insured and you'll be a prosperous and beautiful widow."

Mrs. P. was not easily pacified.

In Roanoke that evening, in order not to attract attention, I registered at the Ponce de Leon Hotel under the name of "A. R. Pearson," which I haven't used for years and which goes back to the name I was christened, "Andrew." Shortly thereafter we were in a huddle with Col. Tom Bailey, chief enforcement officer for Dwight Avis and the Alcohol and Tobacco Tax Unit; also Walter Elmore, his top agent in southwest Virginia, and Harry Lieberman of the Washington office.

Elmore reported that he had located a big 600-gallon still in an old apple-packing barn in the Blue Ridge Mountains about 15 miles from Roanoke and had just come back from inspecting it.

He had found that several vats of mash were bubbling and ready to run.

"They'll have to start running tonight or in the morning," he explained, "or the mash will get too ripe. They inspected their mash early this morning then will come back again tonight."

"One of our lookouts saw a truck go up there to the apple barn just before daylight," Elmore explained, "and it's probably loaded with jars ready to begin work."

Colonel Bailey had originally figured we would raid that night. But Elmore, long versed in the ways of the mountaineers, suggested that we close in at about 4 or 5 the following afternoon.

Colonel Bailey finally decided that it would be better to start in the morning.

Early next day we were up and off by car to a little ravine tucked away in a foothill of the Blue Ridges about 15 miles from Roanoke.

In the party, in addition to the men already named, were A. H. Mucciano, David L. Price, Cecil E. Kline, Thomas B. Stevens, Fred H. Murrell and Raymond Bevins, all of the Alcohol Tax Unit; with the following members of the Virginia ABC (Liquor Control) Board: Wayne Prillaman, George A. Martin, R. P. Richardson and W. W. Moore.

I had not realized before what perfect teamwork exists between the Virginia and other state authorities and the Federal agents. A. L. Fulcher, in charge of Virginia ABC enforcement, was with us and his men worked with the ATU agents as if they were one team.

We split up at the mouth of the ravine, six men together with my cameraman, Bert Spielvogel, and me going up over the mountain ridge to come down on the other side from the rear. The other men were to sneak up a ravine and approach the barn from the front. The raid was timed for 12:30 noon.

It was rough going up the mountainside. And it was cold standing up on top waiting for the other men to skirt around to the rear. I had been up in Greenland a short time before, where it was 10 degrees below; but the Blue Ridges at 10 degrees above somehow seemed colder.

As we stood and waited for the zero hour I learned something about the work of the revenue agents. I had not realized how much rum-running and moonshining still continues despite the most concentrated effort of authorities to stop it.

It's surprising how still it is back in the Virginia mountains. No automobiles, factory whistles, radios, not even a dog barking. All we could hear was a faint put-put of a motor down below, which Walter Elmore, chief revenue agent for Southwest Virginia, explained was operating the moonshiner's pump, inside the old apple-packing barn.

Not a soul was stirring around the barn or anywhere in the valley, and in that eerie stillness Elmore and I descended the mountain ridge.

We couldn't hear the other agents who had gone around to the rear, but we knew they must be there, for it was only five minutes before zero hour, when we were to close in on the barn.

Suddenly there was a shout. The advance revenue agents had gone into the barn five minutes early and the moonshiners made a break out through the rear. They ran right into the arms of Cecil Kline and Donald McLean, who had skirted the ridge and come down in the rear.

They also almost ran into Bert Spielvogel and his TV camera. He slipped, fell, but got a blurred picture.

The two moonshiners were young mountaineers, Ray Shelton and Wilson Hall, both of nearby Floyd, Va., not far from Roanoke. I couldn't help feeling a little sorry for them, though perhaps I shouldn't admit it. One had just come out of jail.

I had quite a talk with them, even interviewed them in front of the camera. At first they were reticent, but eventually seemed rather pleased to talk for television.

It was obvious someone else had put up the money for their operation, for about two tons of sugar was stacked in the barn. There were also 100 or so 5-gallon tin cans and a good many dozen 2-gallon fruit jars. No mountaineer can afford that setup.

The 600-gallon still was a big wooden job with oil drums made into boilers to supply the steam. Vats full of mash were fermenting, ready to be piped in through the still.

Ray Shelton, a man of few words, explained the operation. "It's just rye, sugar and water," he said. "You let it set. Then you run it through the still."

The revenue men told Shelton and Hall to go home and report in Federal Court Monday at 10 a.m. My camera crew drove them back toward their homes.

This may sound unusual. But I learned from Col. Tom Bailey, chief Alcohol Tax Unit enforcement officer, that the Southern moonshiner is a man of his word.

"He won't tell you much, but what he tells you is the truth," explained the Colonel. "He plays a kind of a game with you. He knows we won't shoot except in self-protection, so he runs.

"Most of them can run like jack rabbits. They run right up the mountain, and our men have to be good to catch them. Once I was chasing a moonshiner and told him to surrender.

" 'You ain't kotched me yet,' he said. Finally I 'kotched' him and he went on home and turned up in court at 10 next morning."

The tragedy is that moonshining in some cases, has been passed down from father to son, and in one or two cases teenage boys have been caught operating stills.

Another difficulty is that local Federal judges are not inclined to give heavy sentences. I can understand this; because usually someone else is supplying the cash. However, many

Figure 13 This photo was displayed in the office of Harold Serr, Director of the Alcohol, Tobacco & Firearms Division of IRS. Three youngsters, ages 6–12, are practicing the moonshiners art with a homemade log team still. The still was seized in the Sinking Cove section of Tennessee in 1940. Two of the young boys later grew to the rank of full-fledged adult moonshiners and met their captors again.

sentences have been so light that moonshiners come back again and again.

Moonshining is most heavily concentrated in the South, with the largest number of stills in Georgia, Alabama, and North Carolina. Up around New York and New Jersey is another busy area, but there the trade is carried on by racketeers, usually with industrial alcohol.

Northern bootleg liquor is much more dangerous, and there have been cases of severe poisoning. Southern white mule will almost blow the roof off your mouth, but its poison content is likely to be less.

Most of it is sold only one or two days out of the old garden hose that we saw emptying from the still into another washtub. It sells for about $12.00 a gallon, and since it costs $1 to $2 to make, this is quite profitable. The moonshine raided was going to be sold in West Virginia.

You don't hear the hurrahs and hosannas about Dwight Avis, head of the Alcohol Tax Unit, that you do about J. Edgar Hoover. But he and his men do just as efficient and just as courageous a job. Many have been killed, many more wounded. They don't have enough funds to spend or enough personnel to operate, which is why the men on our raid were working about 60 hours a week. Some had been up all night.

The still raid is the prime function of curtailing moonshine production and putting the daring practitioner out of business. New methods to trap the still man are being put to use with good results. A recent new twist involves the application of ultraviolet paste to components of the still (when found unmanned) and in this way the suspected operators can be identified when their hands are inspected under ultraviolet light. Science will play an increasingly important role as the twentieth century moves toward a close, and as one aging moonshiner expressed it, "Afore long the revenooers will be awiretappin' every tall poplar in the mountain."

If the agents wiretap the trees, they will have to go a step further and do likewise to the uncountable caves of the southland. Caves are still as popular for operation as they were in the 1800's. Investigators of Putnam County, Tennessee, recently trudged through seventeen miles of the most rugged terrain of that mountain state to locate and demolish a still concealed in a three-level cave.

The year 1965 passed with a downward swing in still seizures. The decline was very slight (19,391) from the nearly twenty thousand seizures of the previous year but it was a hopeful sign that Operation Dry-Up was beginning to work in some areas. Georgia pulled ahead of Alabama in leading the nation in illicit distilling. The signs were clear—Georgia would be the recipient of a vigorous Dry-Up campaign in an effort to stem the tide.

National still seizures by 1966 had dropped to 17,774 with Georgia still leading the nation and Alabama and North Carolina running second and third place respectively. The first sign that Operation Dry-Up was working in Georgia came with the 1967 seizure statistics. Still seizures nationally were down to 17,083 and Georgia had dropped from 5,130 seizures in 1966 to 3,725 in 1967. The cutback was impressive, but a red light flashed on the statistical screen. Alabama had jumped into a commanding lead in still seizures with a whopping total of 5,864 for the year. Only the previous year, Alabama had been second in offender states with total seizures of only 4,118. Had the hotly pursued moonshiners of Georgia moved into Alabama to begin anew? It certainly appeared so, or a small new army of Alabama practitioners had set up operations to fill the production void created in Georgia.

Not until the 1968 statistics were in did the biggest downturn of the decade of the '6o's become evident. Nationwide still seizures had dropped to 13,065—the lowest figure in twenty years. A series of things were working. Operation Dry-Up, ineffectual at first and traveling across the southland slowly, was beginning to have a dynamic impact on an awakened citizenry. The increased public awareness, coupled with cooperative educational activities by anti-moonshine councils, zeroed in on the moonshine producer and seller. But all the apparent downturn in illicit activity could not be claimed by the different adversaries of the moonshiner/ bootlegger. Other things were changing in the moonshine belt. Many counties and communities of dry states were changing their status to allow the sale of legal liquor. This issue had long been a focal point in the minds of enforcement authorities and regional government heads. How close was the moonshine problem tied to the wet-versus-dry issue? There were, and are, arguments both ways. Some qualified authorities have long pointed out that the highest number of still seizures occur in dry areas. They point out regions in thirty states with dry areas where the moonshine ped-dler seems more than normally successful. Going still further to exemplify their position, they point out that in some of the states of highest violation of revenue laws, 50 percent of the population live in dry areas. Other issues for consideration come to light upon strict examination: tremendous losses of liquor taxes in the absence of legal sales; high mortality rates from moonshine poisoning; loss of income taxes, social-security taxes, license fees; and a host of other considerations applicable to the legitimate industry and avoided by its illegal counterpart. Opposed to the wet factions are those who point out the massive consumption of illegal liquor in the heart of the industrial North where legal liquor is available everywhere. Price, tax rebellion, and preference seem to be the issue there as stated earlier—with wet or dry sentiment playing no part at all. In the South, part of the issue is still one of morality. Is it better to withhold legal liquor from some of the masses and permit the moonshiner to supply the needs of the thirsty and restricted, or to throw wide the gates of supply, demand, and avail-ability? This too is part of the Southern problem. Liquor avail-able only through state stores or bars has a distinct disadvantage to the potential moonshine buyer. Often he is remote from a legal supply, and his convenient purchasing hours do not coincide with the selling hours of the store. Moonshine salesmen have no such problem. They are in every hill and hamlet—available twenty-four hours a day—and will save the buyer money in the process. There is no problem of rent, payroll, taxes, operating expenses, fringe benefits, payroll withholding, production reports, or year-end income-tax forms. So far in history, the moonshiner has fulfilled a need, and this fact is one of the first rules of successful merchandising.

The South *is* changing. Citizens and legislators who would not have dared to cry wet even ten years ago are taking the more modern approach—not because they are any less moral than the next man, but because they are able to take a realistic approach to an issue that shows no signs of going away. In the past, the majority of Southern opinion has held that it is necessary to keep drinking at an absolute minimum no matter what the cost. Sin and drinking are traditionally synonymous in the fundamentalist mind of the Bible-belt South. Until modern days they have been willing to permit a degree of moonshining, bootlegging, and the like to prevail in the interest of overall temperance. They must now take a close look at the record. Perhaps after so doing they will still determine their course of part wet, part dry, is the right one in spite of the present evils. The trend, however, appears to point in the other direction.

CHAPTER ELEVEN

Travel Among the Moonshiners

After months of travel across several states, visiting still sites and interviewing moonshiners of every type, one man stands out in my memory above all the others. He was the oldest practicing moonshiner I encountered and had just turned eighty-four. He was a robust man with a gorilla-like build and, except for a bushy head of silver-white hair, could have passed for a man of fifty-five or sixty years. The only symbol of declining health was the walking cane he used because of "rhumatiz." The old man had practiced moonshining across three states—Maryland, Virginia, and North Carolina. He had never been caught in any of them. Asked about this questionable good luck, he remarked that he always kept "his relations in order." Gently pushed further on this topic, he explained that he always managed to pass around occasional samples to "the boys." He meant, of course, that he had shared his squeezin's with certain county sheriffs and local law-enforcement officials. He claimed on two occasions to have been tipped off by a county sheriff when federal investigators were in the area.

There was great warmth and personality about the old man, and the simplicity of his life was moving and often humorous. He had few friends except former "business" acquaintances. He had no children, and his wife had a habit of leaving him, sometimes for months or a year at a time. He never worried about her, knowing she "would come in some night with the chickens."

Having given up practice on the big stills, he did do a little stillin' in the spring of each year. He had one favorite product which he liked to make and considered his specialty. This was wild-strawberry brandy. In the spring when the wild strawberries ripened, he would get out the components of a little twenty-five gallon copper pot still and ready himself for the makin'. Into all the surrounding fields of his little mountain farm, boys would be dispatched to pick the wild berries while in their prime. With all their "scratchin' round," forty to sixty gallons was "about their crop" he said, and such a small quantity would only produce five or six gallons of brandy. But it was worth the effort to him. He gleamed with pride in discussing this rare drink. To have the yearly practice and a supply of his own, plus a little for friends, was all that he really expected.

We discussed at length the big distilling operations of his younger days and the varieties he had made and sold. In Maryland he had operated a one thousand-gallon still, making corn liquor and occasionally apple brandy. He scratched his head and added that, "believe I made plum brandy a few times but it's hard to recollect." Before I departed his company he insisted on a tour of the branch where he set up his little still each spring. It was less than one-half mile from his house. The furnace, made of small limestone rock, sat to the side of a flush limestone branch. He paused and looked at me for approval of his setting. It was indeed beautiful, and not a sound disturbed that moment of silence except the trickle of the water and a variety of birds singing in the surrounding trees. It was a perfect hiding spot, with rolling hills to either side of the spring. To the rear, the lofty, bluish mountain separating North Carolina from Virginia loomed in the distance.

As I left him for an interview six miles away, I had a most positive impression: here was a man truly of the old school, one who didn't like to "pilfer" with people and didn't like to be "pilfered" with. It is doubtful he knew the name of the current President of the United States. He did know the current sheriff of his county. His mountain house had electricity but no television set or phone. His last question to me is still memorable: "Do ye reckon the time will iver come agin when we can do our stillin' without hidin'?" The negative answer left him standing in a state of puzzled exasperation.

The next interview was with a man in his sixties who had done time for moonshining. This interview had been set up weeks earlier by a mutual acquaintance. In the beginning, this fellow was a little suspicious but for the most part cooperative. His wife became angry and insisted that he refrain from any discussion of his past life and experience. Her reaction was understandable in view of the fact that her husband had not practiced moonshining since his release from prison. They now had a small but nice mountain house (most likely paid for from his moonshining profits), and she probably hoped they could improve their lot in life still further without more trouble.

There was nothing unusual about the interview with this man —he had operated for about seventeen years and had been caught three times. The first time he had been a part of a large operation requiring the participation of several men. The payment of a fine found him free, and shortly thereafter he had been caught again as a co-operator, running corn liquor on Sunday. The second offense cost him a sizable fine and a few years' probation. After sweating out his probation period and working at a sawmill in the interim, he decided to try the trade again on his own. He was caught again, which wasn't surprising but the manner of his downfall is worth recording.

His probation ended in the winter months and being anxious to try his stillin' art, he did not await the coming of spring and the protective cover of flush green leaves. Purchasing an extra still from an acquaintance soon to "pull time" (a fact which had nothing to do with his being caught), he headed for the thickest area of leafless trees, high in the mountains. Moonshining in the winter is more difficult because in addition to the personal risks involved, it is harder to get the mash to ferment properly in cold weather and the fermenting time is extended. To help overcome that problem, our friend moved a shock of fodder (cut corn) from a field in the lowlands and placed it around the mash barrels, to keep out the cold and help generate a little more captive heat. All went well until the mash was just about ready to run when two revenue men stepped from behind a large grove of oak trees. Our friend's still was destroyed before his own eyes, and not until he sat in the back seat of the agent's car did he learn that the fodder shock had been his undoing. It had been sighted from a small search plane used by the investigators, who thought it strange to see one lone fodder shock high in the mountains and not a cornfield in five miles.

Unusual accidents sometimes happen to give insight into the problems of the mountain moonshiner. A Kentucky moonshiner related an experience somewhat unusual and humorous enough to share. This moonshiner had gathered what he thought to be common field rock for the base and furnace of his still. After being readied, the still was set in place and filled with mash, and a wood fire was built to accomplish the cooking. All went well as the fire got hotter and the steam vapor began its journey through the cap, into the thump keg, and on into the worm. Hardly had the foreshot cleared the worm when shots rang out.

Bullets seemed to be finding their mark at the base of the still, and clouds of dust indicated projectiles digging into the ground around the furnace. The two teen-aged still hands made for the sanctuary of the woods and a ravine beyond. As sure as his employees were that they were indeed being fired upon by the revenooers, the still owner ran in an opposite direction to the top of the hill on which they were stillin'. After several hours of watching and waiting and detecting no sound of axes chopping up the still or the application of dynamite, the still owner returned to the scene. Besides seeing that the run had completed itself and the zinc bucket under the worm spout was full and running over (sending the balance of the run down the hill into the gully), he looked upon the state of the fire in the stone-enclosed furnace. There lay a pile of stone rubble continuing to pop as it cooled, with the still hanging precariously on what little of the stone furnace remained. Still minus two workers, who probably thought their boss under lock and key, he quickly repaired the furnace base and continued his work well into the next day when all the mash was used up and the white lightnin' safely bottled in fruit jars. The next day, after consultation with an older moonshiner, the still owner was sure of his problem: He had used a particular type of flint rock for the still furnace which contained organic matter or minerals that would cause the rocks to explode in extreme heat. One exhausted moonshiner went to bed to rest from forty-eight hours of sleeplessness, and two sheepish-looking still hands sat idly on his porch waiting to start new mash preparations when their boss awakened.

The moonshiner does not always fit his public image. Take the case of a South Carolina moonshiner. This moonshiner is a woman—a very attractive young woman in her midthirties with raven black hair and a figure reputed to equal a Fifth Avenue model. The Saks' dress she would be wearing as she glides gracefully into a white Lincoln Mark III would hardly give away her current occupation. Once a Charleston telephone operator at sixty dollars a week, she inherited a small farm from a bachelor uncle, who seemed always to have more money than what his small farm could possibly provide. At his death the farm and a sizable bank balance were accepted with both gratitude and curiosity. While walking over her new real estate, she discovered the source of her uncle's real income. Sitting in a grove of pine trees, not one quarter mile from the farmhouse, was a skillfully made submarine still of five hundred-gallon capacity, being worked by two still hands. Fearful that she would turn them over to authorities, or at least fire them from a job they had performed for her uncle so long, they trembled, awaiting her judgment. Her decision was to continue the business on shares, and all would profit. The white Lincoln that now frequents the New Jersey Turnpike going north brings back a wardrobe that leaves the eyes of a few South Carolina lasses slightly on the green side.

> Quite often nowadays the moonshiner falls victim to the scientific age. Take the case of the moonshiner's nails for instance. It started when agents moved in fast on a still hidden in a Virginia ravine. The moonshiners slipped out through the brush faster yet. The still and mash boxes weren't even finished; carpenters' tools and nails lay hastily discarded. Down the road a piece the reserve line of revenooers waved over a fast running car. "Just ridin' to Aunt Tillie's to do some fixin' up," the driver said. He had a few tools in the back, sure enough—and a keg of nails. Now the scene shifts to the Washington laboratory of the Internal Revenue Service. Routine checking of legal alcohol was put aside for examination of some nails, under a microscope. The machines that make nails leave marks on their product, marks that are as individual for each machine as the marks on a bullet are for the gun that fires it. The microscope showed them plainly. There was no question— the nails from the keg in the car were identical to the nails found near the still.*

Moonshiners sometimes turn the tables and use some pretty far-fetched gimmicks themselves. More often than not, the mountain moonshiner includes his whole family in some phase of his profession. His wife and daughters often serve as lookouts and sometimes as still hands or bottlers. One such Tennessee moonshiner worked out a near infallible system of early warning. This moonshiner had a collie dog which accompanied him everywhere. If he went to town, the dog sat in the seat beside him. Likewise the dog was his constant companion at the still. Usually the dog would growl at approaching strangers but by then it was too late. Finally an idea for an improvement dawned. The moonshiner presented

* Reprinted courtesy of *Popular Science,* © 1959, by Popular Science Publishing Company, Inc.

his wife and daughters with high-frequency dog whistles, which they wore around their necks at all times. If the women happened to sight a strange car or suspicious-looking pedestrian, a blast on the whistle, above the range of human hearing, would bring the dog to attention a mile away.

Sometimes a moonshiner gets in trouble by just being neighborly. Three Virginia revenue men had been casing a rural Virginia community for several weeks in an attempt to find just which one of three suspected families was moonshining brandy. The surveillance had been done mostly at night and from long hikes in the mountains during the daytime. Getting nowhere, they posed as itinerant cherry pickers in order to get a close-up look at the community and its people. They picked cherries for two days without learning much, but on the third day two neighborhood men stopped and offered to help them. After another day of cherry picking, the two volunteers confessed they were killing time waiting for their mash to work off. Assuming the itinerant pickers were brothers under the skin, the volunteers offered them a gallon of moonshine by the next night if they were still around. The disguised agents were only too glad to stay around one more day, but only a part of the next day saw any cherry picking accomplished, and then only by one man remaining as a lookout. The other two stationed themselves in the woods before daylight in order to watch the direction taken by the two moonshiners, who had a hard day's work ahead of them. The moonshiners appeared just at dawn and were followed to their still. The still was located not down in a ravine beside a mountain stream where the agents had searched previously, but was concealed high up on another ridge with water being conveyed by plastic pipe from a spring located still higher on another ridge of mountain. The water was coming by gravity flow, and the pipe had been buried shallowly under leaves and mountain turf. The agents waited only long enough for the still fire to be built and moved in hurriedly. At first the moonshiners were simply baffled as to how their newfound "friends" had located them. Then it all became only too clear, and two sixty-gallon barrels of fermented cherries started a long slide down the mountainside.

Not every moonshiner claims to be in business by choice. One such man, after being in business only long enough to run six cases, was caught within hours after his still rig was operable. He had gone in business "only after much pressure from a group of businessmen and lawyers," he stated to arresting officers. "These men," he said, "wanted only the highest quality moon and nothing else." He had worked on the still site and distilling equipment for over a year and had ingeniously concealed the whole works underground. "I was just going to make them some for their own use," he pleaded. The next day he witnessed the fruits of his labor flying a hundred feet into the air from a charge of TNT. "This is the first time in my life I have ever seen a still blown up," he commented sadly.

The moonshiner as a rule is not a jovial fellow. Most times he is rather solemn, businesslike, and frequently downright mean. He is almost always inventive, and he can display a sense of humor, especially if such a display can serve a useful purpose. The quick thinking of a northern Mississippi moonshiner is a case in point. This particular moonshiner had hurried down from the hills to a nearby country store for additional sugar he needed for a rotgut run. He had previously taken into the hills all that he needed for his first sugar and second sugar run but decided that the mash would stand one more run through the still, and besides, some itinerant farm workers had moved into the area, and he was sure of a sale for the poor-quality moonshine. Bursting into the store, he immediately came face to face with two agents who were questioning the store owner about his heavy sales of sugar. The moonshiner drank a pop and propped himself against the counter to listen. The questioning turned from sugar to an inquiry about moonshining in the area. The store owner steadfastly maintained that he knew of none and assured the officers that his sugar sales were directly in proportion to the heavy home canning the women of the area were doing in that particular season. At this juncture, the moonshiner stepped up and informed the agents that he had seen something suspicious in a hollow down the road a couple of miles while cutting some saw timber just a month ago. He even offered to take them down the road and point out the spot from the highway. As the three men left, the moonshiner flashed a three-finger signal to the storekeeper and followed meekly behind the two revenue men.

In a short while the agents' car returned, let the moonshiner out, and turned back down the highway. As they disappeared from view, he scurried into his own car and headed in the opposite direction, content in the knowledge that three one-hundred-pound bags of sugar rested securely in the trunk.

Previously we have considered the nationally known terminology for the product made by the moonshiner. In addition to these terms there are often regional names by which the illicit distillate is recognized. Some of these are "cannonball swig" (meaning a hard-hitting drink), "preacher's lye" (meaning a burning drink with spirit), "dead man's dram" (this is doubled alcohol, undiluted, said to give even a completely drunken man a subconscious jolt he can remember when he sobers up—if he does), "swamp root," "shinny," "roasting ear wine," "balm of Gilead" (soothing medicine), "kickapoo joy juice," "who shot John" (drink that brings instant unconsciousness), and "teedum barrel." This last name comes from a small wooden barrel or cask the moonshiner kept in the mountain stream near his still, the container for his private drinking likker, usually the finest moon the practitioner was capable of making. There were no particular size requirements for the barrel or cask—it all depended on the moonshiner's consumption habits. The real connoisseur of moonshine whiskey knew of the existence of the teedum barrel and often paid the premium price required to purchase from this stock. Such was the case with an Alabama moonshiner. He was approached by a frequent customer who insisted on purchasing one gallon at a premium price if it came from the teedum barrel. Since the buyer had never insisted on stock from the teedum barrel before, the moonshiner asked him the reason for his change in habit. The buyer confessed that his purchase was for a "white collar man" and unrolled a fistful of bills to back his claim. Further conversation revealed the absent purchaser's name, and the moonshiner recognized it instantly. He inquired next if the absentee purchaser was aware from whom he was buying. Being assured that "I was told to get it anywhere the quality was good and see that it come from the teedum barrel," the moonshiner wandered off toward the branch with two empty glass jars.

Returning to the other, who kept a faithful watch over the still in his absence, the moonshiner gave his assurance that the two jars had been filled from the teedum barrel. With money in hand and a broad grin of satisfaction, the moonshiner watched his customer wend his way through the laurel thicket and down the mountain.

It had been a score he'd wanted to settle for twenty years. The absentee purchaser was a member of the state legislature, but it had not always been so. Twenty years before, the same man had been a conniving young lawyer who had not only done a poor job of defending the moonshiner in his first scrape with the law, but had charged an outrageous fee and taken half the money from the sale of his confiscated still to a competitor, besides! But now the score was even. The good legislator had his teedum-barrel whiskey all right—topped off with all the urine the moonshiner was able to generate on the spur of the moment.

Sometimes the revenue men, after catching their prey, run into still further obstacles. A story from Mississippi relates such an incident. A woman caught selling white mule couldn't be brought in for a hearing on her offense. Her weight was reputed to be in excess of five hundred pounds, and she was left at home, and the problem of how to get her into court was left to the presiding judge. The judge finally arranged transportation through the Army Engineer Corps, which hauled her to court, still in her bed, on a large truck. The bed and the defendant were unloaded on a loading platform at the back of the courthouse. A small band of muscled men managed to get her to the door of the court chambers by way of the freight elevator. The problem still wasn't solved, for her bulk prevented entry into the court chambers by way of the door. The judge left his chair, strode over to the door, and sentenced her to a term of imprisonment at the federal reformatory at Alderson, West Virginia. She was transported to prison in a rail baggage car, and then a flatbed truck. After her confinement was completed and she returned home, only a short time elapsed before she was again found selling white mule. Another sentencing became stalemated; the Federal Bureau of Prisons requested that she not be sent into custody again for the problems of confining her were insurmountable.

Moonshiners everywhere have, for over a hundred years, bragged of the healing and regenerative powers of mountain dew. There is absolutely nothing which the balm of Gilead will not make sweeter, more pleasant, or more meaningful, and when all the words of praise are exhausted, it's just plain good. It has cured everything from heart trouble to yellow jaundice.

The real test for good moonshine whiskey is described in an old story that has been around for years but continues to be a favorite of the mountain moonshiner. The test consists of placing two live electrical wires of high voltage in a jar of fresh moonshine. If it's really good stuff, not only will the slightest arc be prevented, but the moonshine will drive the electrical current back up the wires. It can be observed causing a whiplash in the lines like a crawling worm, for as far as the eye can see. When the transformer on the fifth ridge in the distance is seen to explode or at least smoke profusely, then it is beyond question that the product is ready for the market.

The anecdotes about accidents occurring to moonshiners could well fill a book by themselves, and restraint needs to be shown. There are some, however, that just should not be passed up. A Wilkes County, North Carolina, moonshiner was known to be a man not only skilled in the nocturnal art but a good businessman extremely tight with the dollar. He had his own still and sold his output from his own café, where his restaurant business was equally successful. A country store a couple of miles away, which he also owned, did a good business as well as supply the needs of sugar, cornmeal, and yeast for his distilling operation. A fourth occupation included farming from which fruit, vegetables, eggs, and meat complemented the needs of the store and café. The accident about which we are concerned, however, happened at the site of the still. He had finished a run of sugarhead and was in the process of bottling the last of it, which sat glistening freshly in the blending tub. As he opened the last case of Mason jars in preparation for the final task, his rabbit dog came bounding up, driving before him—its scent glands wide open and functioning— a full grown skunk. It dashed right through the still yard and over the blending tub, spraying as it went. Being a frugal man, the moonshiner saw no necessity to pause and consider the possibility of throwing the aromatic distillate into the nearest branch. He bottled it but did mark it apart from the first of the run.

Arriving at the café, he told his waitress of the accident and instructed her not to throw the stuff away—but rather to sell it only to customers who might wander in and be too drunk to know the difference. It was near midnight and near closing time, the story goes, before such a customer arrived. The buyer paused just long enough to order a fried-egg sandwich to go before he plunked down the three dollars required for the quart jar. The waitress turned down the lights and began to turn over the day's receipts to her boss when a pounding fist rattled the front door unmercifully. The owner unlocked the door and recognized the defrauded drunk.

"This is the worse damn likker I ever tersted," he lamented.

"My same dependable formula," the moonshiner-businessman insisted.

"It stinks like a whorehouse and swallers like motor il'!" the other bellowed.

"You're just feeling bad tonight, maybe," the owner calmed him somewhat. The drunk stumbled toward the door and took another long drink and a bite of the fried egg sandwich. He gagged noisily, but kept it all down. As he cleared the door frame, the owner started to close the door and breathe a good riddance, but the drunk turned to face him. He ignored the owner and directed his unsteady eyes at the waitress. "Ma'am, I just got one thing ter say. If this damn likker ain't stinkin-rotten, there ain't but one other answer. Somebody's damn skunk 'is been fucking your chickens!"

Judges aren't always noted for their humor, but one such gentleman, in moonshining country of the old days, recalled a light moment. During his first weeks as a judge, the older judge whom he was to replace shared the bench in an advisory capacity. Upon seeing the younger perform the tasks of judgments with skill and dispatch, the older man slumped down in his chair, becoming somewhat sleepy and bored with proceedings he had experienced for forty years. All was going well with the young judge until the case of two men haled into court on a second offense of moonshining. The younger man had not encountered this situation before, and lacking judgment and sure knowledge of the law, he whispered somewhat awkwardly to his older adviser, "What is the law regarding second offense for moonshining?" The older man continued to doze away, and the young judge shifted his papers nervously. Still he was afraid to act on his own. He sensed the spectators were aware of his hesitancy, and he acted quickly by giving the judge a soft poke in the ribs, accompanied by a second request for information:

"What do I give the moonshiners?" The older man rubbed his eyes and sat up briskly, "Not over two dollars a gallon, and it better be damn good stuff at that!"

The most dangerous situation can sometimes turn out to be

prime slapstick material for television. A former revenue agent from Missouri recalled just such an occasion from earlier days of raiding in the southland. The affair had started from a live report pertaining to moonshining operations in a private residence. Suspecting the usual kitchen still, the agent and a fellow agent slipped up to the house under cover of darkness. As they inched nearer the window, the sound of glass breaking could be heard. "I think they know we're coming—they're breaking the fruit jars!" the fellow agent shouted.

With the strength of instinct, the agent plunged through the partially opened window, taking part of the glass with him; sliding clear across the room, he finally came to rest against the blaring television set. Looking up, he saw at least twenty people in the room. Embarrassed and now not at all sure of his right to be there, he tried to make conversation. Words wouldn't come, and he glanced toward the television set. "Are you all watching *Dragnet?*" he asked shyly.

After staring him down, the madam of the supposed distilling establishment answered him curtly: "We ain't watchin' it, but we sho' is living it!"

The wife of a jailed moonshiner in eastern Tennessee holds the record for tricks played on county sheriffs. The sheriff was dumbfounded one afternoon to find his prisoner as drunk as the proverbial monkey. The man had been in jail for three days on an assault charge while under the influence of what was probably his own white mule. He had had no visitors, and no bottle could be found in his cell to explain his drunkenness. Two days later the same thing happened. On guard this time, the sheriff had a deputy maintain close surveillance to make sure someone was not slipping a bottle through the office and on through the cell door. After a watch of one day and still another, nothing happened, but on the third day by sundown the prisoner was again drunk. There was only one other explanation—somebody was tilting a bottle for the prisoner through the outside window of his cell. Another two-day wait. The moonshiner's wife appeared, approaching the rear of the building. Sure he had the culprit, the sheriff demanded she open her purse. She did so with a pleasant smile befitting an expectant mother, which was obviously her advanced condition. With the open purse revealing nothing, the sheriff started to leave when he noticed small drops of liquid appearing at the woman's feet. She noticed his attention and looked down for herself, whereupon she exclaimed excitedly: "Please get me to Dr. Fenner's quick—shore looks like my water has broke."

Complying in the manner of male distress in such situations, the sheriff had the woman at the doctor's doorstep in three minutes flat. As he turned to leave, a mighty gush of liquid splashed to the ground, and he thought for sure another little moonshiner had, for all practical purposes, made his entry into the State of Tennessee. His steps to her aid became less hurried as the aroma of balm of Gilead reached his nose. The woman looked down shyly, raised her skirt, and withdrew a hot-water bag with a rubber tube extension wound tightly at the neck. She didn't have to explain. It was all very obvious that a thirsty moonshiner with a dutiful wife had "nursed" on his own white mule through the bars of his cell.

My visits to moonshiners, ex-moonshiners, judges, and agents added both facts and color to my field research for this book, but nothing can compare with the experience of a visit to an operating still.

You do not "just go" and visit a still any more than you "just go" to visit the President of the United States. After meeting the artful practitioner of the mountains, you still do not "just ask" to visit his still. The subject is avoided altogether with the sort of discretion one might use in the boudoir seduction of a virgin queen. Moonshiner and properly escorted visitor get a "feel" for each other first and speak of the "sweet smell of the honeysuckle" in the mountains. The old moonshiners especially are some of the most perceptive people to be encountered anywhere, and one has the instant feeling his very soul is being surveyed to its innermost depths.

But let us start at the beginning of such an experience, so you, the reader, may go to a place where not one in fifty thousand average Americans has ever been—into the very heart of the moonshiner's domain.

The groundwork for this particular visit began the first week in May 1969. Contact was made with a man who had, himself, been on probation for supplying moonshiners during the rationing period of the 1940's. I only knew him casually, but I was aware of his background and previous activities. Exploratory conversation revealed his knowledge of and acquaintance with moonshiners in an area I had long wanted to visit. He agreed immediately and enthusiastically to a visit, saying, "It's been far too long since I visited the boys."

We decided a dry run into the area was the first move before any contact whatever was to be made. There was a chance the particular moonshiner we wanted to see (who was the king of his particular clan) might be pulling time or that he had moved from the area.

We came into the remote mountain area after a lengthy drive, and my guide asked me to stop the car. I did so, and he looked to the rear to ascertain that no vehicles were following us. His concern was that a resident might start the horn blowing. The blowing of vehicle horns is the modern-day equivalent of gourd-horn blowing of the old days, and still serves as an early-warning system to the moonshiner.

No vehicles passed us in either direction for a distance of about six miles, but our presence in the neighborhood was almost immediately noticed. We drove very, very slowly, but at several houses and shacks we could see people peeping around corners at us with the suspicious mountain stare. On the first pass we did not stop at the house of the moonshiner whom we intended to visit. We continued west, to the end of the ridge road, assuring ourselves that no agent's cars were parked along the road, keeping the area under surveillance, or making exploratory thrusts into the surrounding mountains. After we turned around and headed back east, heads continued to observe us suspiciously. No horn blowing could be heard, and I believe the fact that my automobile could not have been mistaken for the vehicles normally used by the area agents was the explanation.

After we reached the residence of the moonshiner to be visited, we pulled the car off the dusty gravel road to the side of his house and partially out of view. A record player could be heard blaring away with hillbilly music through an open window. We knocked at the front door and waited. Nothing happened. A longer and more vigorous knock still brought no results. We started to walk around the house to the rear door when we noticed the head of a middle-aged woman peering at us from the outside corner of the house. Our arrival in the rear and the expected confrontation with the shy resident was fruitless; the back door was closed (though we hadn't heard it), and the woman was gone. We knocked again with no results. I was foolishly dressed in city clothes, and my guide felt this might be part of the trouble. We assumed the woman to be the wife of the moonshiner, and although the guide knew the supposed husband, he did not know the wife.

We decided to wait out the situation, sure now that the moonshiner was either inside or up in the mountains working at the still. We had not sat under the trees for more than twenty minutes when the moonshiner and two other men drove up in a car. At first, the king of the clan did not recognize my guide (I learned later they had not seen each other for six years) and regarded us with suspicion. In a brief while the reacquaintance was established, and the suspicious glare turned to me. My presence was explained as "a man who likes good, cold limestone water and the scenery of the mountains." The undercover jargon meant, of course, that I liked moonshine liquor and had a great sympathy and appreciation for moonshining. (The truth was that I had at the time never tasted white lightnin' and had only an artistic interest in the trade.)

Conversation fell into a lull after a few moments, and another car arrived on the scene. The new arrivals stayed at a distance, but soon the moonshiner beckoned them inside the house. In a few moments they all emerged from the house, the moonshiner drinking from a pint-sized fruit jar. The last two visitors left with one of the men who had brought the moonshiner home by car. We supposed the three were going up the road to the "warehouse" to get the liquor the two men had paid for, inside the house. (We later learned that this was the case, and the warehouse dispenser was the moonshiner's son-in-law.)

The moonshiner then turned his attention back to us, first passing his fruit jar among my guide, myself (I declined, saying I had an ulcer), and the remaining mountaineer. (He too was later discovered to be a son-in-law.) The fruit jar was empty in ten minutes or so, and the moonshiner went back in the house for a refill. His emergence found him in still better spirits.

Conversation turned to the "beauty of the mountains," which at the time were infested with millions of cicadas, screeching so shrilly the sound was like a dive-bomber attack. My guide started very expertly to pursue my cause, by asking the moonshiner if we couldn't cut a bee-tree sometime soon. Cutting a bee-tree (a hollow tree containing a swarm of wild honeybees and usually filled with excellent sourwood honey) is a favorite pastime with the mountain moonshiner. In most cases he has spent weeks tracking the bees and finding the well-hidden location of such a tree. (The bees are tracked by watching their ascent from a flower, bloom or branch, as they return to the hive. They always fly straight—in a bee line, in fact.) Now, an invitation to a bee-tree cutting carries with it one of two connotations: It can be simply that, period, or it can be the introduction to a more rewarding day—hopefully, the latter.

With the request for an invitation issued by my guide, the moonshiner regarded us severely and motioned my guide aside, where they conferred in hushed whispers. My trustworthiness, apparently assured, brought forth an invitation to attend a bee-tree cutting two weeks hence. There was still no assurance we would do anything more than cut the tree and take the honey; a look at the still, the distilling art, or our moonshiner's participation in the occupation had not been mentioned except by slanted phraseology. We let the situation rest and invited our newfound friends to accompany us to a country store for a lunch of sardines and cheese. To our surprise they accepted, and all five of us climbed into my car for the nine-mile journey to the nearest store. After lunch, something happened that impressed me at the time very deeply and still does.

The store where we had eaten was at a crossroad of a paved state highway. On an opposite corner, a rundown house was being used as a combination antique-junk shop, and displayed in one window an antique lamp which appeared to be a design for which my wife had long been searching. I asked my companions if I might stop long enough to look at the lamp, and they cheerfully agreed to the delay and even followed me into the house, peering over my shoulder at the object. A smile could hardly be retained, as I knew they had passed the place thousands of times without the slightest interest.

I did want the lamp, and the price was a steal at twenty dollars. But when I opened my billfold, six dollars turned out to be the extent of my resources. I explained my dilemma to the clerk, but she refused to accept a check. My guide, from whom I had hoped to borrow, had only a five-dollar bill. At this juncture the older of the two sons-in-law pulled out his old-fashioned purse (it looked like a child's dirty sock with a snap opening as on a woman's handbag) and said he'd be glad to lend me twenty dollars. I was over-come with this display of trust, for he had known me less than two hours. I declined his offer, and the clerk, impressed by this action, too, changed her mind and accepted the check, and we delivered our passengers home.

After the two weeks had passed (too slowly for me), my guide and I returned to the scene. During the journey, my guide had warned me that the whole affair might be off. It was not that the moonshiners would go back on their word, but the time "might not be just right." Moonshiners act a great deal of the time on instinct rather than logic. If their instinct directs that they post-pone a plan (no matter how involved), they will act on this feeling without hesitation. This instinct, I was to find out, is genuine with them and to a great degree explains their freedom from a higher rate of capture. Many an agent has come upon a warm still with the cap and worm removed, and scratched his head questioningly. No, he hadn't been seen or heard, but he had been felt. One other thing I would come to observe: The eyes of a mountain moonshiner are always in motion, moving from left to right and back again. Even *out* of the mountains, this occupa-tional habit is observable. It is not a shifty-eyed action; it is a sweep-ing motion of the panorama in view, the constant radarlike searching of the eyes for a movement in the bushes, a sound among the leaves, or the quick sprint of a wild animal, indicating a human presence.

When we arrived at the house, the matter looked discouraging. No vehicles were in sight, and no activity was observable around the house. With hope dampened, we crawled from the car and knocked at the door. After vigorous poundings, the moonshiner's wife appeared at the door and informed us that her husband had gone to a distant city to visit his sick mother. Her explanation was brief if not curt, and we found ourselves facing a closed door. It was easy not to be angry with her, for I have yet to see a pleasant- or happy-appearing mountain moonshiner's wife.

As we had on the first visit, we decided to wait out the turn of events. Analysis of the situation was hard, since we didn't know whether the moonshiner's wife was ignorant of the plans (likely) and thought our stopping was unplanned, whether he had told her to make up the story, whether the story was true, or if there was a possibility of revenooers in the area, and the moonshiner was protecting both himself and us. Maybe it was simply a case of instinct at work as the guide had anticipated, and the time indeed was not "right."

After we debated the possibilities for almost an hour, who appeared out of the trees behind us but the moonshiner himself. He looked weary, and his drooping eyelids indicated sleeplessness. The picture now became clearer—he had been in the mountains all night working his shift toward getting off a run. We did not ask, nor did he venture an explanation—but we knew. We walked back to the front steps, and he went inside, returning with the familiar fruit jar. We expected him to dismiss us shortly and go to bed, but he started to talk of the equipment we would need for the bee-tree cutting.

The chain saw we would need was at the home of one son-in-law, and we were asked to go to him with instructions to bring the equipment. As agreed previously, he would accompany us on the outing. We assisted him in loading his battered farm truck with the chain saw, smoker (device to neutralize the hostility of the bees), bonnet (net covering for head as protection against bees), ax, gloves, pans for the honey, and extra gasoline.

The moonshining leader of the clan had had a fried-egg sandwich with his "fruit jar coffee" and appeared in unusually good spirits. He too had waited for this day and appeared eager to mix a little sweet lightnin'. Two quart fruit jars of moon were the last supplies we needed, and they were packed into the truck with the other supplies.

We had no idea where the location of the bee-tree might be or the proximity of the still, if indeed we were to see it at all. The subject was still not mentioned in any form, but I felt we were all of one accord. The gravel road was taken for approximately two miles, back toward the paved highway, before the driver turned right onto a less-traveled side road. After following this for only a few hundred yards, he made another right turn onto a log road. It was hardly passable for ruts and treetops, but we continued on for approximately one mile, which was the extent of travel by vehicle. As each man loaded part of the equipment, we discovered that one of the fruit jars had tipped over, spilling all its contents. The moonshiner took this loss with merely a few choice words and asked us to wait for him a few minutes. We did, without knowing what he had in mind. He walked back up the log road out of sight and returned shortly with another jar of moon to replace the lost one. That was another revealing fact of the day. I was to learn that, all over the mountainside and along the route we took, he had planted a few jars here and there, either for his own use or to disperse his supply in unlikely locations in the event of search.

The bee-tree was located after a walk of a few hundred yards (straight up toward the top of a ridge), and we happily dropped our equipment. The tree was a huge, twisted black gum, towering high into the air. Some bees could be observed flying in and out of the small opening, which was located about halfway up the tree.

The moonshiner found a comfortable spot under a poplar tree, pulled healthily on the fruit jar, and prepared to watch his son-in-law at work. The cicadas were shrieking by the millions, and the moonshiner slapped and cursed them intermittently. The buzz of the chain saw echoed throughout the mountains only slightly louder than the cicadas.

The big tree crashed to earth like a clap of thunder, taking with it the tops of two smaller—but still large—trees. (I didn't think we were on his land but drew out of him later that we were.) The falling action of the trees launched in flight a mass of cicadas sufficiently thick to cause a momentary shadow over the sun. In minutes, bees emerged angrily from the fallen tree, and the three of us without bonnets retreated further into the trees.

The sawing of the tree after this point is done more carefully for exact location of the honey deposit is unknown. It is not always as near to the opening used by the bees as one might imagine. The skillful man at the chain saw worked on, using his smoker rarely. The first sawing severed the tree well below the suspected area of deposit; then short blocks of wood were sawed off one at a time, until the honey was exposed. The tree yielded about two gallons of honey, but the upper area of the deposit had been invaded by ants and was worthless.

The moonshiner now had his honey. He equalized the moon by pouring some from the full jar to the now half empty one. Into each jar he put the equivalent of one half pound of honey and shook both jars vigorously. If there had been any doubt the moonshiner was enjoying the day, it was now abolished. He drank more heavily than before, which was already an unbelievable rate of consumption. The guide and the son-in-law had sipped along lightly, but the balance of the liquor had been consumed by the older man. The equivalent of one quart was almost gone, and the moonshiner was not really drunk yet. After the honey was added, curiosity overcame me, and I sipped a small swallow for my education. The honey had not reduced the fiery effect of the liquid, but a sweet taste could be distinguished.

We all sat in the shade and rested as the bees continued to swarm safely out of range. The visit to the still had not yet been suggested, and as the moonshiner showed further signs of drunkenness I became concerned that our outing was being scrapped by default. When I had conveyed my thoughts by a silent glance, my guide broached the question cautiously.

"Why, hell, yes, I'm gonna take you to my still—but whatza' hurry?" he replied.

We all began to store the honey and equipment against a nearby tree, after the example of the son-in-law. He quietly informed me the still was further on into the mountain range. This was the first time that he, too, had mentioned the still, but hearing his father-in-law mention it first, he felt safe in discussing it.

The moonshiner was walking unsteadily by now—not the least unhappily but unsteadily. My guide and I had brought sardines, cheese, and crackers, but nobody had taken time to eat with the events moving along rapidly. I thought, after we started for the still, we would delay to eat and the moonshiner would recover more rapidly that way. But the food had been stored with the honey and equipment, and it was too late for second considerations.

After a walk of what seemed like at least a mile, we passed into a ravine and up the other side. The profuse sweating of the moonshiner seemed to be effective in increasing his sobriety. With the ridge beyond the ravine behind our weary feet, we entered a clearing with a shallow hollow running north and south. A small branch was visible, and a recently used log road crossed it, winding down the hill. The appearance of the road answered a question for me. I knew the supplies for the distilling operation had to come in by a different route from the one we had used. It would have been impossible to transport them over our route except by horse or mule. I suspected we were being deliberately confused. I felt for certain the location had been reached, but the moonshiner walked on. A second hollow was quickly reached, and the moonshiner turned parallel to it and walked only a few yards before stopping. He asked us to wait five minutes and follow him. The son-in-law grinned and waited with us.

In no longer than two and a half minutes we followed. The son-in-law led the way, but we were still within twenty feet of the still before we saw it. It was a 250–300 gallon pot, set right in the midst of laurels. It was fired up and running, and we hadn't even seen or smelled the smoke. Moonshiners claim green leaves in thickly wooded areas will "swallow" (absorb) the smoke—now I believe it, but I didn't before. There was little smoke to be sure —green wood was used for just such advantage—but there was still another reason which the moonshiner explained with a great deal of pride. The still furnace was constructed of stone and cinderblock in such a way as to surround the still and contain it, within two feet of the cap. The only hole emitting smoke was the "clean out" box to the still, and this had been partially plugged with mud. The design forced most of the smoke to circle the air space through a channeled corridor between the still and furnace wall, passing back over the flames a second time where the smoke was burned before passing out the side-mounted flue. It was the most ingenious design I had ever personally seen.

The still was being manned by the missing son-in-law and a younger man who was not introduced. The king of the clan reached for the dipper and helped himself to fresh distillate, while the still hands drank from the fruit jar containing the honey. To the east of the still, twelve to fourteen mash boxes stood. Several cases of half-gallon fruit jars had been filled and stacked to the side. Other cartons had obviously not been opened, and unopened bags of sugar lay on boards covered with a tarp. All of the men bragged on the still and solicited our compliments on the setup. The two men seemed unnerved with our presence, but it might have been their concern with the cicadas. It appeared clear that the shrieking insects were getting to them, possibly because their noise would drown out the sound of approaching investigators. In spite of the noise, the sweeping eyes never ceased, even in the midst of a conversation.

We never knew whether the two men at the still knew we were coming or not. We wondered, of course, if they had known prior to our actual arrival but could not pursue the matter.

The still was running a steady stream of distillate about the thickness of a pencil. They were not using an automobile radiator but a copper coil which was submerged in a square box continually flooded with cool water from the branch over which we had passed. Plastic pipe carried the water by gravity and the overflow wound its way down the mountainside.

We stayed and watched the operation for over two hours, and we still had had nothing to eat. My legs were trembling from fatigue, but my thirst had been revived by the fresh water at the still. Some canned sausages and cans of beans lay in view on top of a still hand's coat, and there were moments when I felt the urge to dive for them. They offered us no food, and the moonshiner was having his in liquid form. He was now getting drunk for certain, and his personality was starting to change for the worse. As fantastic as it might sound, I am sure that in the six or seven hours we were in his presence, he had consumed one and a half quarts and possibly more. His capacity for drink is still unbelievable to me.

We knew beyond doubt it was time to leave. Our moonshining host was too drunk to walk, and with the son-in-law, we started our long journey back. I started to ask if we couldn't take the (I suspected) shorter road back. The guide anticipated my glances in that direction and countered my move with a whisper. It would be "unneighborly" not to help with the equipment and honey-loading duties, he informed me; besides, had the moonshiner wanted us to know about the other road, he would have brought us that way. We knew the road existed, but we would play along and be as lost as he had felt we ought to be.

Before we got the chain saw and equipment back in the truck, I felt for certain someone would need to carry me, but in the truck at last I gobbled my sardines hungrily. The other two were still not worried about eating, but they too had drunk the sweet moon to a considerable degree and had some nourishment from that.

The day was to have one more bonus. When we arrived at the house, we met our present truck driver's two children. We did not see his wife, whom we supposed to be inside with the grandmother, but it is doubtful whether we would have been introduced had she been five feet away. The little boy and girl clung to their father shyly, but I was finally able to draw the little girl of four or five years into conversation about the bee-tree we had cut. (The little boy of about eight listened but refused to talk.) I was carrying the honey (two or three pounds of which I accepted, after they had attempted to force the entire lot upon me), and when I had shown her this and spooned out a quantity with a clean stick, she chatted busily for the reward. A more precious child was not to be found anywhere, though her raven-black locks lacked the freshness of a recent shampoo, and her feet were bare and dirty. Her childhood innocence in all its freshness seemed to make all other things negligible.

We said our adieus and drove away. It had been an unusual day, and my knowledge of that strange breed of men increased fourfold. But the gnawing thought would not leave me; what of the little girl? Would she somehow find her way out of the valley, or would the age of sixteen find her immersed in the chores of motherhood, wife of a young moonshiner, living a life of loneliness, sacrifice, and seclusion like her mother's? Foolish though it was, I felt an urgency to turn, go back, and tell her of the life beyond —but to what use? What tender ears could hear or understand anything save the nighttime call of the whippoorwill, the majesty of a firefly, and a trip with Daddy to the mountains, and while he worked, to watch the long-tailed squirrels play? Somehow I pictured her weary at thirty with no reason to smile anymore; face drawn and wrinkled, paying attention neither to the squirrel nor firefly—seeing nothing save the empty space that separated the dream of yesterday from the reality of her today.

After being home a few weeks, with the memory of more visits to operating stills behind me, it was natural to think in terms of arranging a close-up view of a still raid. I started to lay the proper groundwork with authorities and then thought better of it. Though I could have arranged to be on the scene of a raid far from any distilling sites I had visited, I knew that the moonshiners had an effective grapevine of their own. In short, word passed among them that I had participated in a raid could only leave them with one conclusion. It was a hard decision to make, for passing up the chance to observe a raid at close hand would be the only vital experience pertaining to the book that I would miss.

CHAPTER TWELVE

Types of
Stills
and Their
Application

In preceding chapters, none but the small pot stills of simplest design have been illustrated. From the 1700's to the early 1900's the vast majority of moonshiners practiced their art with such small and simple units. On occasion, capacity and design would be enlarged, but in spite of attempts to make it more productive, the pot still would be found to be losing favor with the coming of the twentieth century. The natural evolution of any industry, illicit or otherwise, was partially responsible for drastic changes in still design. The prohibition era, with the tremendous production demands it brought in its wake, was, however, the biggest single influence. A much more efficient still design was needed—and an army of craftsmen and technicians, both imported and domestic, changed illicit distilling equipment almost overnight.

The reader need not be overwhelmed by the numerous descriptions of stills to follow; keep in mind that the function of each is the same conversion task as that illustrated by the simple pot still in Figure 8. Each still is designed to convert a mixture of mash (of sometimes varying ingredients) into ethyl alcohol. The mechanics of doing this vary from one still design to another, but the biggest, most complex still performs essentially the same task as the small pot still that would fit into the trunk of your car. Vast fermenting tanks, complex exhaust systems, massive steam boilers, water pumps, stills three stories high, sophisticated condensers, etc., are merely to turn out more distillate, more efficiently.

In the picture section to follow, general classifications of still designs will be shown first. Illicit distilling is not, however, restricted to these general equipment classifications; all sorts of cross combinations of these types have been successfully employed. Still design is strictly up to the individual moonshiner, and every conceivable shape, size, and design has been and still is being made by the individual practitioner.

The Pot Still

The pot still is the oldest of all the designs and is the mother Still of moonshining. It is occasionally called the "turnip bottom" still if it is made in the shape of a turnip (rounded bottom with tapering neck). The pot still is not always made in a pot shape and can be box shaped in design and still be within the pot-still family. Figure 14 illustrates a very small pot still with nonremovable cap. A screw-on cap opening serves for filling and emptying, and a pressure release valve is provided for safety of operation. Such a small unit could be used on a kitchen stove or in the mountains. Small stills such as this one, when used in the mountains, are called "mountain teapots." They are normally used for the needs of one or just a few families. Although winemaking for family use is still widespread throughout the United States, whiskey making exclusively for family consumption tends to be confined to pocket areas, primarily in the South, and almost exclusively among families who have a long history of the distilling art in their background.

Figure 15 shows another small pot still designed for indoor use. A basement drain is utilized for carrying away water overflow, doubler drainage, and still drainage. Note the "blisters" on the small doubler between still and worm barrel. Heat in the doubler, no matter how large or small, reaches intense proportions. This little unit would produce approximately three gallons per run and, operated only one day per week, would keep even a heavy-drinking family supplied with plenty of white mule.

The small pot still should not be thought of in terms of small production capability only. Figure 16 illustrates this point dramatically. Mash boxes shown in the picture and those out of view provide storage for approximately three thousand gallons of fermented mash. After the first mash is run, it can be slopped back into the empty mash boxes with a little fresh grain, sugar, and yeast, and the next three thousand gallons will be ready to run in three or four days. The same action can be repeated two or three times until the last rotgut is drained off. Thus, this small still, operated around the clock until the first mash is depleted, then run again in the same manner when the next batch of mash is ready, can produce six hundred gallons of moonshine whiskey weekly. This still is a wood-fired mountain rig, and the tree stumps may be observed where the wood has been cut to fire the still.

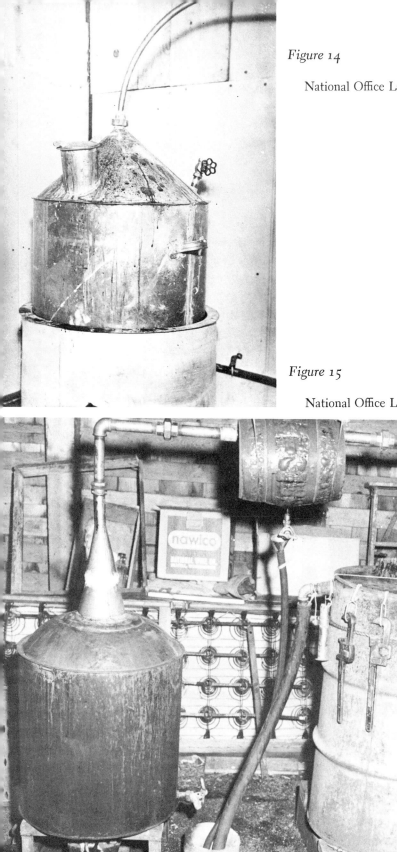

Figure 14

National Office Laboratory, IRS

Figure 15

National Office Laboratory, IRS

Figure 16　　　　　　　　　　　　National Office Laboratory, IRS

Figure 17 shows yet another design of the pot-still family, sometimes affectionately called a mountain teapot. This Idaho moonshiner does it the old way without benefit of a doubler; for high proof he will have to double back (run distillate through the still again). The still is handmade of copper. Snow surrounds the operation, and it is certain that the warm fire under the still was welcome.

Figure 18 pictures one of the smallest stills made. This is a kitchen-type still, designed to fit down into the deep-well fryer of an old-style electric stove. It is complete with a miniature doubler and copper worm. The worm would be submerged in a bucket of cool water (probably with a few cubes of ice added) with the end of the worm penetrating the housing of the bucket so the distillate could be caught. The puncture area would be sealed with caulking compound or bathtub cement. One run from such a small unit would yield approximately one-half to one-quarter pint of white mule.

The Submarine Still

The submarine still has replaced many of the small pot stills of earlier years. The name is derived from the elongated shape of the unit, which is really more like an army tank minus the tracks. The unit is simpler to build than the true copper pot still and less costly. The sides are wood, preferably with a wraparound sheet of copper but often of nothing more than galvanized sheet metal. The majority of submarine stills are built with a capacity of from 250 to 1,500 gallons. As a rough gauge of productivity, a submarine still of the 1,500-gallon size would produce approximately 130–160 gallons of moonshine whiskey from one run. This output varies, depending on the percentage of sugar–grain used and other factors. All components of this type still can be seen in Figure 19. The large cap on top feeds steam vapor into the doubler, where it passes through plastic pipe into an auto radiator for condensing (the radiator is submerged in water backed up by a small dam formed by sand bags). The officer is dumping a zinc tub of pure white lightnin'.

Submarine stills use copper worm coils as often as auto radiators, and contamination of the distillate is less likely with a clean coil.

Figure 17

National Office Laboratory, IRS

Figure 18

Virginia Alcoholic Beverages
Control Board

Figure 19

Morris Stephenson

Figure 20

National Office Laboratory, IRS

ROUNDHOG STILL

FUEL
SOURCE

TO DOUBLER
AND

CONDENSER

MASH

NOTE:
Source of heat may be oil, bottled gas, wood, coal or coke and is applied to the sides of the fermenters when the mash is ripe and after the portable cap is put into place.

Groundhog Still

Like the burrowing mammal from which the name is derived, the groundhog still in Figure 20, sits snugly in a hole in the earth, with only the top exposed. The mash can be mixed and allowed to ferment in the still or mixed and allowed to ferment in barrels and boxes in another location and then emptied into the still. Designs utilizing a wooden bottom and wooden top have the heat for cooking applied to the metal sides of the still. Heat can be supplied by oil, bottled gas, or, on occasion, steam piped directly into the mash. Burying not only partially hides the still, but helps suppress the evidence of smoke.

Figure 21 illustrates an actual installation. The still, in use, is capped with a metal or wooden barrel from which the steam travels to a doubler and on to the condenser. This type of still is used mainly in the deep South. It is impractical to use in geographical areas where the ground is rocky and the still would be hard to bury. This particular still operated in Mississippi.

The Alabama Box Still

The Alabama box (or pan) still (Figure 22) is not altogether limited to one state but seems most prevalent there. It combines the features of simple design, low-cost construction, and quick removal and relocation. Reasonably good production can be expected from the simple unit, and the capacity of the still can be easily altered at the will of the moonshiner. A metal bottom is necessary, for it is worked by direct heat, usually from wood cut nearby. One or more doublers are used, with condensing taking place through a car radiator or worm coil. Mash may be mixed and allowed to ferment in the still or in other mash boxes or barrels located nearby.

Figure 23 shows two box stills of large capacity. Note oil barrels being used for caps. On big stills, double caps can be used to enhance output. Vapor lines from the cap on this huge operation are three-inch hot-air furnace pipes. These lines travel to the big doublers and on to the condenser. Bottle gas rather than wood is sometimes used, particularly if the location of the still is jeopardized by smoke. While the use of gas is more expensive for the moonshiner, the absence of smoke is desirable. These big units operated in North Carolina.

The most dangerous still ever made came into popularity during and after World War II when metals were scarce. This still was made in many designs—pan shape, cone, barrel—and affectionately named the "silver cloud." The metal used for making it was old or new galvanized sheet metal or barn roofing. After being in

Figure 21   National Office Laboratory, IRS

Figure 22   National Office Laboratory, IRS

ALABAMA BOX TYPE STILL

Figure 23   Licensed Beverage Industries, Inc., New York City

use for awhile and getting washed and waxed by the elements, by the light of the moon it would gleam like a mound of polished silver. What made the still so dangerous was the method of making it. The corners and edges were often soldered together rather than riveted. A very small model had over 300 lineal inches of solder seaming on which the hot steam of cooking mash could act. The large models with over 1,000 lineal inches of exposed solder seaming must have turned out at least a teaspoon full of deadly lead salts for every 5,000 gallons of distillate run.

Most moonshiners today know the danger of solder seaming and this type of still is a rare find by enforcment officers. The main danger of lead salts today comes from the use of auto radiators and/or soldered connecting pipes in the still apparatus.

The Georgia Type Still

Figure 24 illustrates a unique type of still, quick to set up and very productive for a medium-sized operation. Steam is utilized by means of a boiler (sometimes this unit is portable and on wheels for quick removal). Steam passes into a double-stacked

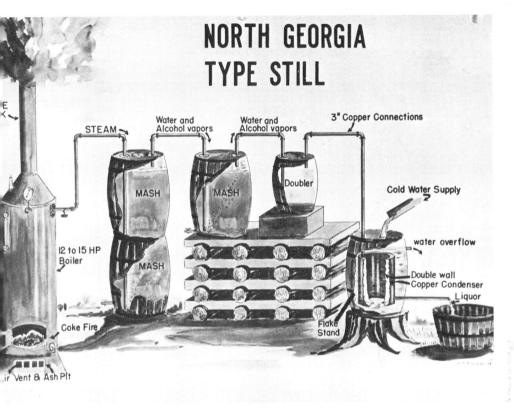

NORTH GEORGIA
TYPE STILL

STEAM

Water and Alcohol vapors

Water and Alcohol vapors

3" Copper Connections

MASH

MASH

Doubler

Cold Water Supply

12 to 15 HP Boiler

MASH

water overflow

Double wall Copper Condenser

Liquor

Coke Fire

Flake Stand

ir Vent & Ash Pit

Figure 24   National Office Laboratory, IRS

mash barrel, heating these units to boiling temperature, where the vapor passes into a third mash barrel. The accumulated vapor and water are of a very high strength and are further doubled in the doubler before reaching the condenser. The condenser in this instance is a double-wall copper shell. Though not as popular as the auto radiator or worm coil, it is frequently used. The reason for having steam pass through three mash barrels rather than one is the combined accumulation of high-strength vapors with the resultant improving of the alcoholic strength of the final distillate. All barrels are heated by steam from the original source.

Figure 25 shows a double boiler unit firing a large moonshining operation. Boilers use coal, coke, and occasionally charcoal. Smoke stacks emitting heavy volumes of smoke must either be very remotely located or near enough to industry not to draw suspicion. This type of operation cannot be moved or dismantled quickly, and some type of camouflage is imperative. Heavily wooded areas will swallow some degree of smoke, but nothing approaching this amount.

Figure 25   National Office Laboratory, IRS

Figure 26   Bufford Pusser

Figure 27   Licensed Beverage Industries, Inc., New York City

The Steam Roller Still

Figure 26 illustrates the smallest segment of illicit distilling. This distilling operation uses no mash and no mixture of any kind. The illicit alcohol is derived by "sweating" or "wringing out" the empty barrels used by the legal industry. This type of moonshiner will take barrels previously charred and used for aging and storage, and recover the whiskey soaked into the wood. He does it by injecting steam into a series of barrels from which the final outlet is fed into a condenser. The condensate, which is the end result, is whiskey extracted from the wood.

Barrel Stills

The barrel still as shown in Figure 27 is the very cheapest of all moonshine operations to construct. Junk oil, or chemical barrels with lard cans or other tin buckets are about all that are needed, except for a copper coil or radiator and a bottle of compressed gas. Plastic pipes are used as connectors. The still itself is nothing more than one barrel turned upside down over another. A tunnel is made in the dirt to allow the gas burner to be placed under the still. In this photo the sugar bag at the bottom right of the picture hides the tunnel. Plastic pipe from the still passes to a tin-can doubler on each side and on into a barrel containing a worm coil. The moonshiner was setting up three multiple units, as illustrated, to operate simultaneously. Plastic pipe is poked through holes in barrels and sealed with clay mud and rye paste to cut down on steam loss. Such an operation is almost sure to suffer from contamination. Barrels are frequently used without cleaning and often contain highly toxic industrial chemicals. Three complete still units, as shown, can be constructed for less than $150.00.

In the barrel-still classification, one thousand- and two thousand-gallon gas-storage tanks have been found being used as stills. Such a big unit will normally be fired with wood under the entire bottom surface or gas burners placed at several locations under the bottom. Sometimes a steam boiler is used, and this method is deemed safer. The danger of explosion from flame heat is very great. Old gasoline-storage tanks retain explosive vapor for years, and perhaps this reason alone explains the fact that their use is limited.

The Mushroom Still

The mushroom still in Figure 28, is a design for producing very high-proof alcohol, deriving its name from the mushroom-shaped components of the stack. Each of these mushrooms or hollow-core disks has the effect of doubling, double doubling, and triple doubling the steam vapors passing up the column. Condensing takes place through a series of coils, which may be cylindrical or "fan folded." The mash may be cooked by steam injected into the mash or by other heat sources under the still.

Figure 29 illustrates an actual model of the mushroom with five disks. Each disk has the effect of increasing alcoholic strength. Note that each disk, in a part of the compartment, has a supply of water for cooling the vapors as they rise. Some degree of condensation takes place in each disk, so that the next higher disk has a higher content of alcohol to act upon further.

The mushroom still is found most often in the Northern metropolitan areas and is fairly expensive to make because of the complexity of design and workmanship. This still operated in Paterson, New Jersey.

Continuous Process Column Still

Figure 30 illustrates a still design that more nearly approximates the modern legal distillery than any others used by the moonshiner. It is a highly efficient operation of high output, utilizing steam and a preheating device. This same device will be shown

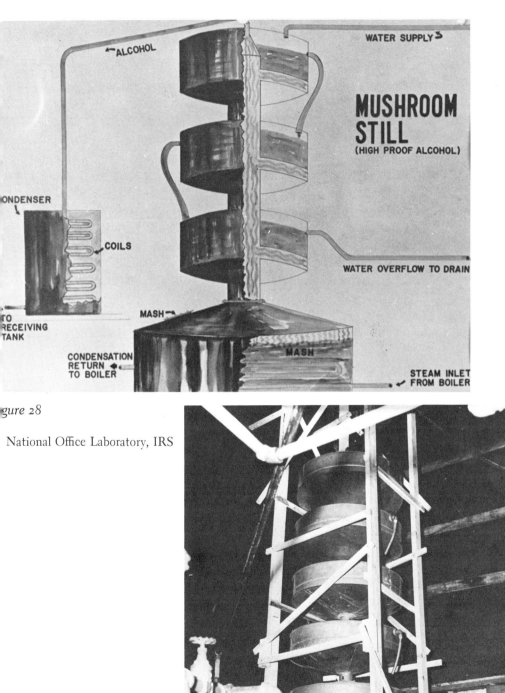

ALCOHOL

WATER SUPPLY

MUSHROOM STILL
(HIGH PROOF ALCOHOL)

CONDENSER

COILS

WATER OVERFLOW TO DRAIN

TO
RECEIVING
TANK

MASH

CONDENSATION
RETURN
TO BOILER

MASH

STEAM INLET
FROM BOILER

Figure 28

National Office Laboratory, IRS

Figure 29

National Office Laboratory, IRS

CONTINUOUS PROCESS COLUMN STILL

DEPHLEGMATOR

COND[

BUBBLE CUPS

TRY BOX

RECEIVING TANK

PRE-HEATER

SUGAR

SUGAR

Figure 30   National Office Laboratory, IRS

on less sophisticated stills also, and its purpose is to raise the mash temperature preparatory to distilling, so that a minimum of time will be lost prior to actual distillation. Mash is pumped into the still continuously and bypasses the older and more crude method of filling the still manually, emptying and refilling, with delays in between actual distilling.

This type of still is normally found indoors and most generally in the metropolitan areas of the North. Such fast producing stills were responsible for the mass output of illicit alcohol during the prohibition era. Of all the stills used by moonshiners, it is the most expensive to build.

The Pot Column Still

Figure 31 illustrates a still type that derives its name from a combination of the column still and the pot still. The design provides a voluminous output but eliminates many of the more com-

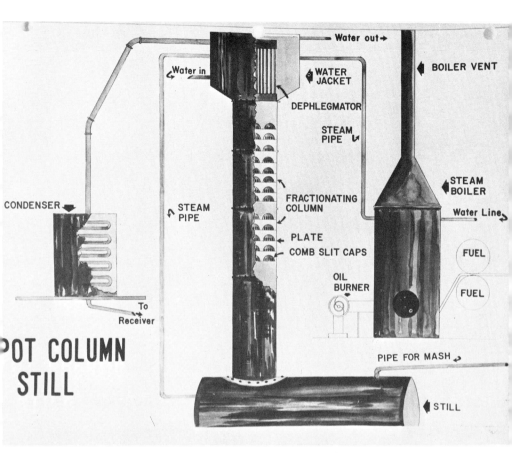

POT COLUMN STILL

Figure 31   National Office Laboratory, IRS

plex and expensive accessory fixtures and devices necessary in the true column still operation. This unit, like the true column still, more closely approximates equipment of the legal industry than do most of the others designed for moonshining. The unit is most often found in the Northern metropolitan areas; it enjoyed its greatest use during prohibition.

The Blackpot Still

"Black pottin'" pertains more to the method of distilling than to the actual equipment used. It is done with a box still, ground-hog still, pot still, or submarine still. In black pottin', the still is used both as the mash box and the still (generally referred to as a fermenter still). The mash is either made, or allowed to ferment, right in the still. When this is accomplished, a fire or gas burner is applied to the bottom of the still, and the operation proceeds. After the still is used several times in this manner, the spillage and accumulation of mash ingredients begin to build up all over the still, and the scum becomes black. The interior of the still builds up an even worse degree of scum and becomes totally black. Under these conditions, the mash in the still during its fermentation period becomes almost black, and the still beer looks as if coal dust has been generously added and stirred well. Repeated running of the same mash until the last rotgut run is extracted from the spent mash makes the still even blacker with residue buildup. From these factors, this type of distilling aptly derives its name.

The blackpot stilling operation in Figure 32 was discovered in Virginia and consisted of eight big submarine stills. Through the cap opening in the bottom still the blackish mash can be seen, ready to be distilled. This illicit operation was caught early, and the individual stills had not been used enough to become black on the outside.

Black pottin' has several advantages to the moonshiner. He eliminates the need of cumbersome mash boxes, and he saves the work of emptying by hand or pumping mash from other boxes into the still. His operation is better concealed, with fewer components covering a large area, and if the stills are not full of mash, he can move the entire operation in a big truck fairly quickly. Timing is all important also. If the mash has fermented without detection, the moonshiner can move in, distill the ripe mash, and move out with his output in a minimum of time. If all goes well, he will come back when the mash is cool, add sugar, water, and fresh yeast, and distill the whole business over in seventy-two to ninety-six hours in warm weather. Depending on the policy of the individual moonshiner, this might be done once, twice, three times, or even four or five, until the mash looks like human sewage in an advanced state of decay. Some moonshiners make no more than one run from a batch of mash, and some no more than two runs; it all depends on who the moonshiner is selling to and what he knows he can get by with, or his individual integrity.

The actual distilling from a string of subs, as pictured here, can take several forms. If caps, doublers, condensers, connecting pipe, water supply, and heat are available for all stills, they can all be put into action at one time. Most times the moonshiner has only accessory components for one or two stills at a time, and the distilling will take place in this manner.

A big sub as illustrated in Figure 33 will sometimes have both a drain cock and a crudely built clean-out opening. Fast drainage

Figure 32

Morris Stephenson

Figure 33

Morris Stephenson

allows the quick filling of the still for another run. Some of these sub distillers use tanks of automobile gasoline, to which they attach a valve stem and pressurize the liquid with a simple, hand-operated tire pump. The pressurized liquid is then fed to a standard gas burner for use under the still.

Still Components and Accessories

In Figure 34 an ATF investigator displays the two most valuable components of a still. Though in many cases the still uses plain sheet metal and wood, the moonshiner sometimes insists on a copper worm and cap. The time required to replace two such lost units is as vital as the cash value of the components. The two pieces shown here operated on an 850-gallon submarine still.

Figure 35 illustrates what is hardly the most modern of boilers for the steam distiller, but the wheels are most useful. If the "move out" command is passed down, a tractor or jeep can have the portable boiler five miles away in thirty minutes, even if it's still hot.

Figure 34   Morris Stephenson

Figure 35

National Office Laboratory, IRS

Figure 36

Morris Stephenson

Figure 36 shows a close-up view of a gasoline-operated water pump. The moonshiner will on occasion pump his water to a high, remote location, even though water is available in a nearby limestone spring from which gravity flow would fulfill his needs. Well-hidden locations are not as plentiful as in an earlier day, and this factor is considered even if it means extra equipment. However, a pump does make a noise. This pump is buried and covered with boards and dirt. When running, it can be heard only a few feet away.

Figure 37 illustrates another method of multiple radiator use. On a very big still, running a heavy output of vapor from the cap, a heavy-duty condenser is advantageous. This illustration shows three radiators welded together in a series to handle rapid condensation from a heavy input of vapor. From an operation of this size, white mule would be coming from the last condenser, in a stream as big as a man's thumb.

 Figure 37   Licensed Beverage Industries, Inc., New York City

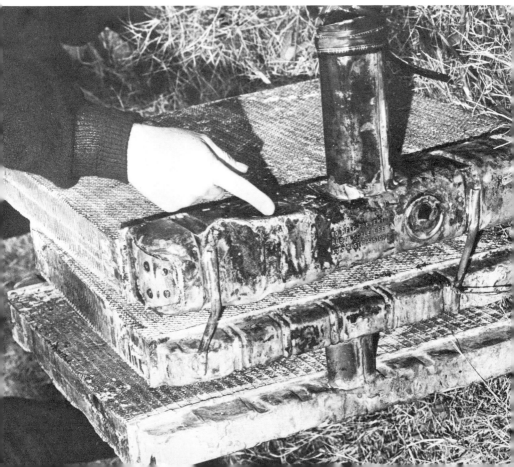

Another fixture of the still is shown at the bottom right of Figure 38. This sacklike device is a filter. Made of a felt material (and sometimes chamois) it filters the distillate, removing foreign particles and some of the fusel oil and other undesirable elements, thus reducing the harshness of the drink. The operation, called leaching, is not practiced by all moonshiners. Some simply bottle the white mule without the least thought of filtering. Old moonshiners sometimes used a filtering process of running the distillate through crushed charcoal in a blanket.

Figure 39 shows the economy method of providing a filter. A wornout, sweat-saturated felt hat is doing the job nicely. Asked about contamination from a dirty hat, a moonshiner will answer, "There ain't no bug ever lived that can swim in my likker and live to tell his family about it—no siree, my stuff is better than sheepdip any day."

Figure 40   Morris Stephenson

Secrecy and Concealment

Figure 40 might look to the Sunday afternoon hiker to be simply a rolling meadow and beautiful grove of trees. A close look at the base of the trees near the center of the picture might rightfully draw a suspicious second look. All looks normal except for the obvious depression. A careful moonshiner would have added more dirt to allow for the settling of the earth.

Approached from the gully side, Figure 41 begins to confirm the suspicions. The cut trees propped against the wall might well have hidden the entrance if it had been summer and the leaves were out.

Figure 42 shows the view inside the underground distilling setup. It is a big boiler arrangement, cooking the mash by steam in a giant cooker. Large timbers hold the earth above. Electricity provides light for a twenty-four-hour operation and electric pump-

Figure 41   Morris Stephenson

Figure 42

Morris Stephenson

ing of water and mash. Smoke stacks from the boiler were the only thing above ground. Such operations frequently have retractable smoke stacks.

To the reader, the hiding of a big distilling operation with all the necessary equipment and supplies would seem next to impossible. In Figures 43, 44 and 45, even with the leaf cover missing, one would have to be within one hundred feet of any of these (if walking) to know what was taking place. With heavy leaf cover, a pass within twenty-five feet would require some pretty observant looking. The number of discoveries would be reduced if revenue agents did not have the assistance of spotters from planes and helicopters in their searches. Considering how well hidden these stills are, one can see the problem in proper prospective by realizing that the agents must cover hundreds and sometimes thousands of square miles of territory as dense as shown here or more so.

The author recalls on one occasion being taken to a still site in the mountains of North Carolina by a guide who led the way directly to the still. The big unit was completely unseen (all the while we were looking, remember) until within twenty feet.

Problems of concealment are just as painstakingly thought out in the city as in the mountains. Even with the best plans, it is much more difficult in the city for a number of reasons: Heavy water use improperly camouflaged is a dead giveaway; heavy elec-

Figure 43   Morris Stephenson

Figure 44   Morris Stephenson

Figure 45   Licensed Beverage Industries, Inc., New York City

trical consumption without adequate reason is another; telltale odors, too much coming and going, disposal of spent mash, and a variety of other reasons make illicit distilling in the city more difficult. All these problems, however, do not deter city moonshiners from plying their trade in every conceivable location, with every method of trickery. Often a city (and rural) moonshiner will tap a natural-gas line or electrical-service cable in such a, way that no meter recording is possible. Water supply also is often diverted to avoid metering, in the cities. Figure 46 illustrates a large indoor setup, which required some extensive remodeling and expensive equipment.

Big Time Moonshining

The city moonshiner/bootlegger, though not as numerous as his rural counterpart, takes the prize for the sophistication of his equipment and the volume of illicit alcohol he can turn out. The mammoth size of the prohibition and post-prohibition distilling operation is dramatically illustrated in the following pictures.

Figure 47 illustrates warehousing space needed for the storage of tons of sugar, barrels, docking facilities, and general work room.

Figure 48 shows a giant fermenting vat with data chart affixed to side. Such an illicit operation utilizes great production-control methods patterned after the procedures of the legal industry. Although working conditions or quality control are hardly comparable to those of the legal distilling industry, equipment and production many times approach it. Note the details of the chart, listing temperature information, date of mash preparation, etc. Time means money and production, and the city moonshiner has become a master of the art of rapid production. He capitalizes on the use of scientific and automated measures of production with every tool at his disposal, and goes a step beyond in some-

Figure 46   Licensed Beverage Industries, Inc., New York City

Figure 47National Office Laboratory, IRS

Figure 48National Office Laboratory, IRS

Figure 49   National Office Laboratory, IRS

times using chemicals to hurry fermentation. A typical mix of mash in this type of big vat (probably ten thousand-gallon capacity) would be seven thousand gallons of water, 2,500 pounds of sugar, thirty-five pounds of yeast, 750 pounds of cornmeal (or in some cases no grain additive at all), and—if a booster chemical was used to hurry fermentation—approximately twenty-five to thirty-five pounds of that would be included in the mixture. From this mix or mash, approximately nine hundred to a thousand gallons of high-proof alky could be distilled.

Boilers in big operations are normally oil- or gas-fired. Large vacuum systems for conveying alcoholic fumes to smoke stacks are mandatory. Sometimes a large blower is used to shoot the fumes high into the air above the smokestack, in hope that they will disperse sufficiently in the atmosphere and leave no telltale odor.

Figure 49 reveals another inventive device to warn of incoming visitors. This is a doorway alarm system, which tells the workmen inside when the outside door is opened.

Figure 50 shows a moonshiner's attempt at automation in speeding up the bottling process. This unit is an electrically driven machine designed to fill ten five-gallon cans simultaneously.

This giant moonshining operation was discovered on a farm near Joliet, Illinois, in 1935. From the barn loft Figure 51 provides a good view of mash fermenting in a huge vat. At the time of seizure all vats revealed a total of 69,400 gallons of fermenting mash ready to be run. Dual timbers provide a track for a dumping car, hauling ingredients to be emptied. Note "snowballs" on surface of mash, indicating fermentative action in advanced states.

Figure 52 illustrates graphically that huge operations are not limited to the metropolitan areas of the North and Northeast. Shown here are nine hundred fifty-five-gallon mash barrels, giving a total mash capacity of 49,500 gallons. At left center of the picture, part of two large stills can be seen. One of the stills was a 3,600-gallon capacity pot still (the largest southern pot known to the author) and another pot still of 1,650-gallon capacity. This big operation was capable of producing 4,500 gallons of illicit

Figure 51   National Office Laboratory, IRS

Figure 52   Licensed Beverage Industries, Inc., New York City

whiskey per day, or more. The big stills used multiple double-decked barrels for caps. The operation was seized in Jackson County, Mississippi, in 1964.

Production Problems

Sanitation around a large or small moonshining operation would seem a problem. But many moonshiners do not even recognize it as such and maintain that cleanliness around the still is a waste of time and energy. It is not unusual to find mash boxes containing dead rodents, birds, snakes, millions of insects, and even dead skunks or opossums. One reason this fails to bother the moonshiner is because he believes that the distilling operation sterilizes contaminated mash. Connections on distilling pipes are sometimes held together by old rags, dirty socks, rubber stripping, or burlap which, saturated and soured, draw flies and rodents. Not all moonshiners are guilty of such practices, but the danger to the purchaser exists just the same. Many still sites after successful operation for just a few weeks take on the look of a garbage dump.

Figures 53 and 54 provide a view of ground conditions around such a successfully operated still. Figure 53 shows mash boxes, some of which are full and some empty, swamped with sugar bags and other trash. Roosting birds in the trees above them contribute a healthy share of droppings. This latter point is not considered unhealthy at all by the moonshiner. In fact, the old, old moonshiners believed in letting their turkeys, geese, ducks, and chickens roost on the mash boxes, hopefully with their tails turned

Figure 54

Morris Stephenson

inward. They believed that fowl manure enhanced fermentation and the quality of the distillate. (The author was dumbfounded to find out, during laboratory research, that this belief does have a solid chemical foundation. The nitrogen in the manure provides a helpful additive, particularly in the moonshine brandies!) Animal manure is used occasionally by moonshiners in two different ways: one, by adding it to the mash in the same age-old belief pertaining to fowl manure, in addition to the belief that bacteria in the manure will assist in fermentation; secondly for an insulator. In winter, various methods are used to keep the mash barrels warm, and stacking manure around them is only one. The moonshiner believes that the manure is not only a good insulator in itself but that the bacteriological content actually provides a heat of its own. Here again the moonshiner knows what he is talking about. Any farmer will verify that even cold manure (several days old) will show a slight visible heat vapor in the coldest of weather. Moonshiners differ on the wisdom of covering mash boxes, either during or after fermentation periods. Some of the more meticulous ones cover the boxes as a sanitary measure, to prevent rainwater weakening or interfering with fermentation, or as a method of retaining captive heat during fermentation. Other moonshiners simply don't bother unless cold weather forces them to cover up in order to operate. Covering is done with almost anything functional: tar paper, old sacks, old tin, blankets or boards.

Figure 54 shows a complete unit rapidly being buried in ungathered trash. The shovel on top of the mash boxes might have been used to clean out the barn in the morning and to stir the mash the same afternoon.

Figure 55 would hardly allow a moonshine drinker to enjoy his favorite tipple, if he could see the prebottling conditions under which his moon might have been processed. Mud around a still is always a problem, and it finds its way onto and into the receiving vessels as well as the shoes of the still hand. For still operations in barns and chicken yards the problem is doubled, for the mud becomes mixed with manure.

Figure 55   Morris Stephenson

Not all stills, however, are operated under such conditions. Many are maintained in the cleanliness of the mountain air, with covered mash boxes, right down to the bottling operation.

The enormous variety of stills and types of operations seem needless. Variations in size are more readily understandable, but it is surprising that the equipment is not more standardized throughout the moonshining states. But this wide variation is due to the individuality of the moonshiner, his preferred practices, and the conditions under which he must operate. How he learned his trade and from whom is often a factor. Where he learned it also has a great bearing. A groundhog still could be easily buried in the soft soil of Mississippi, but the burying would not be so simple in rocky and mountainous West Virginia.

A smokestack steam unit operated successfully in remote North Carolina mountain country would not be so inconspicuous in the flat area of Florida.

The small subs and pots also seem to be found in geographical areas more suited to their use—the high ridges and mountains of Tennessee, Virginia, Kentucky, North Carolina, West Virginia, etc. All in all, we must concede the moonshiner has found the best equipment for his particular area. Where there seems to be a logical point of disagreement, the moonshiner would probably counter: "You'uns tend to your readin' an' ritin', and I'll take care of the stillin'. Don't rightly 'magine you'uns got it altogether figured out no ways."

The moonshiner is a peculiar individual in many, many ways. His reasoning processes and often his actions are those of a man who is totally a unique individual. Rare is the moonshiner who likes legal whiskey. "That store-bought stuff will poison ya," he will say in all seriousness. "It never knowed a still, and it's nothin' but chemicals no way," he will add.

Some moonshiners will not drink even their own product while they are at work distilling. Others will drink legal beer or soft drinks while they are working, and others like the still beer from their own mash boxes. It would not be unusual to see a moonshiner dip a cup full of still beer from a mash box saturated with gnats, flies, and a host of other intruders. Still other moonshiners drink their own product continuously while at work, by robbing a full fruit jar or catching the distillate as it comes out of the worm cock. The real old timer would have his teedum barrel, stashed away in a cool spring nearby.

Fermenting mash has a pleasant aroma to a degree, but large quantities of it, fermenting indoors, will cause asphyxiation if not properly ventilated. Figure 56 shows fermenting mash in an advanced state. Note ventilating fan in the background of the picture. Gaseous bubbles (called snowballs by some moonshiners) can be seen clearly, and the smaller, rounded barrel in the center foreground is yeast, being allowed to attain advanced activation before application to other mash boxes being prepared. Advance activation of the yeast cuts down on the fermenting time.

The moonshiner sometimes gets careless, as demonstrated by Figure 57. This photo was taken by the moonshiner himself. It is a print made from a roll of film found in the moonshiner's car when it was stopped and seized, loaded with illegal whiskey. Note the setting of the distilling operation. The ledge overhang provides a difficult location to find if the smoke is kept under control. The belief of the moonshiner that heavy leaf cover will swallow smoke appears to have some scientific foundation. To a small degree, tree leaves will absorb carbon dioxide. The canopy effect of the trees themselves and the inversion factors of temperature and climate also add substance to the moonshiner's belief.

This still is constructed with the stone furnace built around it, up nearly to the top. This is the most popular design of wood-burning furnaces for the small-and medium-size pot stills—it allows the flame of the wood fire to cover the bottom and sides of the still and hence bring the still contents to a boil more quickly. If the man in the center of the picture stepped backward a few steps and fell over the cliff, he may have landed in another state. As long as he stayed put, he was still in Alabama.

The rural moonshiner doesn't usually have the warehouse drops of his city counterpart. Often, an old log hut, or a barn or deserted building, serves as a temporary storage place. Sometimes he uses a cave or a large, coverable hole in the ground. Many cautious moonshiners will have several such holes, so that if one is discovered all the distillate will not be lost. Any moonshiner gets edgy when he has a large quantity of moonshine on hand. The longer he must store it, the more nervous he becomes. It is not unheard of even for a very small moonshiner to have a thousand to two thousand gallons on hand at one time. Professional bootleggers and wholesalers know this, and have tried on occasion to capitalize on the fear psychology. During such times, if the moonshiner is distraught

Figure 56   John F. Gilbert Studio, Walter Elmore

Figure 57   National Office Laboratory, IRS

Figure 58

Morris Stephens

enough (and has no sales outlet of his own), his entire stock can be bought at a fraction of its worth. A typical squeeze play on the moonshiner will work like this: Bootlegger A (the moonshiner's buyer) will send word that he has been captured or is otherwise indisposed. In a few days another strange bootlegger will attempt to make the entrée with the moonshiner. If he is unsuccessful or untrusted, still a third bootlegger will appear on the scene, offering a still lower price than the second bootlegger offered. The moonshiner, caught between the problems of his vast storage and the doubt about the authenticity of the strange buyer (not knowing they are all of the same bootleg operation), begins to get panicky. The final result is sometimes selling out at a third of the normal price.

As a rule, a bootlegger will try this only on the small independent moonshiner, and only then if he does not need to count on the same man as a regular source of supply. The flimflam does not always work. One Georgia bootlegger made the mistake of assuming his former moonshiner friend didn't know that he (the bootlegger) had set up such a squeeze play. The bootlegger wasn't killed, but it was no comfort to him to receive—as a get well present while hospitalized—a neatly wrapped quart of white mule with his own testicles permanently preserved therein.

The moonshiner does not always get rich by any means. Some of his kind suffer the same lack of business acumen that can

Figure 59   Morris Stephenson

affect a legal enterprise. In numerous instances, illicit liquor is
sold at just a fraction over cost, or the less enterprising moonshiner
has allowed himself to become almost an employee of a bootlegging ring. Moonshining is back-breaking work, and added to the
physical side of the task is the constant mental anguish of possible
imprisonment and the never-ceasing pursuit of the revenue agent.
But with all the woes to be considered, for every moonshiner who
bites the dust, another seems to fill his place at the still.

In Figures 58, 59, 60, and 61, some of the woes of the moonshiner are graphically demonstrated. A moonshiner caught at the
still must stand and watch as his investment, his stock and supplies
disappear before his eyes. In Figure 58, the fruit jars filled with
white lightnin' burst at his feet. In Figure 59, eight thousand
gallons of still beer flood the mountainside. When the agent re-
turns, he wires the entire operation (Figure 60) for the big blowup.

Figure 60

Morris Stephen.

Figure 61

Morris Stephens

Figure 62   Morris Stephenson

Figure 61 shows the aftermath of such an explosion. The moon-shiner will face his defeat calmly He knows his act is illegal, and the old, time-worn excuses even sound trite to him. But there will be another day, he silently vows to himself. If prison faces him, there will be time to think about an improved model of his still and a location that will be better—safer and sure to go unde-tected for years. Maybe not really—but it will be worth the try.

Figure 62 shows another big sub steaming hot, wrecked by a revenue agent. This still illustrates the "key hole" cut, a method of making a still inoperative until the agent can get back with dynamite or TNT to destroy it completely. Sometimes on a routine discovery, the agent has limited tools of destruction. This poses a problem, particularly if the operation is very big, for the destruc-tion by hand is a difficult task. This key-hole cut renders the still useless even if the moonshiner comes back with a spare cap to replace the one which will be destroyed.

Figure 63

Morris Stephenson

Figure 64

Morris Stephenson

The moonshiner does not always wait for the revenue agent to come back and destroy his still with dynamite. In Figure 63, the moonshiner has taken his still away and repaired it while the revenue agent has gone for dynamite. Note the ax hole functionally patched and a new cover to accommodate the cap fitting. An affinity between the moonshiner and revenue agent exists which is almost unbelievable. If a moonshiner promises an agent he will not remove a discovered still, it is rare for him to go back on his word. In this case the still was probably discovered while the moonshiner was absent for supplies. Had his run been completed, the chances are good he would have removed and hidden the cap. Returning to the scene he probably found his still chopped up, removed it to another area in the agent's absence, and repaired it.

In Figure 64, the faces of a moonshiner (in bib overalls) and his son (in checkered shirt) reflect their defeat as they pose with officers, peaceably. The old-fashioned shoot-outs are a rarity in the rural areas nowadays, and in such places the agent and moonshiner understand each other and enjoy a mutual respect no one else could share. It would not have been unusual for this moonshiner to invite the agents home for dinner after they had completed their tasks of destruction. Neither will the moonshiners in this picture be shackled in handcuffs and taken to jail. They would promise to be at court the next day, and the agents would know without doubt that their word would be kept. However, many other moonshiners could not qualify for this expression of trust. The agent would have to take into consideration length of residence, personal recognizance, property ownership, and general reputation of an individual before deciding to trust him.

CHAPTER THIRTEEN

Moonshining
and the
Future

During the closing years of the 1960's, enforcement agents began to witness a preview of what the early years of the 1970's held in store. Some real sophisticated distilling rigs began to make their appearance, utilizing the latest in electronic gadgetry. These new stills needed no battery of still helpers or limestone springs to cool the worm coil. There was no smoke from the still fire either—no fire was needed. The newer design was mobile, heated by an electric coil, and the worm was cooled by air-conditioning. How much of a part scientific technology will play in the illicit business of the future can be but mere speculation. One thing is certain: The moonshiner of history has survived every onslaught, and there is no reason to suppose he will not accept advantages open to him, in innovation of equipment, method of doing business, and support from any faction of the population who will patronize him. Perhaps the moonshiner of the future will be more of a man on the move, with larger and larger mobile distilling rigs. Headlines of tomorrow might reveal the capture of a sophisticated tractor-trailer rig, which loaded up with sugar in southern Florida, mashed in while traveling through Georgia, completed the run and bottled in New York, and made the sale in New England. The return trip wouldn't be wasted either. Sugar could be purchased or previously arranged for in Massachusetts and the whole process repeated in preparation for a second large sale in the South. Seagoing rigs of the same nature are not out of the question and have on occasion been captured in the past. Ultra-high-frequency cooking units, air-conditioned cooling units, more scientific waste disposal, and even the eventual commercialization of laser or atomic energy will most probably make the headlines in connection with illicit distilling of tomorrow. More and more, the suppression of illicit distilling will be everybody's job. Close cooperation among federal and state enforcement agents, local sheriffs, and city police chiefs will play an increasingly larger role as moonshiners as well as bootleggers and transporters become more mobile and widespread in their movements. Public education will continue to be an effective weapon, as will organizations such as the National Council Against Illegal Liquor and stepped-up programs by federal government agencies. It is a time in history when the public at large is in a better listening mood than any period for decades. Pollution of the air, the streams, and the entire environment are now in the forefront of the individual citizen's mind. He is concerned about the food he eats and suspect of any form of contamination, whether it be the air he breathes or the water in which his children swim. There is no reason to believe he is less concerned about what he drinks.

It is a paradox of the times that a man who might scream out at the possibility of a shipment of poisoned tuna fish or recoil at the thought of eating cranberries with an excess of insect spray will drink moonshine by the gallon.

There is much optimism among most authorities on all levels of the enforcement program. Combined seizure efforts from all agencies is stronger and more unified than ever before in history, and still seizures are lower numerically than at any time in more than twenty years. The apparent downturn in illicit distilling, if it is a permanent fixture of the future, depends on more factors than previously mentioned. An inescapable criterion of this success is an upward moving economy, a realistic legal liquor-tax structure, a higher individual living standard, an educated public, and a relentless pressure on the moonshiner by all levels of enforcement and judicial authorities, working in harmony with government and the average citizen.

A grim reminder of the importance of economics was brought home to me during my field interviews. In traveling about the country, it was startling to learn of vast fruit orchards, farms, mountain homes, suburban homes (and some mansions), and businesses that had been acquired—or at least subsidized—through moonshining or related activity. In most cases these things had been acquired during prohibition, the depression, or the World War II era. Realizing the importance of this discovery, I questioned some of those who had long ago retired from the business after profiting: "If hard times and economic ill fortune came to you and you lost all this, would go back into the business?" The answer was too often a firm yes. Those few who said no were mostly men who had spent time in prison or under probation, although some did look back, from the vantage point of age, reflection, and change of heart, with disapproval for an illicit business.

Like all big business, moonshining has had, still has, and will have its kingpin operators. Some of the big ones have been toppled in just the past few years. Some yet operate, with an arrogance and defiance of federal law that is startling. Unfortunately, some exist and prosper with the home support of politicians and men in high places. Perhaps the most despicable of all are those who furnish the bankroll but never get their own hands dirty. Not enough are running scared, but a new day may be dawning. If ever the moonshiner had his back to the wall, it is now.

The moonshiners all across the land would laugh heartily at the first part of this statement. They would be quick to remind us that it is impossible to put a man in such a position that he couldn't make some squeezins'. "Give me a clay pot and a blanket to sleep on—and a city cellar or a mountain ridge—and I'll have you a drink in no time. I'll take some chicken feed or a case of dried prunes, and ferment 'em for a while, and build me a little fire under the pot, and catch the steam in my blanket, and wring it out. No sir, mister, you can't hardly put a man where he can't shine a little if'n he has a mind to. And if you won't give me no blanket, I'll go to the woods and pack a holler log with apples and ferment them. In no time a-tall I'll have a fire going and steam 'em out the other end. Yes sir, that'll just about do 'er, and if'n there's no old tin can around, I'll just catch the juice in my hat."

The more sophisticated moonshiner takes no such antiquated look backward toward his trade. He looks to the future with a great deal of optimism, gall, and guile, and even throws in a little industry propaganda. "We got a new thing coming out now," he says half seriously. "We have worked out a method to freeze-dry hundred-proof white mule. The only problem we got is something to package it in—keeps eatin' holes in plastic and polyethylene, and we want to keep it out of glass—the coin-dispenser idee, you know. The idee is real big . . . real big. The freeze-dried powder chases a couple of ice cubes around in a glass like a shark after a hamburger." I smile disbelievingly. "While we're getting the bugs out of this idee, we got one going that's really selling big even in New York. We're atakin' millions of oranges and asquirtin' them full of white mule. Some of the fellers ain't too steady with them hypo-der-mic needles on Monday, but we're gettin' 'em crated." It was not hard to disbelieve him, but I found myself scratching my head doubtfully as I headed for the car. Could it be that saturated oranges were being added to the 700 billion gallons of moonshine I would guess, if asked, had been consumed by the American public, in the long history of moonshining?

Glossary

The following terms are often a distortion of the strict scientific definitions as applied by the legal distilling industry. The purpose here, however, is to define terminology as used and recognized by the moonshiner.

Age: To mellow, mature, or color illicit whiskey in an attempt to simulate the legal product.

Alembic: An early name for a still.

Alky: Name for high-proof ethyl alcohol, coined by big-city moonshiners and bootleggers during the prohibition era.

Backins': The last part of the run in distilling, during which the alcoholic content of the distillate drops to a very low proof.

Barrel dogging: A moonshining operation wherein barrels formerly used by the legal industry are taken and steamed or sweated out to capture the alcohol soaked into the wood.

Beads: Small bubbles which form on top of a distillate when shaken in a fruit jar, indicating to the moonshiner the presence of alcohol and its approximate strength or proof.

Beading oils: Any mixture or concoction used to falsify the beading affect on moonshine liquor, normally used to upgrade a poor quality distillate or one too watered down.

Blind tiger: Location where spirits can be purchased illicitly.

Blockader: One who transports and sells untax-paid spirits.

Body heat temperature: A temperature range of 90 to 100 degrees F.

Boiler: Any component used to cook mash as a part of the distilling process, most frequently used to indicate cooking by steam.

Bootlegger: A seller of illegal liquor; the term is frequently used to denote the maker, transporter, wholesaler, or seller of illegal liquor.

Brandy: The distillate derived from fermented fruit or the juice therefrom; moonshine brandy is normally from peaches or apples, but cherries, berries, plums, etc., are frequently used, too.

Cap: A component of the still which normally sits on top as a gathering place for steam; pressure buildup in the cap forces steam into the worm for condensation.

Char: To burn the inside of whiskey barrels to improve coloring and aging; used by moonshiners of earlier years but rarely in the latter half of the twentieth century.

Charge: A single filling of a still prior to cooking and distilling.

Condenser: The component of a distilling rig which converts the hot alcoholic vapor into a liquid; moonshiners normally use auto radiators, copper coils, or double-wall copper condensers which are submerged in water for cooling purposes.

Congeners: Minor constituents found in ethyl alcohol after distilling, important to the quality of the drink in correct proportions.

Corn whiskey: Moonshine made from corn mash in the absence of sugar (pure corn); broadly, whiskey made with high percentage of corn mash (with lesser quantities of rye, barley, etc.), but with some sugar additive.

Crazy apple: Moonshine liquor which is a mixture of brandy and grain/sugar liquor; can be mixed after distilling or during distilling for a variety of taste.

Cutting: Reducing the proof strength of distillate by mixing with alcohol of a lower proof, with water, or with any other liquid which will mix (often paint thinner, wood alcohol, antifreeze, etc.).

Distiller's beer: The liquid part of the fermenting mash, frequently called still beer by the moonshiner.

Doubler: A component of a distilling rig placed in series with the still and the worm, or condenser; the purpose of this unit is to boost the alcoholic strength of the distillate and save the necessity of running the distillate through the still twice to obtain high-proof alcohol, as was the custom before the device came into use.

Doubling: Taking the distillate after the first run and redistilling it a second time; the purpose is to increase alcoholic strength.

Double back: To use the same mash from a previous run by adding only a little fresh sugar, water, etc.

Drappin' the bead: Mixing high-proof alcohol with very low proof backin's or water to equalize or lower the proof strength.

Faints: Low-proof distillate at the end of the run; see "backin's."

Fermentation: A state of agitation undergone by the mash as it is being converted to sugar.

Fermenter still: A still in which the mash is mixed and allowed to ferment until ripe for distilling, also called black potting; this method eliminates the more time-honored method of separate mash boxes from which ripe mash is taken.

Flame up: A test by moonshiners to determine the presence of alcoholic content in the distillate near the end of a run; if low-quality distillate is thrown on the fire and doesn't burn, alcohol in sufficient strength for commercial value is missing.

Foreshot: The first appearance of distillate coming through the worm or condenser after the still begins to function.

Frog eyes: The large beads or bubbles observable after the still start producing clear distillate, free of the foreign matter present in the foreshot.

Fusel oil: An oily, acrid liquid found in moonshine distillate in heavy concentrations if not filtered out, and considered undesirable and poisonous.

Go round: To distill from the fermenter boxes in sequence; after each is emptied, it is mashed in again and sits idle until the new mash is ripe or ready for distillation.

Granny fee: Money paid to a law-enforcement official as a bribe to insure his silence and cooperation in allowing a moon-shiner to continue his illicit business unmolested.

Grease spots: Locations during prohibition where financial payoffs had to be made to insure the movement of untax-paid spirits from one town to another.

Gunpowder proofing: A method of testing alcoholic strength by mixing a portion of gunpowder with distillate; when the mixture is set afire, if the liquid burns away and ignites the powder, the distillate is said to be proof spirit; low-proof alcohol in the mixture will contain too much water to allow ignition of the powder.

Heads: The first portion of the distillate following the foreshot as the still begins to function; this first distillate is low in proof and usually full of undesirable foreign matter.

Heater: A unit in distilling to increase production, used by the moonshiner to preheat mash and save the warm-up time when the still is reloaded or recharged.

High wines: Distillate which has been run through the distilling process a second time to boost the proof strength; distilling twice was standard procedure in the early days of moon-shining, before the advent of the doubler; the first distillation produced low proof or low wines.

Hold her cap: Properly functioning equipment; also, a still properly attended with the cap luted on with rye or clay paste to prevent steam leakage around the cap which would be weighted or chained down.

Kicker: A chemical additive used to hurry fermentation of the mash.

Kiln aging: A method used during prohibition to fake-age illicit spirits.

Leaching: Filtering distillate to remove fusel oil and undesirable foreign matter.

Low wines: The first-run distillate through a still not using a doubler; proof strength will be low, and redistillation will be necessary to raise proof strength or to obtain high wines.

Makin': The act of producing nontax-paid spirits for use or resale.

Malt: Sprouted grain, usually barley or corn, ground up and added to the mash ingredients for the purpose of turning starch into fermentable sugar.

Mash: The mixture of ingredients to be distilled and upon which fermenting action will take place.

Mashing in: The act of combining the ingredients to be distilled and preparing the vats or fermenter boxes with the proper formulation of ingredients.

Mash rake: A tool used as a stirring device to mix the mash or break up solid matter.

Mogo: A voodoolike charm used by early deep South moonshiners and distilling helpers; one was usually worn about the neck, and another was buried near the still.

Moonshine: Nontax-paid spirits made and sold illicitly.

Moonshiner: One who produces nontax-paid spirits.

Mountain teapot: A very small moonshine still normally used to supply the single needs of a family or just a few families.

Must: The bloom, or powderlike substance on the peelings of grapes, white and frostlike in appearance, used by early man and early moonshiners for yeast.

Needling: Inserting an electric needle into a keg of liquor to simulate aging of the liquor.

Pickling: Method used by moonshiners to simulate aging, mellowing, coloring, and/or flavoring; hunks of charcoal were sometimes placed in containers of distillate; oak chips were also added for coloring.

Piggy-back doubling: Using two or more doublers in series in a

distilling rig, for optimum boosting of proof strength, sometimes called rabbit footin' or trickin' n' a half.

Proof: Unit of alcoholic strength; actual proof strength is one half
the designation indicated on label of legal spirits—liquor
indicating 100 proof is 50 percent water and 50 percent
alcohol.

Puke: To boil over, said of an operating still, sending solid matter
into the connecting lines, doubler, and worm; this mis-
fortune sometimes requires dismantling the distilling rig
for a cleaning out.

Pummie: Crushed fruit, fermenting, from which moonshine brandy
will be made.

Rotgut: A general term signifying liquor of such poor quality as to
be scarcely fit for human consumption; for the moonshiner
the word has a more specific definition, and generally con-
notes the last run he will make from repeated distillations
of the same mash.

Run: The completed distillation of one charge or stillful.

Run hot: Said of a still producing distillate too fast through
the worm or condenser for proper cooling. Problem might
be an improperly designed worm coil, too great heat under
the still, water surrounding the worm coil not low enough
in temperature to do proper job of cooling, etc.

Runner: A person or persons who transport nontax-paid spirits
from one person or location to another.

Rye paste: A homemade mixture used for sealing the cap to the
still to prevent the escape of steam; clay mud and grass or
straw is sometimes used for this luting on process.

Scald down: To pour boiling water on cornmeal to accomplish
gelatinizing and set in motion the proper making of mash
to be distilled.

Scorch: To allow the charge in the still to become too hot or un-
stirred at the hottest area in the still (where the wood
fire, gas flame, etc., is most closely in contact with the
still itself).

Second sugar: The second run of the same mash used on the original run with nothing added but more sugar.

Singlings: Low-proof liquor which has been run through a still,
not using a doubler, only once; see "low wines."

Sitting of the bead: The condition of the bead after a jar of moonshine distillate has been shaken up to generate beads; moonshiners claim the ability to read proof strength by observing how much of the bead is submerged in the liquid and how much remains above the level of the liquid.

Slop: Spent mash after distilling.

Slopping back: Using spent mash, boiling hot, to scald down a new batch; this is used in preference to fresh water when a run of sour mash is planned.

Smoke swallowing: Action of heavy leaf covering over a distilling site; moonshiners believe leaves absorb evidence of smoke if volume is not too heavy.

Snowballs: Large bubbles appearing on vats of fermenting mash.

Sour mash: Whiskey made by scalding down a new batch of mash ingredients with hot slop or spent mash with the addition of fresh yeast and additional water; hot slop or spent mash used in preference to fresh water gives the distillate a sour rather than sweet taste.

Spent beer: Fermented mash or distiller's beer after it has been distilled or used to exhaustion.

Squeezin's: The end product from distilling; normally refers to the end product of distilled corn.

Still: Any type, size, or shape of unit, made of any material, for the purpose of cooking mash and effecting the separation of water and alcohol, capturing the latter by condensation through a worm coil, auto radiator, or other condensing device; see Chapter 13 for information on general types: pot, box or pan, submarine, groundhog, mushroom, continuous-process column, pot column, steam roller, etc.

Stillin': Operating a still; see "makin'."

Still house: A building housing the components of a distilling rig; these no longer exist in the historic sense; hastily constructed roof coverings over work areas is the modern-day substitute.

Straight corn: Moonshine whiskey made from pure corn and corn malt with no sugar or other ingredient added except yeast; no blending, diluting, or bead drappin' permitted; drinking of it permitted only on level ground while leaning against a very large tree.

Sweet lightnin': Moonshine whiskey with honey or maple syrup added for sweetening.

Sweet mash: Mash made from all new or fresh ingredients; in contrast to sour mash which is made from hot slop or spent mash rather than fresh water; see "sour mash."

Tailin's: See "backin's."

Teedum barrel: Container in which old-time moonshiner kept his private drinking liquor.

Temping bottle: A testing vial in which a quantity of distillate is placed, shaken up, and the formation of beads therein is observed; proof is unscientifically determined by some moonshiners using this method.

Third sugar: Third running of original mash after additional sugar and yeast is added.

Thump keg (or thumper): Same as "doubler"; name derives from thumping sound it makes as steam passes through it.

Tickler: See "kicker."

Toll bridge: The place payment is made before illegal liquor can be delivered.

Toasting: See "kiln aging" and "needling."

Urea: A commercial chemical used by moonshiners to hurry fermentation.

White lightnin: One of the names given illicit spirits and derived from the ancient belief that a fire started by white lightning could not be extinguished.

Wholesaler: One who buys illicit spirits from the producer and resells to the bootlegger.

Whoppin' the cap: A method used by the moonshiner to determine pressure reduction or buildup in the cap of a still. The test is made by tapping lightly on the still cap with a stick and becoming educated to the sound made by the tapping.

Wildcatter: Less frequently used name for a moonshiner.

Worm: A length of coiled pipe used while submerged in water to effect condensation; hot vapor passing through properly cooled worm turns to liquid.

Worm box or flake stand: The container for water into which the coil or worm will be submerged; water in the worm box will fill and run off continually so that fresh, cool water will surround the worm coil at all times.

Yeast: A budding fungus or unicellular vegetable organism containing enzymes which act upon sugar; without this action the fermentation cycle would not be complete.

Bibliography

Acknowledgment is extended to the publishers and the authors, if living, for the following list of books and periodicals used for review. Each entry provided me with helpful background research and, on occasion, a genuine spirit of the times covered in this history.

Abernathy, Arthur Talmage, *Moonshine*. Asheville, North Carolina: The Dixie Publishing Company, 1924.

Adams, Ramon F., *Western Words*. University of Oklahoma Press, 1945.

Alcohol & Tobacco Tax Division Laboratory, *Alcoholic Drinks of the World*. Washington: Internal Revenue Service, 1964.

Alcohol & Tobacco Tax Division, "Distilled Spirits: History of Taxation and Law Enforcement," Internal Revenue Service, Document No. 5574, 1966.

"Alcohol Symposium," *American Anthropologist*, Volume 66, April 1964.

Annual Report of the Commissioner of Internal Revenue, 1875–1969.

Armstrong, E. F., "Alcohol Through the Ages," *Chemistry and Industry*, 1933.

Arnold, John P., *History of the Brewing Industry and Brewing Science in America*. Chicago: 1933.

Asbury, Herbert, *The Great Illusion: An Informal History of Prohibition*. New York City: Doubleday & Company; 1950.

Atkinson, George Wesley, *After the Moonshiners by One of the Raiders; A Book of Thrilling Yet Truthful Narratives*. Wheeling, West Virginia: 1881.

Baron, Stanley W., *Brewed in America: A History of Beer and Ale in the United States*. Boston: Little, Brown, 1962.

Bassett, John Spencer, *A Short History of the U.S.* New York City: The Macmillan Company, 1913.

Bourke, J. G., "Distillation by Early American Indians," *American Anthropologist*, Volume 2, July 1894.

Bruce, Philip A., *Economic History of Virginia in the Seventeenth Century*. New York City: 1896.

Carson, Gerald, *The Social History of Bourbon*. New York City: Dodd, Mead & Company, 1963.

Cherrington, Ernest H., *The Evolution of Prohibition in the United States of America*. Westerville, Ohio: The American Issue Press, 1920.

Coffin, Charles C., *Building the Nation*. New York City: Harper & Bros., 1882.

Collins, Lewis, *Historical Sketches of Kentucky*. Kentucky: 1847.

Coulter, E. M., *The Confederate States of America 1861–1865*. Louisiana: 1950.

Crawley, E., *Dress, Drinks and Drums*. London: Methuen and Co., 1931.

Davis, T. L., "Primitive Science," *Journal of Chemical Education*, 1935.

Dorchester, Daniel, *The Liquor Problem in All Ages*. New York: 1884.

Dowdy, Clifford, *The Great Plantation*. New York City: Rinehart, 1957.

Driver, H. E., *Comparative Studies of North American Indians*. Philadelphia: American Philosophical Society, July 1957.

Droomgoole, William Allen, *A Moonshiner's Son*. New Jersey: Penn Publishing Co., 1898.

Durand, Loyal, "Mountain Moonshining in East Tennessee," *Georgia Review*, Volume XLVI, April 1956.

Elmore, Leonard, *The Moonshine War*. New York City: Doubleday, 1969.

Fisher, Irving, *Prohibition at Its Worst*. New York City: Alcohol Information Commission, 1928.

Flint, George E., *The Whole Truth About Alcohol*. New York City: The Macmillan Co., 1919.

Forbes, R. J., *Short History of the Art of Distillation*. Leiden, Netherlands: E. J. Brill, 1948.

Fox, John, Jr., *The Trail of the Lonesome Pine*. New York City: Grosset & Dunlap, 1908.

Fox, William, *Moonshine Light, Moonshine Bright*. Philadelphia: J. B. Lippincott Co., 1966.

Fox, William P., "The Lost Art of Moonshine," *Saturday Evening Post*, March 26, 1966.

Gault, W. C., *Thunder Road*. New York City: Dutton & Co., 1952.

Grossman, H. J., *Grossman's Guide to Wines, Spirits and Beer.* New York City: Charles Scribner's Sons, 1955.

Halberstam, David, *The Noblest Roman.* Boston: Houghton Mifflin Co., 1961.

Hannum, Alberta Pierson, *Look Back With Love.* New York City: The Vanguard Press, 1969.

Helmick, Leah Stock, "Key Women of the T-Men," *The American Legion,* August 1937.

Hening, William Waller, *Hening's Statutes.* Richmond: 1809.

History and Organization of the Alcohol Tax Unit Bureau of Internal Revenue, Internal Revenue Service, 1949.

Houlett, W., "Rum Trading in the American Colonies Before 1763," *Journal of American History,* 1952.

Johnson, Guion Griffis, *Ante-Bellum North Carolina.* Chapel Hill: University of North Carolina Press, 1937.

Jones, Madison, *An Exile.* New York City: Viking Press, 1967.

Kearins, John, *Yankee Revenooer.* Durham, N.C.: Moore Publishing Co., 1969.

Kingsbury, Susan Myra, Ed., *Records of the Virginia Company of London.* Washington: U.S. Library of Congress, 1906.

Kobler, John, "King of the Moonshiners," *Saturday Evening Post,* August 2, 1958.

Lefler, Hugh Talmage, Ed., *North Carolina History Told by Contemporaries.* Chapel Hill: University of North Carolina Press, 1934, 1948, 1956.

Marshall, Catherine, *Christy.* New York City: McGraw-Hill, 1967.

Maurer, David W., "The Argot of the Moonshiner," *American Speech,* Volume XXIV, February 1949.

Merz, Charles, *The Dry Decade.* New York City: Doubleday, Doran & Co., 1930.

"Moonshine—Big Business Again," *U.S. News & World Report,* September 17, 1954.

"Moonshining: A Big Business in the Shadows," *Business Week,* April 30, 1955.

Operation Moonshine, Licensed Beverage Industries, New York, 1954–69.

Packard, Vance, "Millions in Moonshine," *The American Magazine,* September 1950.

Parker, G. M. N., "The Mountain Massacre," *Callers to Country Life,* West Virginia, 1930.

Payne, E. J., *History of the New World Called America*. Oxford: Oxford University Press, 1899.

"Records of York County, Virginia," Virginia State Library, 1675–1684.

Ross, Irwin, "The Moonshiner's Still in Business," *The American Mercury*, November 1950.

Schreiner, O., *History of the Art of Distillation and of Distillation Apparatus*. Milwaukee: Pharmaceutical Science Series, 1901.

Scomp, H. A., *King Alcohol in the Realm of King Cotton*. Georgia, 1888.

Simon, A., *Drink*. New York City: Horizon Press, 1953.

Sharp, Bill, *A New Geography of North Carolina*. Raleigh, North Carolina: Sharp Publishing Co., 1958.

Stapleton, Isaac, *Moonshiners in Arkansas*. Independence, Missouri: Zion Printing & Publishing Co., 1920.

Starr, John, *The Purveyor*. New York City: Holt, Rinehart & Winston, 1961.

Stimpson, George, *A Book About a Thousand Things*. New York City: Harper & Bros., 1946.

Stoner, R. D., *A Seed-Bed of the Republic*. Virginia: Commonwealth Press, 1962.

Taussig, Charles W., *Rum, Romance & Rebellion*. New York City, Minton, Balch & Co., 1928.

Taylor, Frank J., "The Wine Ghost Walks," *Colliers*, September 19, 1931.

Thomas, Jean, *Blue Ridge Country*. New York City: Duell, Sloan & Pearce, 1942.

"T-Men's New Tricks," *Popular Science Monthly*, November 1959.

Warburton, Clark, *The Economic Results of Prohibition*. New York City: Columbia University Press, 1932.

Washburne, C., *Primitive Drinking*. New Haven: College and University Press, 1961.

Weiss, Harry B., *The History of Applejack or Apple Brandy in New Jersey from Colonial Times to the Present*. New Jersey: N.J. Agricultural Society, 1954.

Whitener, D. J., "The Dispensary Movement in North Carolina," *South Atlantic Quarterly*, January 1937.

Whitman, Howard, "How We Trapped Capone," *Collier's*, April 26, 1947.

Whittle, Conway, *The Conquest of Virginia: The First Attempt.* Sams-Keyser-Doherty Corp., 1924.

"Why You Can't Have Enough Sugar," *Fortune,* October 1945.

Wiley, B. I., *The Life of Billy Yank: The Common Soldier of the Union.* Indiana: 1952.

Wiley, B. I., *The Life of Johnny Reb: The Common Soldier of the Confederacy.* Indiana: 1943.

Wilkinson, Sir I. Gardner, *The Manners and Customs of the Ancient Egyptians.* New York City: Scribner and Welford, (3 Vols.), 1879.

Williams, Cratis D., "Moonshining in the Mountains," *North Carolina Folklore,* Vol. XV, May 1967.

Wiltse, Henry M., *The Moonshiners.* Chattanooga: 1895.

Wingfield, Marshall, *An Old Virginia Court.* West Tennessee Historical Society, 1948.

Wolf, A., *History of Science, Technology and Philosophy in the 16th and 17th Centuries.* London: Allen and Unwin, Ltd., 1936.

Woodmason, Charles, *The Carolina Backcountry on the Eve of Revolution.* Chapel Hill: University of North Carolina Press, 1953.

Statistics regarding still seizures and related information were taken from official government records, primarily the annual report of the commissioner of Internal Revenue, enforcement agency reports, and/or documents, and official records of Licensed Beverage Industries. Records of Licensed Beverage Industries, Inc., provided nationwide statistical data on illicit distilling on the federal, state and local levels. While it must be acknowledged that there may be some duplication of seizure records when both state and federal sources are used, the statistics cited are believed to be the most accurate available.

Index

A

Accessories and components for stills, 200–204
After the Moonshiners, by One of the Raiders (Atkinson), 42–48
Aging, 112–13, 230
Alabama, 31, 33, 38, 96, 129, 142, 156
Alabama box still, 188–90
Alaska, 87, 96
Albukassen, 4
Alcohol Tax Unit of Internal Revenue, 112, 135
Alembics (stills), 4–5, 230
Alexander of Aphrodisias, 4
Alexandrian still, 5
Alky, 28, 29, 230
American Indians
    alcohol distilling of, 9–10
    selling of whiskey to, 27–28
Amnesty to moonshiners, 36–37
Anecdotes about moonshiners, 159–181
Anderson, Sherwood, 113–19
Antijug laws, 86
Anti-Saloon League, 70–71
Applejack, 13
Application and types of stills, 182–229
Aqua vini, 4
Aqua vitae whiskey, 4
Arika, 3
Aristotle, 4
Arizona, 105
Arkansas, 31, 33, 38, 129, 142
Arnaldus Villanovanus, 4
Arrack, 3
Asiatic Tartary, 3
Atkinson, George W., 42–48, 54–57, 67–69
Atlanta, 133, 138, 141
Automobiles, shootouts and, 97
Avis, Dwight, 152
Ayres, Lee L., 44
Aztecs, 10

B

Babylon, 2
Backin's, 78, 230
Bailey, Tom, 152
Balm of Gilead, 166–67
Baptists, 21
Barley, 2
Barrel dogging, 230
Barrel stills, 193–94
Basement moonshiner, 136
Bathtub gin, 96
Beading oils, 230
Beads, 230
Bee-tree cutting, 64, 173–78
Beer, 2, 13
Belshazzar (King of Babylon), 1
Ben-hadad (King of Syria), 1
Bevins, Raymond, 152
Bhutan, 5
Bible, 1
Big time moonshining, 208–14
Blackpot still, 197–200
Blacks, moonshine and, 49
Blind tiger, 230
Blockader, 27, 230
Boas, 2
Body heat temperature, 230
Boiler, 230
Bootlegger, 230
    origin of word, 27–28
Bourbon, 16, 23
Box (worm barrel), 74
Brandy, 3, 13, 32, 74, 127, 230
Brooklyn, 25
Bureau of Internal Revenue, 92, 112
    See also Office of Internal Revenue
Burke, John G., 9–10
Butler, Smedley, 106

C

Cahita Indians, 9
Cake yeast, 76, 80–82
Calcium sulphate, 98
California, 93, 96, 143
Campus peddler, 136